GENDER AND MIGRATION IN SOUTHERN EUROPE

Law and Migration

Series Editor
Satvinder S. Juss, King's College London, UK

Migration and its subsets of refugee and asylum policy are rising up the policy agenda at national and international level. Current controversies underline the need for rational and informed debate of this widely misrepresented and little understood area.

Law and Migration contributes to this debate by establishing a monograph series to encourage discussion and help to inform policy in this area. The series provides a forum for leading new research principally from the Law and Legal Studies area but also from related social sciences. The series is broad in scope, covering a wide range of subjects and perspectives.

Other titles in this series:

Migration, Work and Citizenship in the Enlarged European Union
Samantha Currie
978-0-7546-7351-4

Refugee Law and Practice in Japan
Osamu Arakaki
978-0-7546-7009-4

International Migration and Global Justice
Satvinder Juss
978-0-7546-4671-6 (Hbk)
978-0-7546-7289-0 (Pbk)

Gender and Migration in 21st Century Europe

Edited by

HELEN STALFORD
University of Liverpool, UK
SAMANTHA CURRIE
University of Liverpool, UK
and
SAMANTHA VELLUTI
University of Lincoln, UK

Routledge
Taylor & Francis Group
LONDON AND NEW YORK

First published 2009 by Ashgate Publishing

Published 2016 by Routledge
2 Park Square, Milton Park, Abingdon, Oxfordshire OX14 4RN
711 Third Avenue, New York, NY 10017, USA

First issued in paperback 2016

Routledge is an imprint of the Taylor & Francis Group, an informa business

British Library Cataloguing in Publication Data
Gender and migration in 21st century Europe. -- (Law and migration)
1. Women immigrants--Europe--Social conditions--21st century. 2. Emigration and immigration--Sex differences.
3. Women alien labor--Europe. 4. Immigrants--Government policy--Europe--History--21st century. 5. Europe--Emigration and immigration--Social aspects.
I. Series II. Stalford, Helen. III. Currie, Samantha, 1982-
IV. Velluti, Samantha.
304.8'4'0090511-dc22

Library of Congress Cataloging-in-Publication Data
Gender and migration in 21st century Europe / by Helen Stalford, Samantha Curie and Samantha Velluti.
p. cm. -- (Law and migration)
Includes index.
ISBN 978-0-7546-7450-4 1. Europe--Emigration and immigration--Social aspects. 2. Europe--Emigration and immigration--Sex differences. 3. Migration, Internal--Social aspects--Europe. 4. Migration, Internal--Sex differences--Europe. 5. Emigration and immigration law--Europe. I. Stalford, Helen. II. Currie, Samantha, 1982- III. Velluti, Samantha.
JV7590.G462 2009
304.8094--dc22

2009005393

ISBN 13: 978-1-138-27955-1 (pbk)
ISBN 13: 978-0-7546-7450-4 (hbk)

Contents

List of Figures

List of Tables

Notes on the Authors

Heli Askola is Senior Lecturer at the Faculty of Law, Monash University in Melbourne. She gained her PhD from the European University Institute, Florence, in 2005. She is a specialist in European Union law, with emphasis on the rights of migrants in the Area of Freedom, Security and Justice. Her publications include *Legal Responses to Trafficking in Women for Sexual Exploitation in the European Union* (Oxford: Hart Publishing, 2007). Before joining Monash in 2008 she worked at Cardiff Law School in the UK. She has been a consultant on migration law and criminal law for the European Commission and the International Organization for Migration and has held visiting research posts at several law schools, including Toronto and Emory (Atlanta).

Laura Bernardi is Associate Professor at the Institute of Biographic Trajectories, Sociology of the Life Course at the Faculty of Social and Political Sciences at the University of Lausanne and Head of the Independent Research Group 'Culture of Reproduction' at the Max Planck Institute for Demographic Research in Germany. Her research ranges from fertility and family demography, to life course sociology, social networks, and transnational migration. She has co-directed a number of international projects which explore fertility and family changes in a comparative European perspective integrating qualitative and quantitative approaches. She is part of the directorial board of the interdisciplinary Centre PaVie (University of Lausanne and University of Genève) and member of the Scientific Review Board of the journals *Demographic Research, Population Research and Policy Review* and *Genus.* She has published in major international journals, among others the *European Journal of Population, Journal of Mixed Methods Research, Demographic Research*, and the *Population Research and Policy Review.* She is co-editor of the Special Collection 'Beyond National Boundaries: Transnationalism and migration in Europe' to appear in *International Migration.*

Paul J. Boyle is Professor of Human Geography and Head of the School of Geography and Geosciences at the University of St Andrews. He is President of the *British Society for Population Studies* (BSPS). He directs the *Longitudinal Studies Centre – Scotland* (LSCS), which has established and continues to maintain and support the *Scottish Longitudinal Study* (SLS), which is one of the world's largest longitudinal datasets for health and social science research. He is co-Director of the recently funded ESRC *Centre for Population Change* (CPC); co-applicant on the recently funded ESRC *Administrative Data Liaison Service* (ADLS); and co-applicant on the Wellcome Trust *Scottish Health Informatics Programme* (SHIP). Paul has published widely in demography and epidemiology.

Thomas J. Cooke is a Professor in the Department of Geography at the University of Connecticut where he has most recently Chaired the Urban & Community Studies program. He is the immediate past-President of the Population Specialty Group of the Association of American Geographers and has been appointed a Work-Family Leader for the Sloan Work and Family Research Network. Thomas has published widely in demography and urban studies and on family migration.

Samantha Currie is a Lecturer in Law at the Liverpool Law School. Her research interests include migration in the context of European Union enlargement, the development of Union citizenship in European Community law and the international posting of workers. She has recently published *Migration, Work and Citizenship in the Enlarged European Union* (2008, Ashgate). She completed her PhD on the legal status and experiences of Polish migrants in the UK, also at Liverpool, in 2007.

Giuseppe Gabrielli is a Research fellow at the University of Bari, specializing in Demographic and Economic Regional Differences in the Mediterranean Area. Previously he held a number of international research posts, at the Max Planck Institute in Rostock (Germany), at the Brown University in Providence (Rhode Island, USA), at the University 'G. D'Annunzio' of Pescara (2004–2005) and at the University of Macerata (2007–2008). He has participated in a range of national and international demographic research projects. His research interests include transition to adulthood, second generation of migrants, mixed couples, international migrations, internal mobility, household formation, fertility patterns, infant malnutrition.

Vernon Gayle is Professor of Sociology at Stirling University and the Institute for Social and Economic Research, Essex University. His main substantive interests are in the sociology of youth, with a particular focus on education and higher education and social stratification. He also undertakes research in the areas of information technology and society, e-social science, population, migration and fertility. Vernon is an honorary fellow at the Centre for Applied Statistics, Lancaster University and the Longitudinal Studies Centre – Scotland, St Andrews University. He is a Vice President of Research Committee 33 Logic and Methodology, of the International Sociological Association and an Associate Editor of Survey Research Methods.

Ruth Lamont is a Lecturer in Law at the University of Sheffield Law School. She completed her PhD on gender equality and international child abduction in European Union law at the Liverpool Law School. Her major research interests are in the field of private international family law, particularly within the European

Union context, and she has recently published on the subject of child abduction in European law, and on the definition and interpretation of the concept of habitual residence.

Gabriella Lazaridis is Senior Lecturer in the department of Politics and International Studies, University of Leicester. She has published extensively and managed a number of funded research projects in the fields of migration and gender.

Clara H. Mulder is Professor of Spatial Demography at the Department of Geography, Planning and International Development Studies of the University of Amsterdam. She is the principal investigator of the research programme 'Residential choice in a family and socio-spatial context', which is funded by the Netherlands Organization for Scientific Research. She is president of the Netherlands Demographic Society. Her research interests include households and housing, leaving the parental home, household formation and dissolution, home-ownership, residential mobility and family relations.

Elizabeth Oliver is a Postdoctoral Research Fellow within the European Law and Policy Research group at The Liverpool Law School. Her socio-legal research focuses on various aspects of migration into and within the EU. Dr Oliver has experience as lead researcher on a number of funded research projects that investigate various relating to highly skilled migration. At present she is a postdoctoral researcher on a study developed within the consortium 'Researching Inequality through Science and Technology (ResIST)', funded by European Commission. This study explores the migration of scientists from third countries into the EU. She completed her doctoral thesis at the University of Leeds on the topic of 'Gender Equality and Career Progression in Science: Managing Work and Family Life on Fixed Term Contracts'. The study sought to identify barriers to career progression associated with an expectation of geographic mobility and a high incidence of fixed term employment from the perspective of women working in academic science.

Anna Paterno is Professor of Demography at the Faculty of Political Sciences, University of Bari (Italy). She is on the editorial board of the 'Italian Review of Economy, Demography and Statistics' and referee of the 'International Migration' Review. She is also currently elected member of the scientific committee of the 'Italian Association of Population Studies' a sub-group of the 'Italian Statistic Association'. Her main research interests relate to the features, determinants and consequences of demographic dynamics, gender roles in migration processes; the socio-economic characteristics of migrants in the EU, and poverty diffusion among the migrant population.

Parvati Raghuram is a Lecturer in Geography at the Open University. She has published widely on migrant entrepreneurship and development studies. Much of her more recent work explores the migration of skilled and lesser skilled women, particularly those moving from the Indian subcontinent as doctors and IT workers. She has co-authored *The Practice of Cultural Studies* (Sage), and *Gender and International Migration in Europe* (Routledge) and co-edited *South Asian Women in the Diaspora* (Berg) and *Tracing Indian Diaspora: Contexts, Memories, Representations* (Sage). She also co-edits the Journal of South Asian Diaspora with the Centre for Study of Diaspora, Hyderabad.

Dianne Scullion is a final year PhD candidate at the Liverpool Law School, University of Liverpool. Her research explores the International, European and domestic legal framework relating to child trafficking, with a specific focus on the UK as a destination country for child domestic workers. Issues considered within this context are the gendered nature of child trafficking and the role played by both women and the child's family in perpetrating and facilitating trafficking of this nature. The practice of private fostering which is potentially abused by traffickers is considered in terms of the difficulties this presents for the law in the identification of children as trafficked children. Her research also critically considers some of the questions trafficking poses in relation to normative children's rights concepts such as agency, autonomy and best interests.

Catherine Sherlock trained as a Social Worker in 1994 and has worked as a social worker in a variety of settings for over 11 years. Her experience is mainly in the area of child protection social work in UK and Ireland, working with refugees and asylum seekers in Denmark and Ireland, and in medical social work (maternity and oncology settings) in Australia and Ireland. Since 2005 she has been a lecturer at the National University of Ireland Galway, teaching on the MA in Social Work and on undergraduate sociology programmes. She has given workshops and provided training on the themes of cultural diversity in practice and for organizations in the community. She completed an LLM in International Human Rights Law from the Irish Centre for Human Rights in 2006. She has published in the area of child rights and social work practice and has a research interest in children in migration and culturally responsive social work practice.

Helen Stalford is a Senior Lecturer at the Liverpool Law School. She has researched and published widely on child and family rights in the EU, particularly in a migration context. She is co-author (with Louise Ackers) of *A Community for Children?: Children, Citizenship and Migration in the European Union* (2004, Ashgate). Other relevant publications explore the impact of migration on women's family life and caring responsibilities, and the status and experiences of children involved in cross-national custody and access disputes. She is joint general editor of the Journal of Social Welfare and Family Law and is a member of the International Family Law Committee.

Salvatore Strozza is Professor of Demography at the Faculty of Political Sciences, University of Naples Federico II. He is a Fellow of the Research Institute on the Population and Social Politics (IRPPS) of the National Council of Research (CNR) and of the International and European Forum of Migration Research (FIERI). He is on the editorial boarding of two international journals: Genus and Studi Emigrazione/Migration Studies. His main research expertise lies in the international migration and, in particular, foreign immigration in Italy.

Helen Toner is Associate Professor in the School of Law at Warwick University. She has written on EC law and migration law, with a particular interest in EU Citizenship and family reunification. Her publications include *Partnership Rights, Free Movement and EU Law* (Hart 2004), and *Whose Freedom, Security and Justice* (Baldaccini, Guild and Toner, (eds), Hart 2007).

Samantha Velluti is a Lecturer at Lincoln Law School. She has researched extensively in the area of EU governance, open method of co-ordination and gender equality. Her current research focuses on New Governance, gender mainstreaming, gender equality and migration. Velluti's recent publications include: 'What European Union Strategy for Integrating Migrants? The role of OMC soft mechanisms in the development of an EU immigration policy' (2007) 9 European Journal of Migration and Law 53; 'Promotion of Gender Equality at the Workplace: Gender Mainstreaming and Collective Bargaining in Italy' (2008) 16(2) Feminist Legal Studies, 195–214. She is co-editor (with Fiona Beveridge) of Gender and the Open Method of Coordination. Perspectives on Law, Governance and Equality in the EU (Dartmouth: Ashgate, 2008).

Introduction

Helen Stalford, Samantha Currie, and Samantha Velluti

The idea for this edited collection arose out of a series of interdisciplinary workshops entitled 'Gender and Migration in 21st Century Europe' hosted jointly by the Migration Unit and the Feminist Legal Research Unit at the University of Liverpool between October 2006 and April 2007. The same title is adopted for this collection which draws on the presentations and discussions that took place during the workshops coupled with additional invited contributions from notable scholars in the field. In referring to 'gender' the aim is to explore how social, economic, legal, political and cultural processes implied by migration govern and reinforce relations between the sexes – not just between men and women, but between female and male children, and between girls and women. Our interpretation of 'migration' is also broad to encompass a range of geographical, economic and personal trajectories into and within Europe as well as the emergence and effectiveness of new regulatory mechanisms to address issues of 'forced' migration (notably trafficking), cross-national family breakdown and employment migration in an expanding European Union.

The collection follows an already distinguished body of work assessing the interaction between gender and migration processes in Europe and beyond, much of which emerged at the turn of the millennium (e.g. Ackers 1998, Boyle and Halfacree 1999, Kofman et. al. 2000; Anderson 2000, Willis and Yeoh 2000). Collectively, this work captured trends and themes relating to the influence of gender roles and relations, geographical context, multi-levelled legal and policy regulation, and globalization on migration processes. The current collection adds to this literature in a number of respects. First, it offers up-to-date reflections on the legal, social, political and economic currency of migration in Europe today, and on the extent to which these processes (continue to) produce gendered outputs. In line with previous work, the family and employment are adopted as key contexts within which to locate this analysis. The collection adds a further dimension to research in this area, however, by incorporating more explicit and substantial analysis of the international, European and national regulatory framework. In particular, the collection reflects the significant changes in the legal framework which have shifted the parameters of the European migration space. In a European Union (EU) context, new legislative developments have altered the residence status and related rights of both migrants with nationality of a Member State and those with nationality of a third-country.[1] The EU has also introduced a more robust framework to regulate the recognition and enforcement of divorce and parental responsibility judgments cross-nationally in recognition of the correlation between family breakdown and migration (with the latter acting as both a trigger and a consequence of the former).[2] The post millennium enlargements of the European Union (in 2004 and 2007) have also had a dramatic impact on the mobility landscape in Europe. Nationals of the 12 newer Member States have experienced a shift in their legal status from that of third-country national to the 'privileged' category of EU national, carrying more immediate and tangible benefits for some than others. Similarly, the fluid migration space generated by the erosion of internal migration borders has led to an unprecedented co-ordination of external border policing as well as a distinct alteration in the social, cultural, economic, political and, of course, legal status of many non-EU migrants, particularly those who are more economically vulnerable.

In addition to the legal and constitutional changes to have taken place since 2000, significant developments of a social and demographic nature have prompted a fresh look at the topic of gender and migration in Europe. For example, the recognition of the progressively ageing nature of Europe's population – with predictions that deaths will outnumber births from 2015 onwards and that the ratio of pensioners to working-age people will increase to up to 60 per cent in 2060 (EUROSTAT, 2008) – have prompted calls for enhanced migration from external regions as a means of sustaining welfare states and social care systems in the future.[3] Expectations of the professional and personal opportunities generated by migration are still distinctly gendered, but have evolved also in response to higher levels of educational and professional attainment among women leading to, among other things, a re-alignment of caring responsibilities in the home, not necessarily between women and men, but between women and other (often migrant) women. Contrasted with this image of opportunity and accomplishment, however, is the soft underbelly of European migration systems – the more sinister and exploitative manifestations of gendered migration such as trafficking in

1 Such as, Directive 2004/38 on the free movement and residence entitlement of Union citizens and their family members OJ [2004] L158/77; Directive 2003/109 on the status of third-country nationals who are long-term residents OJ [2003] L16/44; Directive 2003/86 on the right to family reunification OJ [2003] L251/12; Directive 2004/83 on minimum standards for the qualification as refugees or as persons in need of international protection OJ [2004] L304/12.

2 Regulation 2201/2003 concerning jurisdiction and the recognition and enforcement of judgments in matrimonial matters and matters of parental responsibility OJ [2003] L 338/1–29.

3 For example the Commission has proposed a Council Directive on a single application procedure for a single permit for third-country nationals to reside and work in the territory of a Member State and on a common set of rights for third-country workers legally residing in a Member State: COM(2007) 638 final.

women and children, and the persistent and embedded racism, xenophobia and social exclusion experienced by many migrant groups.

All of these factors illustrate the dynamic and multidimensional nature of migration and reinforce the need to adopt an interdisciplinary perspective.

Structure of the Book

The resulting collection is not intended to explore a single coherent theme within the context of gender and migration in contemporary Europe. Instead, the contributions address a range of issues pertinent to an understanding of how gender is manifested in migration processes and frameworks and approach them from a wide variety of disciplinary and methodological perspectives. Certain concepts, ideas and themes recur in several of the chapters allowing for the more nuanced and multi-disciplinary exploration that the subject matter demands. As such, the collection is grouped into three main parts each of which are comprised of contributions drawing on a range of approaches and perspectives. The first part (chapters 1–3) addresses the impact of migration on family life. Part II (chapters 4–7) examines the impact of migration on women's labour market participation and career progression, and Part III reflects on the gender implications of immigration systems (chapters 8–11). The collection comprises a diverse but complementary mix of empirically-grounded and conceptual pieces, drawing on a range of qualitative, quantitative and more orthodox doctrinal research projects. Together, these provide a rich and unique insight into the gendered impact of migration in Europe today.

The first chapter of Part I, by Boyle, Cooke, Gayle and Mulder, explores the impact of family migration on personal relationships and offers fresh insights into the specific consequences of this for women. Their previous work had attributed some of the more injurious effects of migration to the typical notion of the 'trailing spouse', a phenomenon that essentially implied a woman relinquishing much of the personal, familial support, and often her own employment, in favour of relocating elsewhere in support of her husband's career. Drawing on longitudinal data from the British Household Panel Survey this analysis reviews this theory in the light of changing patterns in women's education and employment, and the consequent refinement of roles in the home. Surprisingly perhaps, the research reveals that in spite of these changes, family migration continues to carry disproportionately negative effects for women, impacting in negative ways on their professional progression, their ability to achieve an effective balance between work and family, and on their sense of social and cultural isolation. Unsurprisingly, such pressures converge to place an unremitting strain on relationships, and the authors identify a clear correlation between the number of moves a couple undertakes and the likelihood of dissolution.

Ruth Lamont's chapter complements this analysis with a detailed review of the legal framework governing one of the more distressing features of international relationship breakdown; that of cross-border parental child abduction. Locating the discussion within the specific context of domestic violence, her analysis reflects the limitations of EU and private international law to effectively accommodate the needs of mothers who abduct their children out of genuine fear for their own safety and the safety of their children. She argues that the law is gendered in that it is premised on an outdated and inaccurate model of a male abductor. Moreover, the law's avowal to secure the immediate return of the child to their habitual residence reinforces abusers' control over women since a decision to return the child will inevitably necessitate the return of the mother thereby exposing her to the threat of further abuse. Lamont's discussion also points to the contradictions in the law; in seeking to separate out and attend to the best interests of children, the needs and interests of women may be sidelined, and the practical and emotional interdependency that exists between mother and child disregarded.

Dianne Scullion's chapter shifts the focus onto child trafficking, exploring the motivations behind trafficking for the purposes of child domestic labour and the consequences for children. Specifically, the author highlights the gendered nature of this process, in that it affects predominantly girls and reflects and reinforces female stereotypes in the domestic sphere. Particular consideration is given to the role of the family – and particularly of mothers – in facilitating child trafficking, both as 'senders' and 'recipients' of child domestic labour. While a range of legal instruments have been enacted to address this issue at international, European and national level, this chapter illustrates the limitations of the law in regulating forms of trafficking that are perpetrated by private individuals operating within closed informal networks. The analysis also highlights the law's tendency to categorize trafficked children into a fixed homogenous 'victim' category while failing to acknowledge the distinct needs and experiences of children within that group depending on the type of trafficking they endure, and the gender variables at play.

In the first chapter of Part II (chapter 4), Elizabeth Oliver reflects on the employment experiences of women engaged in the science and technology sector, an area of development prioritized by the EU in its quest to develop the world's leading knowledge-based economy. This seemingly narrow frame of analysis exposes some of the challenges facing highly skilled women more generally. In particular, her discussion points to the expectations placed on such women to gain international experience in order to progress in their careers. Added to this, however, are the pressures generated by the increasingly widespread use of fixed-term contracts in the UK which enhance the allure of migration to more permanent positions abroad. This 'mobility imperative', Oliver argues, presents particular challenges to those with children, since migration often demands significant social, economic and cultural upheaval for the whole family, or, if they migrate alone, long periods of absence from children and partners.

Parvati Raghuram's chapter continues in a similar vein, this time focusing on the impact of highly skilled migration on the sending regions. In an endeavour to offer a gendered perspective of 'brain drain'– a phenomenon typically represented as a male-dominated practice – Raghuram's analysis seeks to identify the presence of highly skilled women in brain drain trends. In the process, she teases out the distinctive experiences of such women within the migrant and non-migrant population and how they diverge in response to cultural, ethnic and class variables. This chapter also touches upon the need to adopt a multi-levelled perspective to fully appreciate the many factors that control and influence migration. While regulation at the national and international level remains critical, more subtle forces at the sub-national, professional and personal levels are also highly influential. By way of illustration, Raghuram asserts that changes in patterns of female mobility among the highly skilled have yet to be reflected in administrative and professional structures that facilitate brain drain migration; professional accreditation bodies, administrative agencies, funding councils and academic boards are exposed as relentlessly hierarchical and patriarchal and yet they exert a significant influence over the role of and opportunities available to women within both the sending and receiving countries.

Chapter 6 by Samantha Currie offers a valuable insight into the impact of EU enlargement on women's migration and employment status. She argues that the accession of the Central and Eastern European states – and the proposed opportunities for migrants implied by this process – are undermined by the residence and employment restrictions imposed at national level. Such restrictions, rather than enhancing the social and professional ascendance of migrants, can serve to lock them into irregular, poorly paid and highly insecure jobs. Drawing on EU and national data, as well as a series of in-depth interviews conducted with Polish migrants in the UK following the 2004 accession, the discussion reveals a significant incongruity between the high qualifications and skills levels of migrants and the employment they undertake on arrival in the UK. Currie argues that this 'downward occupational mobility' affects new EU migrant women particularly acutely. She attributes this to both cultural and systemic factors, which reinforce and perpetuate female stereotypes and which remain impervious to legal regulation.

Chapter 7 by Strozza, Paterno, Bernardi and Gabrielli provides a detailed insight into the geographical and sectoral positioning of migrants in the Italian labour market. The authors draw upon two complementary statistical data-sets (the Italian Labour Force Survey and a survey conducted by the Fondazione ISMU, an independent migration organization). The discussion highlights how region-specific labour market demands impact on both the ability of migrants to access work and the type of work (in terms of sector and immigration status) they can access. The authors observe that migrant women often face greater disadvantage than migrant men in terms of their employment opportunities, with female migrants often finding work in more precarious and irregular sectors of employment. The use of quantitative analysis in this chapter sits nicely alongside the qualitative and legal approaches embodied in other chapters.

Moving on to Part III, chapter 8 by Heli Askola explores the scope and effectiveness of the law in addressing the global problem of trafficking in women. Legally binding EU measures, the so-called UN Trafficking Protocol and a 2005 Council of Europe Convention, together make up an impressive and far-reaching cocktail of legal measures which support a three-stranded approach to trafficking: prosecution of traffickers, protection of victims, and prevention. Taking us on a historical journey through the development of this framework, Askola questions whether the current approach (with its emphasis on criminalization and migration control) is truly equipped to address the reality of trafficked women's needs and experiences. By the same token, she challenges the appropriateness and effectiveness of an exclusively 'victim'-led approach to trafficking which makes presumptions about and, in many respects, serves to augment women's vulnerability. These limitations, it is argued, stem from the fact that the regulatory framework surrounding trafficking has become a repository for a multitude of political, economic and human rights issues. The end product is a vague, elective and somewhat dysfunctional framework that achieves little in the way of actually promoting the welfare of women.

Chapter 9 by Helen Toner focuses on the treatment of foreign national prisoners, considering, in particular, the gender implications of foreign incarceration. She examines, on the one hand, the family status of men who are in custody or facing deportation proceedings following a conviction for a criminal offence. Many seek to establish a right to remain in the host state on the grounds that their family members are resident there and the European Court of Human Rights has frequently rejected such claims where it is deemed reasonable for the family to relocate with the offender to their country of origin. Toner argues that such an approach is based on gendered assumptions as to the patriarchal dynamics of family life which automatically presume that the wife will willingly abandon any connections she might have in the host state in pursuit of her partner.

Toner's analysis then shifts to foreign nationals who are imprisoned in the UK and compares the treatment and experiences of men with that of female foreign detainees. The former, she points out, are portrayed as violent, sexually deviant and predatory, such that deportation is the only safe and responsible option. The latter, on the other hand, face a raft of different challenges which relate less to their status as foreigner prisoners, and more to their status as mothers and carers, separated involuntarily from their children. This issue is exacerbated in a migration context, where detention in a foreign prison makes contact with family all the more difficult.

Chapter 10 by Gabriella Lazaridis explores the notion of boundaries – social, symbolic and institutional – within the context of Albanian migration to Greece over the last two decades. In doing so, the discussion distinguishes between the (favourable) treatment of ethnic Greek Albanians, on the one hand, and the (unfavourable) stance the Greek government has taken towards 'other' Albanians, on the other hand. Lazaridis integrates into the discussion extracts from a series of qualitative interviews carried out in Athens with migrants (both Albanians and ethnic-Greek Albanians) as well as with civil society actors, state agencies and other key informants. It begins with an analysis of national immigration policies in Greece since the early 1990s. In tracing the subtle changes in emphasis that have occurred in the policy framework over time, Lazaridis explores the malleable boundary between 'legal' and 'illegal' status. She highlights how regularization does not always result in any actual transition from informality to formality and argues that migrant women are particularly likely to remain excluded from the regular economy due to the specific (often hidden) types of work many of them carry out. The chapter moves on to consider how xenophobia and racism have influenced the experiences of migrants and, in line with the general approach of the chapter, draws out the specific implications of racialized boundaries for men and women respectively. Lazaridis also draws attention to the way in which these newcomers ultimately have a broader impact on the host national identity as a whole by, over time, crossing the divide between 'us' and 'others'.

The final substantive chapter by Catherine Sherlock examines gender, family unity and migration. It develops some of the themes highlighted by Lazaridis; how gender and nationality can both act as exclusionary forces, and how migrant women are at particular risk of being rendered 'invisible' in the process of migration. This contribution uses a human rights framework to explore family unity within the context of migration focusing on those who have been granted refugee status in Ireland. Central to Sherlock's analysis is the manner in which international human rights documents and the European Court of Human Rights conceptualize family unity and the resulting gender implications. She demonstrates, through her evaluation of national policies, particular problems faced by migrant women when exercising family choices at various stages of the migration process. A particularly compelling argument put forward relates to the perception of women as more resource intensive than men in terms of the demands they place on social and welfare systems. The perceived greater 'burden' imposed by women migrants shapes the way in which host countries select family members for entry, limiting, in some cases, opportunities for family reunification.

References

Anderson, B. (2000), *Doing the Dirty Work? The Global Politics of Domestic Labour* (London: Zed Books).

Ackers, L. (1998), *Shifting Spaces: Women, Citizenship and Migration within the European Union* (Bristol: The Policy Press).

Boyle, P. and Halfacree, K. (1999), *Migration and Gender in the Developed World* (London: Routledge).

EUROSTAT Regional Yearbook 2008, Statistical Office of the European Communities.

Kofamn, E., Phizacklea, A., Raghuram, P, Sales, R. (2000), *Gender and International Migration in Europe: Employment, Welfare and Politics* (New York: Routledge).

Willis, K. and Yeoh (eds) (2000), *Gender and Migration* (Cheltenham: Edward Elgar).

PART 1

Gender, Migration and Managing Family Life

Chapter 1
The Effect of Family Migration on Union Dissolution in Britain

Paul J. Boyle, Thomas J. Cooke, Vernon Gayle and Clara H. Mulder

The negative influence of 'family migration'[1] on women has been well documented. Beginning in the 1970s, with work influenced by neoclassical economic perspectives, it was shown that women are less likely to be employed, earn lower wages and work shorter hours than otherwise equivalent women following long distance, intra-national moves with the family (Sandell 1977; Mincer 1978; Spitze 1984; Morrison and Lichter 1988). Explanations for this were derived from human capital theory, with the expectation that families move to improve *overall* household circumstances. Although a gender-neutral theory it was found consistently that women's careers were less likely to benefit from such mobility while men tended to gain, with the expectation that such gains would offset the losses made by women in the medium- or even short-term. Hence, women were commonly referred to as 'tied migrants' or 'trailing spouses' in this literature.

In the 1990s and 2000s researchers have returned to this topic to explore whether, some decades later, women continue to 'suffer' from family migration. Given that women are now more likely to have higher qualifications, to be working, and to have career-focused jobs, it raises the question of whether they remain less likely to benefit from family moves. Perhaps surprisingly, the overwhelming consensus in the more recent literature is that women's labour market position continues to suffer from family migration and this finding is consistent in a range of national contexts including the UK, the US and the Netherlands (Smits 1999; Boyle, Cooke et al. 2001). As a consequence, many have moved beyond relatively crude human capital approaches arguing for a more nuanced approach which recognizes the influence of gender roles and family resources (e.g. Shihadeh 1991; Bielby and Bielby 1992; Halfacree 1995; Jurges 1998; Bailey and Boyle 2004; Jurges 2006; Cooke 2008; Cooke 2009). For example, Boyle, Cooke et al. (1999) showed that women are more likely to be unemployed or economically inactive following long-distance family migration even in those cases when the women had a higher status occupation than their partner and these results do not appear to be explained by decisions related to child-bearing (Cooke 2001; Boyle, Cooke et al. 2003).

---

1 Defined here as the geographical movement of couples with or without children within nations.

There has also been a growing recognition that longitudinal methods are required to tease out the complex relationship between life course events, mobility, and labour market outcomes. Panel data analysis comparing the UK and the US shows that the effects of moving as a couple on women's wages appears to be nearly as great as that of giving birth (Cooke, Boyle et al. 2009) and certainly has a long-term impact. Longitudinal analysis also shows that the negative effects of family migration on women's employment status are not purely a result of the selection of previously unemployed women into family migration (Boyle, Feng et al. 2009).

Overall, then, many of the results to date do not seem to accord with a simple gender-neutral human capital model and point to more deep-rooted gendered social structures as reflected in traditional gender roles. One consequence of such gender inequity within the family is that it could lead to tension between partners, raising the question of whether family migration may have an influence on couple separation. This was recognized as a possibility early on in the family migration literature. Mincer (1978) argued from an economic perspective that the 'utility' from remaining married can be affected by (im)mobility if individuals are forced into 'tied migration' or, alternatively, become 'tied stayers'. If the personal loss to moving, or staying, exceeds the gains from marriage, then dissolution may occur and he did indeed show that marriage breakdown was more common in the 12 months bracketing a long distance move than in years that involved no migration (Mincer 1978: 769). Unfortunately, that approach did not distinguish between moves that stimulated separation and moves which were caused by separation. Here we explore this question using longitudinal panel data which allow us to sequence moving and separation events to get closer to a causal explanation of the relationship between moving and union dissolution.

Of course, the gendered labour market consequences of long distance moving may be only part of the explanation why moving may cause couples to separate. We also need to recognize that family mobility is a stressful event in its own right even when the move is over a short distance and the underlying reason for the move was not employment-focused (McCollum 1990). For example buying a first home and the subsequent relocation can be an extremely stressful event in the life cycle of a family. This is hypothesized to be particularly true since the media and popular culture characterize these events as joyful and relatively stress-free. Most families, therefore, are not prepared for the widespread disruption to their everyday rituals and lives (Meyer 1987: 198).

Indeed, the difficulties associated with moving are even reflected in websites designed to help with the moving process. From the minute the 'For Sale' board goes up outside your house, to the minute you put the key in the lock of your new home – moving house can be a stressful business. When the British public was questioned about which life event they found most stressful, moving home came top. A total of 44 per cent found it most stressful compared to 15 per cent who identified changing jobs as their most stressful experience, according to the survey in 2000 carried out for the health and disability insurance company Unum Ltd (Inman 2008).

The pressures associated with such mobility have even influenced recent government policy, with the British Government introducing a new system of house purchase in England, of which major aim of which being to reduce the stress associated with the moving process (Office of the Deputy Prime Minister 2004). 'Sellers' packs' now have to be produced before a house is put on the market and include a survey, a draft contract and details of local authority searches. By making homeowners provide essential information up front, the government hopes to cut down on the time it takes to sell the property and reduce the likelihood of 'gazumping', where a buyer accepts a higher offer after already having agreed a price with an earlier buyer.

Of course, it is women who usually have to deal with much of the stress associated with moving as they are more likely to have to cope with the practicalities of the move (Weissman and Paykel 1972; Makowsky, Cook et al. 1988; Brett, Stroh et al. 1993). They are more likely to be relied upon to make the arrangements for the move, to organize child-centred activities such as child care, and to purchase the various new possessions which may be required following a change of house (Magdol 2002). As with employment-related moves, therefore, there may be gendered outcomes which mean that partners may have different views about the desirability of moving and its effects (Wiggins and Shehan 1994).

The stresses associated with longer distance moves may be greater than more local moves and an extensive literature documents the potential implications of international migration on mental health (Vega, Kolody et al. 1987; Bhugra 2004). Even longer distance moves within a country will likely disrupt local family and friend networks (Sluzki 1992; Magdol 2002) and there is evidence that children's behaviour may be effected negatively by such disruption, with migrant children apparently suffering higher school dropout rates (Astone and Mclanahan 1994), poorer educational attainment (Ingersall, Scamman et al. 1989), more delinquent behaviour (Adam and Chase-Lansdale 2002), and higher rates of substance abuse (DeWit 1988). Such outcomes for children will inevitably impact upon the parents and may contribute to problems in any relationship, and frequent long- or short-distance moving is only likely to exacerbate such potentially negative effects (DeWit 1988; Wiggins and Shehan 1994).

In addition, as Boyle, Kulu et al. (2008) argue, factors related to the origin and destination of the moves may also influence union dissolution. The destination may offer new opportunities that affect partners differently. Quite simply, one partner may be happier with the new location than the other (Flowerdew and Al-Hamad 2004) and moves which separate partners for a period of time during the settling in period may be particularly difficult (Green and Canny 2003). Movers may also meet new potential partners (South and Lloyd 1994; South, Trent et al. 2001; Trent and South 2003), or may be exposed to different cultural contexts where separation is more socially acceptable. From an international migration perspective, Hirsch (2003) suggested that the feelings of anonymity that Mexican women in the US felt helped them break free from some of the gender norms prevalent in their home communities with resulting higher rates of separation.

Moving from a particular origin may also influence dissolution. Some live in communities that discourage separation and leaving such areas may reduce the social pressure to remain partnered. Such influences may be especially relevant for women (Rosenthal 1985).

There have even been some aggregate, ecological studies which compare divorce rates with mobility rates. These early geographical studies in Canada and the US (Cannon and Gingles 1956; Fenelon 1971; Makabe 1980; Wilkinson, Reynolds et al. 1983; Trovato 1986; Breault and Kposowa 1987) argued that population turnover, driven by migration, in the 'frontier' west could be related to the higher divorce rates observed there (although see Weed 1974; Glenn and Supancic 1984). The instability of these communities was hypothesized to influence individualism and to weaken social control over the actions of individuals – hence divorce which may have been frowned upon in more stable communities became more common. However, such ecological studies were unable to determine whether population turnover influenced union dissolution because of changes in community-level cohesion, or because the migrants themselves were more susceptible to separation.

Various other factors influence union dissolution beyond migration and mobility, which we consider in this study. The 'independence hypothesis' suggests that women who are employed and are more able to support themselves may have less to gain from remaining married if the relationship is deteriorating (Becker, Landes et al. 1977), although the evidence for this hypothesis remains mixed (Mason and Jensen 1995; Oppenheimer 1997; Chan and Halpin 2003). Cohabiting relationships have been argued to involve less 'investment' and are therefore expected to be easier to terminate than married relationships. (Bennet, Blanc et al. 1988; Hoem and Hoem 1992; Diekmann and Engelhardt 1999; Kiernen 1999; Jenson and Clausen 2003). A number of authors suggest that the presence of dependent children discourages union dissolution (Morgan and Rindfuss 1985; Waite and Lillard 1991; Berrington and Diamond 1999; Manning 2004), although Chan and Halpin (2003) suggest that children may actually increase the risk of union dissolution in Britain (see also Boheim and Ermisch 1999). Higher educational status among women is also expected to reduce the likelihood of separation (Morgan and Rindfuss 1985; Hoem 1997). And, the geographical location has also been examined, with rural dwellers being less likely to separate than urban dwellers (Balakrishnan, Rao et al. 1987; Dieleman and Schouw 1989; Lillard, Brien et al. 1995; South, Crowder et al. 1998; South 2001).

Our analysis therefore contributes to both the family migration and the union dissolution literatures. In a previous study, we explored the effects of moving on union dissolution using retrospective event-history data from Austria (Boyle, Kulu et al. 2008). The results from this analysis suggested that couples who moved frequently had a significantly higher risk of union dissolution than similar otherwise comparable couples. Here, we extend this literature by exploring whether similar effects exist in Britain, taking advantage of longitudinal panel data from the British Household Panel Study (BHPS). We are particularly interested in the effect of within nation migration of families on union dissolution, while controlling for other influential factors. Our hypotheses can therefore be divided into two sets of factors.

The first set relate to factors identified in the literature that are expected to be associated with union dissolution:

1. Cohabiting couples are more likely to separate than married couples.
2. The length of partnership will be negatively correlated with separation.
3. Older women will be less likely to separate.
4. The presence of dependent children will reduce the likelihood of separation.
5. Those in urban areas are more likely to separate than those in rural areas.
6. Women with higher qualifications will be less likely to separate.
7. Women in work will be more likely to separate.

More specifically, though, we are interested in the role of family migration, and we identify three hypotheses:

8. Migrants are more likely to separate than non-migrants.
9. Frequent movers are more likely to separate than less frequent movers.
10. Long distance migrants are more likely to separate than short distance migrants or non-migrants.

Data and Methods

The longitudinal data used in this analysis were drawn from the British Household Panel Survey (BHPS). We extracted information from waves A-K (1991–2002) for all individuals aged 16 and above who were in a couple (married or cohabiting) at wave A, or who formed a couple in subsequent waves. Individuals were dropped if the partners separated, as we were interested in the effect of moving together, but individuals were reintroduced if new unions were formed. The resulting dataset included 4,619 couples and 31,821 couple/wave observations. We modelled the women in these couples, and captured in the data were 772 separations and 2,503 moves.

The dependent variable in the modelling was whether a couple separated (1) or not (0) and the independent control variables included: cohabitation (at t–1); the duration of the partnership; age; the presence of dependent children; whether the woman had higher qualifications; whether the woman was in work; and whether they lived in an urban or rural area (Table 1). Of particular interest was the effect of within country moves as couples on dissolution. The independent mover variables included: moves in the previous 1–3 years; the frequency of moves; and the distance of moves. All of these mover variables excluded moves in the year that a couple formed or separated.

Table 1.1 Variables

Variable	Values
Cohabitation one year ago	0 = married 1 = cohabiting
Duration of partnership	measured in years
Age	measured in years, for a random member of the couple
Presence of dependent children	0 = none 1 = dependent children present
Non-metropolitan	0 = metropolitan / urban 1 = rural
Higher qualifications	0 = none 1 = HND, HNC, teaching degree or above
Employment status	0 = not in work 1 = working
Number of moves	0 = none 1 = one 2 = two 3 = three or more
Number of long-distance moves	0 = none 1 = one 2 = two or more

The modelling approach was a random effects logit model which deals efficiently with clustering of individuals in panel data (the repeated observations at each wave cannot be treated as independent of one another, so a standard logit model is inappropriate) and the results are presented as odds ratios. First, we fitted univariate models for each explanatory variable and then two separate multivariate models which focused on the number of moves and the number of long-distance moves, controlling for other variables expected to influence separation.

Results

The results from the various models are displayed in Tables 1.2–1.4. Table 1.2 provides the univariate modelling results for each explanatory variable, showing that a number of these had a significant influence on separation. Cohabiting relationships were more likely to dissolve, older women were less likely to separate and the duration of the relationship was also negatively associated with separation. The presence of dependent children was positively and significantly related to separation for women, offering some support for Chan and Halpin's (2003) finding. Some variables were not significant. Women with higher qualifications were actually more likely to separate, but this was marginally insignificant. A similar result was found for women who were working compared to those who were not – working raised the odds of separation, but not significantly. And those

Table 1.2 Univariate modelling results

Variables	Odds ratios
Cohabitation one year ago	7.029*
Duration of partnership	0.926*
Age	0.920*
Presence of dependent children	1.502*
Non-metropolitan	0.956
Higher qualifications	1.371
In work	1.221
Number of moves (1)	1.508*
Number of moves (2)	2.187
Number of moves (3)	9.683*
Number of long distance moves (1+)	1.150

* Significant at 95%

living in rural areas were less likely to separate, but not significantly so. Moving (once or three or more times; two moves was marginally insignificant) appears to be positively related to dissolution, while one or more long distance move was not significant.

The results in Table 1.1 treat each variable independently. In Table 1.3, we explore the effect of moving on union dissolution, controlling for the other explanatory variables in a multivariate model. Cohabiting relationships remained significantly more likely to end, with nearly three times the odds of married couples. Relationships that were longer or involved older women were significantly less likely to fail. Note that, controlling for these other variables, the presence of dependent children reduced the odds of a relationship ending, although this variable was no longer significant; controlling for other factors, our results do not support those of Chan and Halpin (2003). Living in rural areas, having higher qualifications or being in work had no significant effect on dissolution. Controlling for these other variables, we find that moving three or more times remained significantly associated with union dissolution with almost seven times the odds of non-movers. In Table 1.4, we explore the effect of moving a long distance on union dissolution, controlling for the other explanatory variables. This suggests that long distance moves do not have an influence on union dissolution, once other factors have been controlled.

Table 1.3 Multivariate modelling results: number of moves

Variables	Odds ratios
Cohabitation one year ago	2.800*
Duration of partnership	0.970*
Age	0.950*
Presence of dependent children	0.810
Non-metropolitan	0.838
Higher qualifications	0.796
In work	1.013
Number of moves (1)	0.790
Number of moves (2)	0.911
Number of moves (3)	6.893*

* Significant at 95%

Table 1.4 Multivariate modelling results: long-distance moves

Variables	Odds ratios
Cohabitation one year ago	2.755*
Duration of partnership	0.969*
Age	0.951*
Presence of dependent children	0.754
Non-metropolitan	0.767
Higher qualifications	0.873
In work	0.856
Number of long distance moves (1+)	1.029

* Significant at 95%

Discussion

Few studies have considered the relationship between residential mobility and union dissolution. Mincer (1978) raised the possibility of such a relationship some time ago, although this was not tested rigorously. Since then various dimensions of the family/work nexus have changed as women's roles in the labour market and at home have been refined, and we would expect these changes to influence migration decisions and patterns. As women's roles in the labour market have strengthened we have seen a significant rise in dual career households, many of whom struggle to accommodate two journeys to work alongside other family commitments (Green 1997). In these scenarios, neither partner is assumed to be 'tied' to the other's work. For such couples it can become impractical to move often as finding suitable opportunities for both partners may be difficult, hence reducing the number of couples who are moving on behalf of one partner more than the other. Indeed, it is increasingly likely (although still less common) that the woman will have a more prestigious and financially rewarding job than her partner and we might therefore expect more households to move on behalf of the woman's, rather than the man's, job; the trailing spouse could be a man. In fact, this seems to remain a relatively uncommon practice even when the female partner has a higher-ranking occupation than the male partner (Boyle, Cooke et al. 1999). And, in some areas of work, where once contracted moves within the organization were a prerequisite for career progression, the expectation that families will move frequently has diminished (Brett et al. 1993; Boyle, Halfacree et al. 1998; Green and Canny 2003).

Overall, then, there are good reasons to suppose that women's roles have changed enough so that they are less likely to be left out of the migration decisions of households. Unfortunately, our previous studies continue to demonstrate that women's employment, wages and hours of work do still suffer from family migration. As a result, we aimed to explore whether family migration could also impact on relationship dissolution.

The first comprehensive study that linked family migration and union dissolution considered this relationship using event history analysis of retrospective data collected in Austria as part of the Family and Fertility Surveys (Boyle, Kulu et al. 2008). The results confirmed that moving twice or more had a significant effect on separation rates. A follow-up study using data from Russia (Muszynska and Kulu 2007) broadly confirmed these results.

Here, we extend this literature by focusing on the British context, using data drawn from the BHPS. These panel data allow us to identify mobility histories within couples and relate these to subsequent separations. We explored a series of hypotheses, some of which were supported. To summarize, in the univariate analysis we did indeed find that cohabiting couples were more likely to separate than married couples; those in longer partnerships were less likely to separate; older women were less likely to separate; those living in rural areas were less likely to separate; and working women were more likely to separate. On the other hand, some variables were not in the expected direction: the presence of dependent children appeared to increase the risk of separation and women with higher qualifications appeared to be more likely to separate. In multivariate analyses, though, some of these variables retained their significance, while others did not. Cohabiting couples continued to be more likely to separate, while those in longer relationships and older women were less likely to separate. Having dependent children, living in rural areas, being highly qualified and being in work all became insignificant.

Of most interest in this study were the variables relating to migration. In univariate models we found that the number of moves was positively and significantly related to union dissolution, although only those who moved three or more times had significantly raised odds of separation in the multivariate analysis. On the other hand, we found no evidence that long distance moves were associated with separation, although the small number of such moves in our dataset may have influenced this result.

Overall, our results are consistent with the small number of studies that have examined this question previously in different countries (Muszynska and Kulu 2007; Boyle, Kulu et al. 2008) and they have implications for both the family migration and the union dissolution literatures. We speculated that various processes may underlie the relationship between mobility and separation, arguing particularly that the gendered nature of migration may have a strong influence on relationship deterioration. Moving frequently, even over short distances can be stressful and many argue that women bear much of the burden of such moves. Not only are employment-related moves more likely to be to support the man's job, but even shorter distance residentially motivated moves are likely to impinge on women as they are more likely to be involved in arranging the move, acquiring new household items and organizing child care and other child-centred activities (Magdol 2002). Decisions to move frequently may indicate that the couple is dissatisfied with their circumstances generally, while for others moves may be forced, perhaps because of difficult financial circumstances which could themselves contribute to union instability. Certainly, our results have implications for companies who expect their employees to move frequently during their careers.

There are, of course, limitations to this study as it is not possible with these data to test which of these various explanations may be most pertinent. We have not been able to examine the reasons for couple dissolution, nor who led the decision to separate. This would appear to be an interesting question which could be explored using qualitative methods. Even so, this analysis contributes to a small but consistent literature which shows that family migration does appear to be associated with union dissolution, even today when women's roles have become an increasingly important aspect of family decision-making.

Acknowledgements

Funding to support this collaboration was provided by the *British Academy* and the *Netherlands Organisation for Scientific Research (NWO).*

References

Adam, E.K. and Chase-Lansdale, P.L. (2002), 'Home Sweet Home(s): Parental Separations, Residential Moves, and Adjustment Problems in Low-Income Adolescent Girls', *Developmental Psychology* 38: 792–805.

Astone, N.M. and Mclanahan, S.S. (1994), 'Family Structure, Residential Mobility, and School Drop Out: A Research Note' *Demography* 31: 575–84.

Bailey, A. and Boyle, P.J. (2004), 'Untying and Retying Family Migration in the New Europe', *Journal of Ethnic and Migration Studies* 30: 229–41.

Balakrishnan, T.R., Rao, K.V. Lapierre-Adamcyk, E. and Krotki, K.J. (1987), 'A Hazard Model Analysis of the Covariates of Marriage Dissolution in Canada' *Demography* 24: 395–406.

Becker, G.S., Landes, E.M. and Michael, R.T. (1977), 'An Economic Analysis of Marital Instability', *Journal of Political Economy* 85: 1141–87.

Bennet, N., Blanc, A. and Bloom, D.E. (1988), 'Commitment and the Modern Union: Assessing the Link between Premarital Cohabitation and Subsequent Marital Stability', *American Sociological Review* 53: 127–38.

Berrington, A. and Diamond, I. (1999), 'Marital Dissolution among the 1958 British Birth Cohort: The Role of Cohabitation', *Population Studies* 53: 19–38.

Bhugra, D. (2004), 'Migration and Mental Health', *Acta Psychiatrica Scandinavica* 109: 243–58.

Bielby, W.T. and Bielby, D. (1992), 'I Will Follow Him: Family Ties, Gender-Role Beliefs, and Reluctance to Relocate for a Better Job', *American Journal of Sociology* 97: 1241–67.

Boheim, R. and Ermisch, J. (1999), *Breaking Up: Financial Surprises and Partnership Dissolution.* ISER Working Papers. (Colchester: University of Essex).

Boyle, P.J., Cooke, T.J., Halfacree, K. and Smith, D. (2003), 'The Effect of Long-Distance Family Migration and Motherhood on Partnered Women's Labour-Market Activity Rates in Great Britain and the USA', *Environment and Planning A* 35: 2097–114.

– (2001), 'A Cross-National Comparison of the Impact of Family Migration on Women's Employment Status', *Demography* 38: 201–13.

– (1999), 'Gender Inequality in Employment Status Following Family Migration in GB and the US: The Effect of Relative Occupational Status', *International Journal of Sociology and Social Policy* 19: 115–33.

Boyle, P.J., Feng, Z. and Gayle, V. (2009), 'A New Look at Family Migration and Women's Employment Status', *Journal of Marriage and the Family,* 71: 417–431.

Boyle P.J., Halfacree KH and Robinson, V. (1998), *Exploring Contemporary Migration*. (London: Longman).

Boyle, P.J., Kulu, H., Cooke, T.J., Gayle, V. and Mulder, C. (2008), 'Moving and Union Dissolution', *Demography* 45: 209–22.

Breault, K.D. and Kposowa, A.J. (1987), 'Explaining Divorce Rates in the United States: A Study of 3,111 Counties, 1980', *Journal of Marriage and the Family* 36: 549–58.

Brett, J.M., Stroh, L.K. and Reilly, A.H. (1993), 'Pulling up Roots in the 1990s: Who's Willing to Relocate?', *Journal of Organizational Behavior* 14: 49–60.

Cannon, K.L. and Gingles, R. (1956), 'Social Factors Related to Divorce Rates for Urban Counties in Nebraska', *Rural Sociology* 21: 34–40.

Chan, T.W. and Halpin, B. (2003), 'Union Dissolution in the United Kingdom', *International Journal of Sociology* 32: 76–93.

Cooke, T.J. (2001), 'Trailing Wife' or 'Trailing Mother'? The Effect of Parental Status on the Relationship between Family Migration and the Labor-Market Participation of Married Women', *Environment and Planning A,* 33: 419–30.

Cooke, T.J. (2008), 'Gender Role Beliefs and Family Migration', *Population, Space and Place,*14: 163–75.

Cooke, T.J. (2009), 'Migration in a Family Way' *Population Space and Place.*

Cooke, T.J., Boyle, P.J., Couch, K. and Feijten, P. (forthcoming), 'A Longitudinal Analysis of Family Migration and the Gender Gap in Earnings in the United States and Great Britain', *Demography,* 46: 147–167.

DeWit, D.J. (1988), 'Frequent Childhood Geographic Relocation: Its Impact on Drug Use Initiation and the Development of Alcohol and Other Drug-Related Problems among Adolescents and Young Adults', *Addictive Behaviors* 23: 623–4.

Diekmann, A. and Engelhardt, H. (1999), 'The Social Inheritence of Divorce: Effect of Parent's Family Type in Postwar Germany', *American Sociological Review* 64: 783–93.

Dieleman, F.M. and Schouw, R.J. (1989), 'Divorce Mobility and Housing Demand', *European Journal of Population* 5: 235–52.

Fenelon, B. (1971), 'State Variation in United States Divorce Rates', *Journal of Marriage and the Family* 33: 321–7.

Flowerdew, R. and Al-Hamad, A. (2004), 'The Relationship between Marriage, Divorce and Migration in a British Data Set' *Journal of Ethnic and Migration Studies* 30: 339(13).

Glenn, N.D. and Supancic, M. (1984), 'The Social and Demographic Correlates of Divorce and Separation in the United States: An Update and Reconsideration', *Journal of Marriage and the Family* 46: 905–12.

Green, A.E. and Canny, A. (2003), *Geographic Mobility: Family Impacts*. (Bristol: Policy Press).

Green, A. (1997), 'A question of Compromise? Case Study Evidence on the Location and Mobility Strategies of Dual Career Households', *Regional Studies* 31: 641–57.

Halfacree, K.H. (1995), 'Household Migration and the Structuration of Patriarchy – Evidence from the USA', *Progress in Human Geography* 19: 159–82.

Hirsch, J.S. (2003), *A Courtship after Marriage: Sexuality and Love in Mexican Transnational Families*. (Berkeley: University of California Press).

Hoem, B. and Hoem, J.M. (1992), 'The Disruption of Marital and Non-Marital Unions'. In *Contemporary Sweden. Demographic Applications of Event History Analysis*. Trussel, J., Hankinson, R. and Tilton, J. (Oxford: Clarendon Press), 61–93.

Hoem, J.M. (1997), 'Education Gradients in Divorce Risks in Sweden in Recent Decades', *Population Studies* 51: 19–27.

Ingersall, G.M., Scamman, J.P. and Eckerling, W.D. (1989), 'Geographic Mobility and Student Achievement in an Urban Setting', *Educational Evaluation and Policy Analysis* 11: 143–9.

Inman, K. (2008), 'Channel 4's Stress Survival Guide To ... Housebuying', <http://www.channel4.com/health/microsites/0–9/4health/stress/cws_housebuying.html>, accessed 7 July 2008.

Jenson, A.M. and Clausen, S. (2003), 'Children and Family Dissolution in Norway – the Impact of Consensual Unions', *Childhood: A Global Journal of Child Research* 10: 65–81.

Jurges, H. (1998), 'Vocationally Motivated Migration Behavior in Double-Income Households. An Empirical Analysis Using Gsoep-Data', *Zeitschrift Fur Soziologie* 27: 358–77.

Jurges, H. (2006), 'Gender Ideology, Division of Housework, and the Geographic Mobility of Families', *Review of Economics of the Household* 4: 299–323.

Kiernen, K. (1999), 'Cohabitation in Western Europe', *Population Trends* 96: 25–32.

Lillard, L.A., Brien, M.J. and Waite, L.J. (1995), 'Premarital Cohabitation and Subsequent Marital Dissolution: A Matter of Self-Selection?' *Demography* 32: 437–57.

Magdol, L. (2002), 'Is Moving Gendered? The Effects of Residential Mobility on the Psychological Well-Being of Men and Women', *Sex Roles* 47: 553–60.

Makabe, T. (1980), 'Provincial Variations in Divorce Rates: A Canadian Case' *Journal of Marriage and the Family* 42: 171–6.

Makowsky, P.P., Cook, A.S., Berger, P.S. and Powell, J. (1988), 'Women's Perceived Stress and Well-Being Following Voluntary and Involuntary Relocation', *Lifestyles* 9: 111–22.

Manning, W.D. (2004), 'Children and the Stability of Cohabiting Couples', *Journal of Marriage and the Family* 66: 674–89.

Mason, K.O. and Jensen, A.M. (1995), 'Introduction'. In *Gender and Family Change in Industrialized Countries*. Mason, K.O. and Jenson, A.M. (Oxford: Clarendon Press), 1–14.

McCollum, A. (1990), *The Trauma of Moving: Psychological Issues for Women.* (Newbury Park, London and New Delhi: Sage Publications).
Meyer, C.J. (1987), 'Stress: There's No Place Like a First Home', *Family Relations* 36: 198–203.
Mincer, J. (1978), 'Family Migration Decisions', *The Journal of Political Economy* 86: 749–73.
Morgan, S.P. and Rindfuss, R.R. (1985), 'Marital Disruption: Structural and Temporal Dimensions', *American Journal of Sociology* 33: 1055–77.
Morrison, D.R. and Lichter, D.T. (1988), 'Family Migration and Female Employment: The Problem of Underemployment among Migrant Married Women', *Journal of Marriage and the Family* 50: 161–72.
Muszynska, M. and Kulu, H. (2007), 'Migration and Union Dissolution in a Changing Socio-Economic Context: The Case of Russia', *Demographic Research* 17: 803–20.
Office of the Deputy Prime Minister (2004), *Home Information Packs*. Wetherby, ODPM Publications.
Oppenheimer, V.K. (1997), 'Women's Employment and the Gain to Marriage: The Specialization and Training Model', *Annual Review of Sociology* 23: 431–53.
Rosenthal, C.J. (1985), 'Kinkeeping in the Familial Division of Labour', *Journal of Marriage and the Family* 47: 965–74.
Sandell, S.H. (1977), 'Women and the Economics of Family Migration', *The Review of Economics and Statistics* 59: 406–14.
Shihadeh, E.S. (1991), 'The Prevalence of Husband-Centered Migration: Employment Consequences for Married Mothers', *Journal of Marriage and the Family* 53: 432–44.
Sluzki, C.W. (1992), 'Disruption and Reconstruction of Networks Following Migration/Relocation', *Family Systems Medicine* 10: 359–63.
Smits, J. (1999), 'Family Migration and the Labour-Force Participation of Married Women in the Netherlands, 1977–96', *International Journal of Population Geography* 5: 133–50.
South, S.J. (2001), 'The Geographic Context of Divorce: Do Neighborhoods Matter?', *Journal of Marriage and the Family* 63: 755–66.
South, S.J., Crowder, K.D. and Trent, K. (1998), 'Children's Residential Mobility and Neigborhood Environment Following Parental Divorce and Remarriage', *Social Forces* 77: 667–93.
South, S.J. and Lloyd, K.M. (1994), 'Spousal Alternatives and Marital Dissolution American Sociological Review', *American Sociological Review* 60: 21–35.
South, S.J., Trent, K. and Shen, Y. (2001), 'Changing Partners: Toward a Macrostructural-Opportunity Theory of Marital Disruption', *Journal of Marriage and the Family* 63: 743–54.
Spitze, G. (1984), 'The Effects of Family Migration on Wives' Employment: How Long Does It Last?', *Social Science Quarterly* 65: 21–36.
Trent, K. and S.J. South (2003), 'Spousal Alternatives and Marital Relations', *Journal of Family Issues* 24: 787–810.

Trovato, F. (1986), 'The Relationship between Migration and the Provincial Divorce Rate in Canada, 1971 and 1978', *Journal of Marriage and the Family* 48: 207–16.

Vega, W.A., Kolody, B. and Ramon, V.J. (1987), 'Migration and Mental Health: An Empirical Test of Depression Risk Factors among Immigrant Mexican Women', *International Migration Review* 21: 512–30.

Waite, L.J. and Lillard, L.A. (1991), 'Children and Marital Disruption', *American Journal of Sociology* 96: 930–53.

Weed, J.A. (1974), 'Age at Marriage as a Factor in State Divorce Differentials', *Demography* 11: 361–75.

Weissman, M. and Paykel, E.S. (1972), 'Moving and Depression in Women', *Society* 9: 24–8.

Wiggins, F.M. and Shehan, C.L. (1994), 'Work and Well-Being in the Two-Person Career: Relocation Stress and Coping among Clergy Husbands and Wives', *Family Relations* 43: 196–205.

Wilkinson, K.P., Reynolds, R.R., Thompson, J.G. and Ostrech L.M. (1983), 'Divorce and Recent Net Migration in the Old West', *Journal of Marriage and the Family* 45: 437–45.

Chapter 2
International Child Abduction and Domestic Violence in the European Union

Ruth Lamont

The abduction of a child by their parent across an international border represents a significant challenge for legal regulation because it may cause harm to the welfare of the child concerned and permanently affect their relationship with one parent, potentially terminating it. The complexity of this situation is compounded when a woman abducts her child from the jurisdiction in an attempt to escape a relationship in which she was subjected to domestic violence. Domestic violence is a problem within all patriarchal cultures, including the Member States of the European Union (EU), encompassing physical abuse, but also sexual and verbal abuse, economic coercion and social isolation (Schneider 2000: 65). Feminists argue that this form of abuse is based on male dominance in the relationship, which is a microcosm of the social structures of gender, and, although men may also experience violence in intimate relationships, this does not have the same gendered social basis as violence against women (Schneider 2000: 72).

Worldwide, 68 per cent of unlawful abductions dealt with under the Hague Convention on the Civil Aspects of International Child Abduction 1980 (Hague Convention 1980) are carried out by women, although the proportions vary between States (Lowe and Horosova 2007: 67). Abduction may be motivated by a variety of factors but, in some cases, women are removing their children across international borders in an attempt to escape a violent relationship in their habitual residence (Weiner 2000). This form of international migration highlights the interface between law, international family formation and dissolution, and the effects of gender. The role of gender forms an increasingly important issue in analysing international migration (see Calavita 2006) and this contribution will examine its effects in the context of the legal regulation of international child abduction motivated by domestic violence in the EU.

The EU has recently legislated in relation to international child abduction in Regulation 2201/2003[1] which complements the Hague Convention 1980. This contribution will consider the difficulties of regulating migration motivated by

1 Council Regulation (EC) No. 2201/2003 concerning jurisdiction and the recognition and enforcement of judgments in matrimonial matters and matters of parental responsibility OJ [2003] L 338/1–29, 27 November 2003. This repealed and replaced Regulation (EC) No. 1347/2000 on jurisdiction and the recognition and enforcement of judgments in

domestic violence through an examination of these two instruments, and their operation in England and Wales, a jurisdiction which is regarded as successful in effectively implementing the Hague Convention 1980 (Lowe and Perry 1999: 142). The analysis of the child abduction provisions of Regulation 2201/2003 exposes the effect of EU action in regulating family dissolution across international borders on women and children exposed to domestic violence, and the capabilities of EU law to address this gender issue. The situation which leads women to abduct their child to escape domestic violence will be examined first. The international child abduction provisions under Regulation 2201/2003 and the relevant case law will then be examined to demonstrate that the role of gender in this phenomenon is largely ignored. However, although Regulation 2201/2003 does not explicitly address abductions motivated by domestic violence, it will be argued that its provisions do have the potential to assist women and children in this situation.

Regulating Migration following Family Dissolution in the EU: The Problem of International Child Abduction Caused by Domestic Violence

EU interest in the family has largely developed through its competence to regulate the free movement of workers and their families within the European space under Article 39 EC. The free movement of workers under Article 39 EC, and now the free movement of Union citizens under Article 18(1) EC, has required the EU to regulate the cross border movement of families as it was recognized that a worker's migration would be facilitated if they could be accompanied by their family.[2] This policy has encouraged both the movement and formation of families across EU borders, so the partners to the relationship are not in their home State, and/or may not be of the same nationality (Dethloff 2003: 37). However, as well as family formation, the free movement of workers within Europe has also resulted in the dissolution of international families.

It has been acknowledged that international migration is not just motivated by economic imperatives but that the nature of family relationships can play an important role in migration behaviour (Bailey and Boyle 2004: 236; Boyle et al., this collection). International family dissolution has implications for international migration of the former partners of a relationship. Migration to fulfil caring obligations or restricted movements following family dissolution due to

---

matrimonial matters and in matters of parental responsibility for children of both spouses, OJ [2000] L 160, 30 June 2000.

2 The regulation of the free movement of workers and their families was primarily addressed in Regulation 1612/68 on the freedom of movement for workers within the Community: Regulation (EEC) No. 1612/68, OJ Sp. Ed. 1968, No. L 257/2 475, 15 October 1968. Now the right of citizens of the Union to move is governed by Directive 2004/38/EC on the right of citizens of the Union and their family members to move and reside freely within the territory of the Member States OJ [2004] L229/35, 29 April 2004.

family commitments and children are increasingly common factors in migration decisions, particularly for women (Bailey and Boyle 2004: 237). International families are more likely to migrate on family dissolution and the majority of those moving with children after the dissolution of a relationship in the EU appear to be women (Morano-Foadi 2007: 17). Parental relocation following the dissolution of the relationship may also entail the relocation of any children to another State, particularly if the mother is migrating. Women remain the primary carers of children in society and they may desire support networks to help to provide such care. This may involve international migration if their family and support networks are in another State (Morano-Foadi 2007: 14). However, international migration may also represent an extreme attempt to escape a relationship with a violent partner (see Weiner 2000).

The regulation of the dissolution of the relationship between the parties and any resulting familial migration across international borders represents a significant challenge for private international family law. The difficulties may potentially be compounded if a woman migrates with her child from a host Member State back 'home' in an attempt to escape a violent relationship. In these circumstances women may attempt to create geographical distance between herself and her abuser because this has been shown to reduce the risks of violence (Fleury et al. 2000: 1378). Women may escape the violence abroad, sometimes returning to the State they have migrated from, returning 'home' to supportive family and social networks. Women who are abused by their partner outside the State of their nationality may experience social and cultural isolation, partly due to the abuse itself, but this is intensified if they are also distanced from family and community making it difficult for them to access either informal or formal support networks (Dobash and Dobash 1979: 167; Menjivar and Salcido 2002: 903).

For example, in *Re M (a child) (abduction: child's objections to return)*, [2007] 2 FLR 72 the mother had removed the child, M, from Serbia to England. The mother was British and her relationship with the Serbian father had broken down. She alleged that he had been violent towards her both while the relationship subsisted and, following their separation, when they met to facilitate his contact with M. She had sought protection from the violence but felt that the father had influence over the local police. The harassment of the mother was continuing and had included several incidents where cocaine had been planted in her car and the police informed, as the court found, by the father. M had witnessed incidents of violence inflicted by the father on the mother and described Serbia as 'scary'. Neither the mother nor M wished to remain in Serbia. M had expressed views both to the court and to the father which indicated her fear of living in Serbia and of the father. The father, however, still wished to have contact with M, to develop a relationship with her and be involved with her upbringing. There was evidence of the father's abuse of the mother, but not directly of M, and of his continuing harassment of the mother which was partly aimed at controlling and monitoring her care of the child.

In these circumstances, finding a legal 'solution' which satisfies and protects all of the parties' rights and interests represents a significant challenge. The mother and the child should be protected from further incidences of violence, yet the father apparently wishes to be able to develop a relationship with his child. In determining the outcome the child's interests should remain central and their relationship with their primary carer, in this case the mother, is particularly important as they are typically the most appropriate person to facilitate their development (Freeman 2001: 145).

Regulating Parental Child Abduction Across EU Borders

Relocation with a child may be lawful, but in some circumstances, the removal or retention of a child to or in a State other than their habitual residence constitutes an unlawful abduction. In these circumstances the Hague Convention 1980 is regarded as a successful international instrument providing a civil remedy whereby the child is quickly returned to their habitual residence following an abduction. This has recently been supplemented in the EU by Regulation 2201/2003 which now operates to return the child following an abduction across internal EU borders, as well as regulating jurisdiction and the recognition and enforcement of judgments in matrimonial and parental responsibility matters. It is part of the EU's legislative attempts to address the legal effects of international family dissolution, including international child abduction, which have been encouraged by the free movement of persons within Europe.

The structure of international child abduction law is complex because of the co-existence of two instruments regulating the same event. The Hague Convention 1980 is a global instrument with 80 signatories (Hague Conference) and all EU Member States had signed the Hague Convention 1980. The widespread success of the return remedy meant that the incorporation of rules relating to international child abduction for use in intra-EU abductions was politically controversial (McEleavy 2004: 509). It was clear from the proposals that some Member States and the Commission wanted to include provisions relating to child abduction to address this issue within the European Union framework (Commission 2001). However, not all Member States felt that EU intervention was necessary given that the Hague Convention 1980 was in force in all the Member States (Lowe 2003: 473).

Despite the controversy a compromise was reached and the relevant provisions are found in Articles 2(11), 10, 11, 60 and 62 of Regulation 2201/2003. Rather than creating a new EU remedy for international child abduction, Regulation 2201/2003 adopts the Hague Convention 1980 remedy of returning the child to their habitual residence as the basis of EU action. The Hague Convention 1980 remains in force between the Member States under Article 62, Regulation 2201/2003. However, according to Article 60, Regulation 2201/2003, the two instruments co-exist, so the operation of some of the Hague Convention 1980 rules are altered, or in some instances replaced by Regulation 2201/2003, which is intended to build on and complement the operation of the Hague Convention 1980 (see McEleavy 2005). Regulation 2201/2003 came into force on the 1 March 2005, so Hague Convention practice is still relevant and is likely to influence the interpretation of Regulation 2201/2003. To highlight how the Hague Convention 1980 and Regulation 2201/2003 operate alongside each other, the following section will consider the application and effects of the return remedy in cases where women have abducted their child in an attempt to escape domestic violence in the EU.

Under Article 3, Hague Convention 1980 a child is abducted when they have been wrongfully removed or retained in a State other than that of their habitual residence in breach of another's custody rights, arising either by court order, operation of law or through a legal agreement. Article 12, Hague Convention 1980 provides a civil remedy of returning the child to their habitual residence as fast as possible following an abduction. Any dispute over custody will then be decided in the State of the child's habitual residence, which is presumed to be the appropriate forum (*forum conveniens*) for this dispute (Schuz 1994: 783).

The return remedy is subject to only limited exceptions and return can be refused where the child has been in the State to which they were abducted for more than a year and they have settled in their new environment (Article 12(2), Hague Convention 1980). Where the individual with custody rights has consented or acquiesced in the removal or retention, return will also be refused (Article 13(a)). Furthermore, the return of the child can be refused where there is evidence that to do so would be exposing them to a grave risk of physical or psychological harm (Article 13(b)), and where a child of appropriate age and maturity objects to being returned (Article 13(2)). There is also provision for the return order to be refused where it would infringe the fundamental principles relating to the protection of human rights in the requested State (Article 20). These exceptions have been construed narrowly by the courts so the principle of return is not undermined and, even where an exception to returning the child has been established, the courts retain a discretion to return the child (see *Re M and another (children)* [2007] UKHL 55). It is presumed to be in the best interests of all children to be returned to their habitual residence; the individual child's welfare is therefore not the paramount consideration, even where an exception to return is engaged. The best interests of the child will always be weighed against the return policy of the Convention (*Re R (Child Abduction: Acquiescence)* [1995] 1 FLR 716, 730).

Regulation 2201/2003 largely preserves these rules and the return remedy and the exceptions to return established by the Hague Convention 1980 continue to operate under Regulation 2201/2003. However, Regulation 2201/2003 contains new provisions requiring the child to be heard in the return application if they are of an appropriate age and maturity (Article 11(2)) and sets a fixed six week deadline for the issuing of a decision on the return application (Article 11(3)).

The Hague Convention exceptions to the operation of the return remedy are retained in Regulation 2201/2003, but Articles 11(6) – (8) of Regulation 2201/2003, (hereafter 'the Article 11 mechanism'), implement a new procedure when the return of the child is refused under Article 13, Hague Convention 1980. Under the Article 11 mechanism, the courts of the child's habitual residence prior to the abduction can still consider the issue of the custody of the child following a refusal to issue a return order. The decision of this court on the issue of custody may or may not require the return of the child under Article 11(8). These changes are largely aimed at reinforcing the obligation to return the child following an unlawful retention or removal and strengthening the exceptional nature of refusals to return the child (Schulz 2004: 25).

Both Regulation 2201/2003 and the Hague Convention 1980 are instruments aimed at protecting rights of custody in relation to children, preventing the parents from unilaterally changing the custody provision in relation to the child by removing them to another jurisdiction and returning the child 'home'. Of course, there are many reasons for the removal of a child by their parent beyond domestic violence, including a desire to manipulate the 'left behind' parent on the breakdown of a relationship (Sagatun and Barrett 1990: 439). Neither instrument has abductions by the primary carer of a child 'in focus' nor is there explicit acknowledgement that abductions may be accomplished by women escaping a violent relationship (Freeman 2001: 144).

As observed above, for migrant women in particular, returning to their State of origin to escape violence may appear to be the most appropriate course of action (Weiner 2000: 626). However, there is also increasing evidence that domestic violence causes harm to children, even if they do not directly experience the violence themselves. Children may be incidentally exposed to the violence and, in addition, there is evidence of a co-occurrence between domestic violence and child abuse (Mullender and Morley 1994: 32; Appel and Holden 1998: 596). The continuing risk of violence to a child who associates with a violent father has been acknowledged in domestic law on child contact in *Re L (a child) (Contact: Domestic Violence)* [2000] 2 FLR 251.

Despite this evidence, Lowe and Horosova argue that even violence does not justify the unlawful removal of a child across a State border and the best court to protect both the child and their mother is the court of their habitual residence prior to the abduction (Lowe and Horosova 2007: 71). In these cases there is a tension between the mother's ability to migrate and escape a violent relationship, the child (and father's) right to a relationship with one another, and the desire to protect the jurisdiction of the courts of the child's habitual residence to determine longer term solutions for the family. Applications for the return of the child under the Hague Convention 1980 and Regulation 2201/2003 do not establish where the child's best interests lie in these circumstances, instead leaving that to the courts of the child's habitual residence. In England and Wales, the return principle under the Hague Convention 1980 has been strictly enforced by the courts, even where there are allegations of domestic violence against the parent requesting the return of the child to their habitual residence (Bruch 2004: 534). This approach is embodied by Thorpe L.J.'s comment in *Re W (a child) (abduction: conditions for return)* [2004] EWCA Civ 1366, [2005] 1 FLR 727, that: '… the robust construction and application of the Convention will serve to militate against the risk and dangers of the wrongful removal or retention of children'.

The operation of the return remedy in cases where domestic violence has been alleged against the individual requesting the return of the child has been questioned. If women leave a violent partner with their child and cross an international border and their partner has custody rights (See *Re V-B (Abduction: Custody Rights)* [1999] 2 FLR 192), within the EU, the child should be returned within six weeks unless one of the exceptions described above can be made out (Article 11(3)). If the return of the child is ordered, in most cases the child's mother will return with the child (Weiner 2000). These women and children are then returned to litigate custody in a post separation situation, where the abuser's violence and intimidation may continue and even increase (Fleury et al. 2000). Thus, Weiner (2000) argues that: 'The simplicity and the speed with which the Convention operates ... helps make the remedy of return a particularly powerful weapon for batterers.'

The operation of the return remedy effectively leaves the mother in the position of choosing between being separated from the child and safeguarding her personal safety. The return remedy can therefore provide a legal avenue through which violent men can continue to control women's actions, adding legal status to their desire to control the woman's movements (Weiner 2000: 630-631).

To remove the child legitimately women must therefore seek the consent of the other holder of custody rights or a court order allowing them to relocate outside the jurisdiction. An individual who holds a residence order has the right to remove the child without permission from the jurisdiction for up to one month (section 13(2), Children Act 1989). For longer periods of time in England and Wales, if a residence order is in force in relation to the child, consent to remove the child from the jurisdiction must be obtained, either in writing from the other individual holding parental responsibility or from the court (section 13(1)(a), Children Act 1989). The court will consider the request to relocate in the light of the welfare of the child (section 1(1), Children Act 1989). The Court of Appeal in *Payne v Payne,* [2001] 1 FLR 1052, gave guidance on approaching this question which arguably favours applications made by primary carer mothers as the child's welfare is closely associated with that of the mother (see Hayes 2006). This is in marked contrast to the situation following an abduction, where the individual child's welfare is not assessed and the risk of harm to the mother, and thus to the child, is not a factor in the issuing of a return order.

Women who are exposed to abuse have their choices constrained by a complex web of oppression which means that they are unlikely to seek court permission to relocate. Although leave to remove the child permanently from the jurisdiction is likely to be granted to primary carer mothers in England and Wales it is often unrealistic to expect them to pursue these legal avenues because of the fear of detection, and the time element involved in seeking permission to relocate. Since accessing injunctions against their abuser can be difficult because of financial problems, the abuser's threats and other family or cultural pressures (Humphreys and Thiara 2003: 203) gaining court leave to remove the child will also be difficult.

Despite these issues, the English courts are reluctant to refuse return on the basis that the exceptions to return, if widely used, would undermine the principal aim of the Hague Convention 1980 to return the child. The courts of the State of the child's habitual residence are felt to be the *forum conveniens* for the custody dispute and there is a desire to restore the *status quo* for the child prior to the abduction. The nature of the international obligations created by the Hague Convention 1980 and reinforced by Regulation 2201/2003 requires a high degree of mutual trust and reciprocity to operate effectively and the courts regard it as important to comply with these obligations. Finally, return applications are heard in summary proceedings making it very difficult to substantiate allegations of domestic violence occurring in another State. The commitment to ensuring the child's return has meant that, in most cases, even where serious violence has been alleged, children, and, by implication their mothers, are returned to their habitual residence.

The Hague Convention 1980 and Regulation 2201/2003 effectively act as a restriction on women's right to move and potentially endangers their personal safety if they choose to return with their child. Migration to escape violence without a child within the EU would be legitimate, yet if a child is also removed the risk of harm to the child posed by the abduction is usually regarded as greater than the risk of violence to the mother and, by proxy, to the child. However, in more extreme cases, the Hague Convention 1980 defences based on the child's objections to return (Article 13(2)) and the existence of a grave risk of harm to the child on return (Article 13(b)) have assumed greater importance under Regulation 2201/2003. The role of these defences in cases where abductions are alleged to be motivated by domestic violence in the context of Regulation 2201/2003 will be examined in the next section.

The Potential Effect of Regulation 2201/2003 on Abductions Motivated by Domestic Violence – Defences to the Remedy of Return

In cases under the Hague Convention 1980 women who have alleged that they have removed the child to another State in an attempt to escape domestic violence have attempted to utilize the defences under Article 13 to prevent the return of the child. These attempts have been largely unsuccessful in England and Wales because the courts are concerned that the use of the defences in such a way will lead to exploitation of the defences which will undermine the consistent use of the return remedy. Thorpe J. (as he then was) stated in *N v N (Abduction: Article 13 defence),* [1995] 1 FLR 107, 113, that: 'In this province it is obviously of primary importance that abducting parents should not be empowered to defeat the Convention manipulation or even by the expression of genuine fears and sincerely held feelings.'

Even a genuine fear of violence is not enough to prevent the return of the child on this interpretation of the Hague Convention 1980. However, the defences continue to be utilized in these circumstances and will be considered in the context of Regulation 2201/2003.

If the child objects to returning to their habitual residence following an abduction these objections can form the basis for a refusal to return (Article 13(2), Hague Convention 1980). In *Re M (a child) (abduction: child's objections to return),* [2007] 2 FLR 72, the child strongly objected to returning to Serbia following the father's violence towards the mother and his continued harassment of her. The child regarded Serbia as 'scary' and was fearful of her mother's arrest if they were returned. The Article 13(2) defence was therefore allowed.

The views of the child in cases where domestic violence is alleged is likely to continue to be relevant, particularly since Article 11(2), Regulation 2201/2003 now requires a child of appropriate age and maturity to be heard in the return application. It has been made clear that this is a requirement of Regulation 2201/2003 following *Re F (Abduction: Child's Wishes)*, [2007] 2 FLR 697. Although the child of appropriate age and maturity has the right to be heard, this does not mean that their views are determinative of the outcome of the return application since this is still a judgment for the court (see Lowe 2007 and Lamont 2008).

In *Klentzeris v Klentzeris,* [2007] EWCA Civ 533, decided under Regulation 2201/2003, the children's extreme reactions to the idea of return to Greece, where their mother had experienced domestic violence, were important to the decision to refuse their return. Unusually it was not the mother who had removed the children, but an elder sister who was followed by their mother. In this case, the younger child had threatened to kill himself if he was returned to Greece and was suffering from panic attacks. Both *Re M* and *Klenzeris v Klenzeris* are instances where the children concerned were significantly affected by the violence and were of a sufficient age and maturity to have their views taken into account.

Despite the availability of this exception, the child's expressed views and welfare will always be weighed against the Convention's policy of returning the child and the courts retain a discretion to order the return of the child despite their objections *(Re R (Child Abduction: Acquiescence)* [1995] 1 FLR 716). Although Article 11(2) provides an appropriate focus on hearing the child, this defence does not have the scope to acknowledge the effect of the violence on the mother and on her ability to care for the child in that environment. The mother's interests are effectively collapsed into those of the child and the risks to her only acknowledged to the extent to which the child perceives them, potentially placing an undue burden on the child and shifting the focus further away from the behaviour of the abuser.

Alternatively, Article 13(b), Hague Convention 1980 allows judges a discretion to refuse the return of the child where they will be exposed to a grave risk of physical or psychological harm on return. Article 13(b) was thought to be the basis of too many refusals to return the child so, under Article 11(4), Regulation 2201/2003, a court cannot refuse to return the child under Article 13(b), Hague

Convention 1980 if it established that there are adequate arrangements in place to protect the child after their return. The concerns about the abuse of Article 13(b) are not borne out by an examination of the operation of the defence which still only accounts for 3 per cent of all cases worldwide (Lowe and Horosova 2007: 84).

The Article 13(b) defence may be pleaded by women who have abducted their child, claiming that returning the child to a State where she has experienced domestic violence places the child at risk of harm. Following *Re C (Abduction: Grave Risk of Physical or Psychological Harm),* [1999] 2 FLR 478, the child will not be returned if the abduction was motivated by one parent's legitimate concerns about a family situation in the child's habitual residence which is harmful to the child's development. In practice, however, the risk of harm to a child associated with domestic violence, including the trauma associated with witnessing harm to the mother, is usually not sufficient for the Article 13(b) defence to succeed in the English courts (See *Re C (a child) (abduction: settlement)* [2006] EWHC 1229 (Fam)).

For example in *Re W (a child) (abduction: conditions for return),* [2005] 1 FLR 727 there was extensive evidence at first instance (*Re W (Abduction: Domestic Violence)* [2004] 2 FLR 499) that the father was violent towards the mother, who had unlawfully removed the child from South Africa to England. The alleged abuse included physical violence, threats with a firearm, controlling behaviour and demeaning sexual practices. There was also evidence of the father's attempts to influence witnesses and legal professionals. However, the Court of Appeal felt that it was not possible to conclude that the father was violent or posed a risk to the mother and child concerned. It was argued that there was no independent evidence of the father's violence as she had never obtained any injunctive orders in relation to the father.

The summary nature of return applications means that allegations of domestic violence are difficult to assess for reliability and truth and official interventions and court orders are independent evidence of abuse. However, reliance on this type of evidence displays a lack of insight into the effect of domestic violence on women and the availability of legal remedies. The private nature of domestic violence means that there is often no official intervention. In return applications, the lack of such evidence means that the focus remains firmly on the mother's actions in removing the child across an international border, rather than on the motivations for her doing so.

Article 11(4), Regulation 2201/2003 requires the court to establish that there are adequate arrangements in place to protect the child. The Practice Guide to Regulation 2201/2003 suggests that the assistance of the Central Authorities in the Member States will be required to establish what level of protection is available, (Commission 2003: 33), but a great deal of co-operation is needed between the Member States to provide enough information to allow for a properly informed decision by the court. The court must therefore be active in establishing whether there is protection in place, and assess whether the arrangements are adequate

(McEleavy 2005). Presumably this will require liaison between both the courts of the Member State to which the child was abducted and those in the State of the child's habitual residence to work effectively, otherwise the court assessing the adequacy of the protection of the child may be seen to be judging the systems and practices of another Member State (McEleavy 2005: 26).

There is no definition of what will constitute 'adequate arrangements' under Article 11(4). The Practice Guide (Commission 2003: 32) states that: 'it must be established that the authorities in the Member State of origin have taken concrete measures to protect the child ...'.

The Practice Guide gives little guidance on what standard of protection is to be reached by the arrangements and who is to put them in place. In addition, both Article 11(4) and the Practice Guide focus on measures to protect the child without mentioning the possibility that their parent may also require some form of protection. Although in practice it is likely that arrangements to protect the child would also encompass a degree of protection to their primary carer, the connection between the risk to the child and the risk to the mother posed by an abuser is not explicitly acknowledged.

Article 11(4), Regulation 2201/2003 only requires the arrangements made to be 'adequate'. Adequate arrangements need not be effective arrangements. Even if an injunction aimed at protecting a woman and her child against further violence has been obtained in the State of the child's habitual residence, this may not be effective to secure the protection of a women and her child when they return (McCann 1985: 88). It must also be noted that a court may be unwilling to suggest that the courts of another Member State cannot adequately protect children from harm, returning a child for fear of offending another Member State, despite a lack of effective mechanisms being in place.

Under the Hague Convention 1980 the courts in England and Wales have largely assumed that women and children can be effectively protected from continuing violence in the State of their habitual residence. For example in *Re H (Children: Abduction),* [2003] 2 FLR 141, where the children were removed by their mother from Belgium to England in an attempt to escape a violent father, it was stated by the President of the Family Division, Dame Butler-Sloss, that: 'I do not consider that we are entitled in England to assume that either the father is an uncontrollable risk or that the Belgian authorities would be unable to manage the problem.'

This means that the Article 13(b) exception to the return of the child, which is reinforced by Article 11(4), Regulation 2201/2003 will not be established as the assumption of effective protection on return negates any associated risks, arguably placing unrealistic faith in the legal system to protect those who have suffered from violence at the hands of a partner (Kaye 1999: 198).

Under the Hague Convention 1980, the English courts, in the interests of comity, may instead return the child with undertakings on the part of the applicant parent to try and ensure the safety and viability of the parent and child on return. Undertakings are voluntary statements of intent that the individual seeking the return of the child gives to the court before the order for the return of the child is made. They are not enforceable in the State of the child's habitual residence and they do not form an official part of the Hague Convention 1980. As such the English courts have been criticized as departing from the scheme of the Convention as well as being naïve, as abusers are often capable of flouting legal orders (Bruch 2004: 541-544). Undertakings are particularly vulnerable to this as they depend on goodwill and are not enforceable outside of the jurisdiction. They are also not understood in civil law systems and are often broken, even where a mirror order has been obtained in the child's habitual residence (Freeman 2001). In a study conducted by Reunite, a child abduction charity, undertakings were given in twelve out of twenty one cases studied. 50 per cent of the undertakings concerned violence and were mirrored in five of the cases. The undertakings were broken in eight out of the 12 cases, and non-molestation undertakings were broken in all the instances in the study. It was also clear that undertakings were difficult to enforce and were not necessarily respected by the authorities in the child's habitual residence (Reunite 2003: 30-34).

Undertakings have not been explicitly incorporated into the operation of Regulation 2201/2003. However, Article 11(4) may encourage the continued use of undertakings with conditions for the return of the child, as these may be deemed to be 'adequate arrangements' to ensure the protection of the child on return. Reunite suggests that Regulation 2201/2003 may make conditions attached to return more effective within the European Union. They would have to take the form of enforceable conditions attached to return, which are 'more substantial than undertakings and appropriate inter-court co-operation' (Freeman 2006: 40). However, once back in the State of habitual residence, the problem of obtaining enforcement of a judgment arises, particularly if there are limited financial resources available. So in terms of Article 11(4), Regulation 2201/2003 the protection that these conditions provide may look adequate, but are unlikely to be effective, even if they are enforceable.

However, in cases of abduction due to domestic violence it is possible that the Article 11 mechanism may have unexpected effects. If the return of the child is refused, Article 11(7), Regulation 2201/2003 means that the custody dispute is likely to be conducted with the child and their mother in the State to which the child was unlawfully removed. There is no formal arrangement within Regulation 2201/2003 to facilitate this process, although there is other EU legislation that may be relevant in this context, for example Regulation (EC) No. 1206/2001 on the co-operation between the courts of the Member States in the taking of evidence in civil or commercial matters OJ [2001] L174, 27th June 2001. However, litigating from abroad is clearly advantageous for a woman who abducts a child because the risk of abuse from the woman's former partner is greatly reduced because of geographical distance (Fleury et al. 2000: 1377). Custody can be litigated from a position of safety in the State to which the child was abducted, although Regulation 2201/2003 is not explicit as to where the child will be during the hearing of a custody dispute under the Article 11 mechanism. In the English cases thus far, the child has remained in the State to which they were unlawfully removed during the hearings and this would appear to be the implication of the Regulation. (See *Re A (custody decision after Maltese non-return order)* [2007] 1 FCR 402; *Re A (a child) (custody)* [2007] EWHC 2016 (Fam)).

If the courts are aware that issues of custody will be litigated in the State of the child's habitual residence it is suggested that they may perhaps be more willing to refuse the return of the child under the Article 13 defences. The child's habitual residence is presumed to be the *forum conveniens* for the custody dispute (Schuz 1995: 780). The Hague Convention 1980 is trying to ensure that the child is returned to a familiar environment, their 'home', but if that environment is a place where the child's mother has been exposed to abuse this may not be appropriate. The new Article 11 mechanism under Regulation 2201/2003 would allow both of these considerations to be accommodated by allowing litigation in the appropriate forum but with the parties protected by geographical distance during the litigation process. This would require a less restrictive approach to the interpretation of the Article 13 defences than is currently in evidence in the English courts. This interpretation could now be regarded as in line with our international obligations under Regulation 2201/2003 as the jurisdiction of the courts of the child's habitual residence remains protected. In a substantive hearing there will be an opportunity to establish the credibility of the allegations and, if appropriate, the child may still be returned to their State of habitual residence prior to the abduction under Article 11(8), Regulation 2201/2003.

In *Re A (custody decision after Maltese non-return order)* [2007] 1 FCR 402 the return of the child from Malta was ordered by the English High Court despite the initial refusal to return the child. However, in *Re A (a child) (custody)* [2007] EWHC 2016 (Fam) the refusal to return the child from France by the French courts, in part because of the father's violence towards the mother, was confirmed by the custody decision in the English High Court. It has already been observed that in *Klentzeris v Klentzeris,* [2007] EWCA Civ 533, the Article 13(b) defence was, unusually, allowed to succeed. However, Thorpe L.J. made it clear in his judgment that the case 'fell into a most exceptional category' so, as yet, this approach has not been routinely adopted. However, the judgment of the House of Lords in *Re M (children: abduction)* [2007] UKHL 55, a Hague Convention 1980 case, suggests that establishing that a case is 'exceptional' is not necessary for the exceptions to the return of the child to be established under the Convention, an approach which has been adopted for cases under Regulation 2201/2003 in *Re F (children)(abduction)* [2008] EWHC 272 (Fam).

Following the reasoning in *Klentzeris v Klentzeris,* would require cases to be exceptional for the Article 13(b) defence to succeed and cases where domestic violence is alleged rarely do so. If allegations of domestic violence were regarded as posing a grave risk of harm to a child on return under Article 13(b), Hague Convention 1980, the Article 11 mechanism under Regulation 2201/2003 could provide a way of accounting for the refusal to return the child in the appropriate forum. This interpretation of the role of the Article 11 mechanism is perhaps not in accordance with its intended purpose within Regulation 2201/2003, but it may provide a new element of flexibility when dealing with the difficult issues associated with abductions caused by an attempt to escape a violent partner.

Conclusions

Migration with a child to escape domestic violence provides a particularly acute example of the relevance of gender to international migration and the difficulties of regulating such migration behaviour through law. This situation places the mother's desire to migrate and escape violence at odds with the child's right to a relationship with both parents, is potentially harmful to their welfare and infringes the jurisdiction of the courts of the child's habitual residence to hear decisions affecting the child. The operation of the return remedy under the Hague Convention 1980 in England and Wales has meant that mothers in such situations have returned with their child to their habitual residence, despite the potential risks. The cases under Regulation 2201/2003 may continue this approach, particularly since the Regulation was aimed at reinforcing the application of the return remedy in Europe. However, Article 11(4) Regulation 2201/2003 may help to ensure that courts take a more active role in establishing 'adequate protection' for children, and possibly also their mother, on their return to their habitual residence. In addition, the Article 11 mechanism may provide a new approach to interpreting the exceptions to return under Article 13, Hague Convention 1980. This could allow women and children to remain in the State to which the child was removed whilst custody is litigated, and the substance of the allegations of violence to be assessed, in the appropriate forum.

This analysis of the child abduction provisions of Regulation 2201/2003 demonstrates that the EU, when dealing with family dissolution and migration, is regulating a gendered phenomenon with significant implications for the women and children involved when they are attempting to escape a violent relationship. Acknowledging the role of the family in migration decisions includes consideration of issues such as domestic violence, and means that the gendered nature of family relations becomes an important factor in the law related to international migration. The EU's intervention in the legal regulation of cross-border family dissolution means that it will increasingly have to address the resulting issues of gender and migration. The interface between law, gender and family migration is complex and contested, but with a creative approach, Regulation 2201/2003 has the potential to resolve some of the difficulties where women abduct their children in an attempt to escape domestic violence.

Acknowledgment

I am grateful to Sue Nott for her invaluable assistance on earlier drafts. Any errors or omissions remain my own.

References

Appel, A. and Holden, G. (1998), 'The Co-Occurrence of Spouse and Physical Child Abuse: A Review and Re-Appraisal', *Journal of Family Psychology* 12:4, 578–99.

Bailey, A. and Boyle, P. (2004), 'Untying and Re-Tying Family Migration in the New Europe', *Journal of Ethnic and Migration Studies* 30:2, 229–41.

Boele-Woeki, K. (ed.) (2003), *Perspectives on the Unification and Harmonisation of Family Law in Europe.* (Antwerp: Intersentia).

Brophy, J. and Smart, C. (eds) (1985), *Women-in-Law: Explorations in Law, Family and Sexuality.* (London: Routledge & Kegan Paul).

Bruch, C. (2004), 'The Unmet Needs of Domestic Violence Victims and their Children in Hague Child Abduction Convention Cases', *Family Law Quarterly* 38:3, 529–46.

Calavita, K. (2006), 'Gender, Migration and Law: Crossing Borders and Bridging Disciplines', *International Migration Review* 40:1, 104–32.

Commission (2003), 'Practice Guide for the application of the new Brussels II Regulation (Council Regulation (EC) No 2201/2003 of 27 November 2003)'.

Commission (2001), 'Proposal for a Council Regulation on jurisdiction and the recognition and enforcement of judgments in matters of parental responsibility.' COM(2001) 505 final.

Dethloff, N. (2003), 'Arguments for the Unification and Harmonisation of Family Law in Europe', in Boele-Woeki, K. (ed.), *Perspectives on the Unification and Harmonisation of Family Law in Europe.* (Antwerp: Intersentia).

Dobash, R. and Dobash, R. (1979), *Violence Against Wives: A Case Against the Patriarchy.* (New York: Free Press).

Fleury, R. et al. (2000), 'When Ending the Relationship does not End the Violence', *Violence Against Women* 6:12, 1363–83.

Freeman, M. (1998), 'The Effects and Consequences of International Child Abduction', *Family Law Quarterly* 32:3, 603–23.

Freeman, M. (2001), 'Primary Carers and the Hague Abduction Convention', *International Family Law* September, 140–50.

Freeman, M. for Reunite (2006), 'International Child Abduction: The Effects' May 2006 <http://www.reunite.org/page.php?alias=research20>, accessed 13 November 2006.

Hague Conference on Private International Law 'Table of Contracting States' (2008), <http://www.hcch.net/index_en.php?act=conventions.status&cid=24>, accessed 15 May 2008.

Hayes, M. (2006), 'Relocation Cases: Is the Court of Appeal Applying the Correct Principles?', *Child and Family Law Quarterly* 18:3, 351–72.

Humphreys, C. and Thiara, R. (2003), 'Neither Justice nor Protection: Women's Experiences of Post-Separation Violence', *Journal of Social Welfare and Family Law* 25:3, 195–4.

Kaye, M. (1999), 'The Hague Convention and the Flight From Domestic Violence: How Women and Children are Being Returned by Coach and Four', *International Journal of Law, Policy and the Family* 13:2, 191–212.

Lamont, R. (2008), 'The EU: Protecting Children's Rights in Child Abduction', *International Family Law* June, 110–112.

Lowe, N. (2007), 'The Current Experiences and Difficulties of Applying Brussels II Revised', *International Family Law* December, 182–97.

Lowe, N. (2003), 'The Growing Influence of the European Union on International Family Law – A View From the Boundary', *Current Legal Problems* 56, 439–80.

Lowe, N. and Horosova, K. (2007), 'The Operation of the 1980 Hague Abduction Convention – A Global View', *Family Law Quarterly* 41:1, 59–103.

Lowe, N. and Perry, A. (1999), 'International Child Abduction: the English Experience', *International and Comparative Law Quarterly* 48:1, 127–55.

McCann, K. (1985), 'Battered Women and the Law: the Limits of the Legislation', in Brophy, J. and Smart, C. (eds) *Women-in-Law: Explorations in Law, Family and Sexuality.* (London: Routledge & Kegan Paul).

McEleavy, P. (2005), 'The New Child Abduction Regime in the European Union: Symbiotic Relationship or Forced Partnership?', *Journal of Private International Law* 1:1, 5–34.

McEleavy, P. (2004), 'Brussels II bis: Matrimonial Matters, Parental Responsibility, Child Abduction and Mutual Recognition', *International and Comparative Law Quarterly* 53:2, 503–12.

Menjívar, C. and Salcido, O. (2002), 'Immigrant Women and Domestic Violence: Common Experiences in Different Countries', *Gender and Society* 16:6, 898–920.

Morano-Foadi, S. (2007), 'Problems and Challenges in Researching Bi-National Migrant Families Within the European Union', *International Journal of Law, Policy and the Family* 21:1, 1–20.

Mullender, A. and Morley, R. (eds) (1994), *Children Living With Domestic Violence.* (London: Whiting & Birch).

– (1994), 'What do we know from Research?', in Mullender, A. and Morley, R. (eds).

Reunite (2003), 'The Outcomes for Children Returned Following Abduction', September 2003 <http://www.reunite.org/WEBSITEREPORT.doc> last accessed 17 July 2007.

Sagatun, I. and Barrett, L. (1990), 'Parental Child Abduction: The Law, Family Dynamics and Legal System Responses', *Journal of Criminal Justice* 18:4, 433–42.

Schneider, E. (2000), *Battered Women and Feminist Lawmaking.* (New Haven: Yale University Press).

Schulz, A. (2004), 'The New Brussels II Regulation and the Hague Conventions of 1980 and 1996', *International Family Law* March, 22–30.

Schuz, R. (1995), 'The Hague Child Abduction Convention: Family Law and Private International Law', *International and Comparative Law Quarterly* 44:4, 771–803.

Schuz, R. (1994), 'The Hague Child Abduction Convention: Family Law and Private International Law', *International and Comparative Law Quarterly* 44:4, 771–803.

Weiner, M. (2000), 'International Child Abduction and the Escape from Domestic Violence', *Fordham Law Review* 69:2, 593–706.

Worwood, A. (2005), 'International Relocation – the Debate', *Family Law* 35:8 621–7.

Chapter 3
Gender Perspectives on Child Trafficking: A Case Study of Child Domestic Workers

Dianne Scullion

Trafficking of children is a growing social phenomenon which affects children from countries throughout the world (ECPAT 2004:9). Often various forms of exploitation are involved, including sexual exploitation, drug trafficking, forced marriage and domestic work (ECPAT 2001: 22). There is also evidence of children being used for street crime or for work in restaurants (ECPAT 2004: 9-10) as well as for the purpose of cannabis cultivation and other forms of labour exploitation (CEOP 2007: 6). Traffickers use a variety of methods to control children including violence or threats of violence to the child and/or their family or debt bondage with inflated sums of money which are impossible to repay. There have also been reports of African children being controlled by threats of the use of voodoo with the child being told that their family would die unless they did as they were instructed, although the frequency of the use of this method of control is uncertain (ECPAT 2004: 9-10).

A multi-faceted legal and policy response is needed to acknowledge and tackle the various methods used by traffickers to traffic children into Europe. In the United Kingdom (UK), research by the children's rights organization, 'End Child Prostitution, Child Pornography and the Trafficking of Children for Sexual Purposes' (ECPAT 2001: 22), found that children enter the UK as unaccompanied minors claiming asylum. Alternatively they are accompanied by an adult claiming to be a relative and then subsequently disappear. Some children arrive by air whilst others are stowed away on ferries, in cars or lorries and arrive using fraudulent passports or on student visas as language students or on tourist visas (ECPAT 2001). Children are sometimes trafficked through a transit country before their arrival in the country of destination, whilst others travel directly from their country of origin (UN.GIFT 2008: 13).

When trafficking is discussed from a gender perspective the focus is often on trafficking of women for the purpose of prostitution or sexual exploitation (Anderson 2000). However, children from different countries throughout the world are trafficked for different forms of exploitation and the importance of the gender of these children will vary depending on the intended form of exploitation. UNICEF raised this issue in their report 'End Child Exploitation: Child labour today' which focused on children who are trafficked into the UK (UNICEF 2005). Children from Eastern Europe were often found to be trafficked for the purpose of begging on the streets or exploited within the sex industry. Chinese children (predominately boys) enter the UK illegally, fail to apply for asylum status and remain undiscovered within close-knit Chinese communities. These boys are subsequently subjected to forced labour in restaurants or factories (particularly the garment industry) and are often subjected to debt-bondage forcing them to remain with the traffickers. By contrast, the research found that West African children (usually girls)[1] are trafficked into a life of prostitution, benefit fraud or domestic slavery.

Private fostering is a common method used by parents to provide a 'better life' for their child. However, there is evidence that this process is being abused by traffickers to exploit children. The term 'private fostering' is used to describe a situation when a child up to 16 years of age (18 if disabled) is in the care of someone who is not his or her parent or relative for a period exceeding 28 days (Children Act 1989: s 66). Under English law, a relative is defined as grandparents, siblings, stepparents, aunts or uncles or other persons with parental responsibility (Children Act 1989: s 105(1)). It is estimated that there are between 15,000 and 20,000 children in private foster care in the UK, the majority being from West Africa (UNICEF 2005: 49-50).

Often trafficking of children is viewed in terms of the exploitation experienced by the child without always explicitly recognizing the gendered nature of this phenomenon. Trafficking for sexual exploitation of the child is the main exception, which is presumed to affect predominately females. The impact of gender is generally overlooked in the existing research and literature relating to child trafficking for the purposes of forced labour. In an attempt to address this vacuum, this chapter will focus on one particular form of forced labour, that of domestic work. The discussion will consider the legal status and experiences of girls who are sent from their home and country of origin, with their parent(s) consent and often with adults who are complete strangers, to undertake domestic work in a household within Europe. Specific consideration will be given to the role of the family – and particularly of parents – in facilitating child trafficking.

To set the context for the discussion, the chapter will begin by identifying the link between domestic work and child trafficking. This will include an examination of the cultural practice of private fostering arrangements used by parents and the subsequent abuse of this practice to force girls into domestic work. Migration for domestic work has been viewed through the lens of 'gender and women' and the aim is to illustrate that domestic work undertaken by children who have been trafficked is also gendered. Parallels will be drawn between gender theorizations of female migration in the context of paid domestic work and female children who are trafficked for this purpose.

Child domestic work will be discussed as part of the broader category of forced labour and an overview of the legal definition of trafficking in human beings will expose the law's limitations in addressing the complex gender dynamics that

1 References to 'girl' is used to describe a female child under the age of 18.

shape child trafficking. The chapter will conclude with a discussion of the short- and long-term consequences for female children who have been trafficked for domestic work.

Domestic Work and Trafficking

UNICEF have defined child domestic workers as 'Children under the age of 18 who work in other people's households, doing domestic chores, caring for children and running errands, among other tasks. [This includes mainly] live-in child domestics, that is children who work full-time in exchange for room, board, care and sometimes remuneration' (UNICEF 1999). The concern with child domestic work revolves around the 'relative lack of freedom, vulnerability to abuse, the relatively high numbers of very young children, lack of payment and lack of contact with family and friends' (Black 2002: 4-8). The International Labour Organization's International Standard Classification of Occupations (1990) defines domestic work under the category of 'domestic helper/cleaner' as including roles such as washing, ironing, cooking, and sweeping. However, as Anderson (2000:15) points out, this definition does not include childcare even though this is usually a key element of domestic work.

Domestic work in the context of child trafficking also falls under the broader description of forced labour which has been a concern of non-governmental organizations such as Anti-Slavery International as well as the International Labour Organization (ILO). The ILO Forced Labour Convention 1930 defines forced labour as 'all work or service which is exacted from any person under the menace of any penalty and for which the said person has not offered himself voluntarily' (Article 2 ILO C29 Forced Labour Convention 1930). The Worst Forms of Child Labour Convention 1999 (ILO C182) is particularly relevant to the issue of trafficking for the purpose of child domestic work, demonstrating the link between these phenomena. The worst forms of child labour as defined in the Convention include 'all forms of slavery or practices similar to slavery, such as the sale and trafficking of children, debt bondage and serfdom and forced or compulsory labour' (Article 3 (a) ILO C182). It also includes 'work which, by its nature or the circumstances in which it is carried out, is likely to harm the health, safety or morals of children' (Article 3 (d) ILO C182). Significantly, the Convention requires States to 'take account of the special situation of girls' although there is no elaboration on what this obligation entails (Article 7 (e) ILO C182).

Children who are trafficked and exploited in domestic work are often brought into Europe accompanied by someone claiming to be a relative. These children are not always registered with social service departments as privately fostered children and are often not in contact with schools or other authorities (ECPAT 2004). When a child is trafficked and subjected to forced labour in the form of domestic work this amounts to exploitation of the child. There are millions of children in forced labour throughout the world and research suggests that more girls under 16 are employed in domestic service than in any other form of work (ILO – IPEC 2004: 14). Of course these figures only provide a vague indication of how many children are in forced labour and domestic work as a result of trafficking, because the clandestine nature of trafficking means that accurate statistics are not available. Nor are there accurate statistics revealing the extent of the problem in Europe as compared to the rest of the world.

Of course, children who are involved in domestic work within a household in Europe have not necessarily all been trafficked. There may be children who are above the legal minimum age to enter employment, as defined by the International Labour Organization Minimum Age Convention 1973 (C138),[2] who decide of their own volition to migrate to undertake domestic work and who are not subjected to exploitative conditions in the receiving household. The Minimum Age Convention 1973 requires State parties to set a minimum age for children to undertake any form of employment with a requirement that it shall not be before the age of completion of compulsory education and not less than 15 years old (Article 3). Additionally, no child under the age of 18 years may be permitted to undertake any type of employment which is likely to jeopardize their health, safety or morals (Article 3) which is determined in accordance with national law and policy guidelines. However, where a State's economy and educational facilities are insufficiently developed they may be permitted to specify a minimum age of 14 years (Article 2(4)). The Convention also allows children between the age of 13 and 15 (12 and 14 if Article 2(4) applies) to undertake light work (Article 7). Again, the term 'light work' is not fully defined within the Convention and national laws decide the circumstances in which this is permitted (Cullen 2007: 138).

Not all domestic work is unequivocally exploitative and not all children who are sent from their families to another household are abused and exploited. Children may actually benefit from such arrangements if it is, in reality, providing opportunities such as access to education and better life opportunities that they would not have otherwise had. If the child is able to maintain contact with their family on a regular basis and is treated as a child of the family in the receiving household rather than a domestic worker then this is distinct from the situation where a child under the age of 18 has been trafficked and forced into domestic work, with their parents' consent, and subsequently exploited in the receiving household. The former situation lacks the exploitative conditions recognized as part of the definition of trafficking (see below), which includes, 'at the minimum, the exploitation of the prostitution of others or other forms of sexual exploitation, forced labour or services, slavery or practices similar to slavery, servitude or removal of organs' (Article 3 Trafficking Protocol).

The fact that a child is sent to another household by their parents is not in itself exploitative. Private fostering is a tradition used by many families as a means of securing a better future for their children, particularly girls. These private fostering

2 Ratified by 150 countries as of 15 October 2008. It came into force 19 June 1976.

arrangements are often seen as a normal and positive tradition in the culture and community from which the child originates. It is also questionable whether communities within countries of origin would view the sending of their child to work within a household as trafficking. Traditions may have evolved which mean that sending children to work within another household in another country is normal practice within the particular community concerned and may even be seen to be an important part of a girl's training for later life (Blagbrough 2008: 179). It may also mean that the level of work and the demands subsequently placed on the child are also seen as normal (Surtees 2005: 491).

Social issues such as poverty and lack of education and employment opportunities are also factors that motivate child trafficking (ECPAT 2001: 21). The social and cultural norms of the receiving country also have a bearing, including those that revolve around gender stereotypes. Within Europe, for instance, caring roles and domestic work are primarily occupied by women and such stereotyping undoubtedly impacts on the demand for and acceptability of trafficking in girls for such purposes.

A comparison can be made between child domestic work and paid domestic work undertaken by adult women who have voluntarily migrated by considering the concept of the 'global care chain'. This concept has been previously examined in terms of the relationships between women and the gendered nature of domestic work. The following section will consider this phenomenon in relation to female children who have been trafficked for the purpose of domestic work in order to highlight the equally gendered nature of child trafficking for this form of exploitation.

Child Trafficking, Domestic Work and the Global Care Chain

The concept of the global care chain was introduced by Hochschild to refer to 'a series of personal links between people across the globe based on the paid or unpaid work of caring' (Hochschild 2001: 131). In order to consider the relationship between child trafficking, domestic work and the global care chain, it is necessary to explain the current application of the concept. All of the research and literature on this issue has focused on migrant women with little attention paid to the situation of younger females, but similar critiques reveal new tensions and significantly more controversy when applied to female children.

Women have for many years migrated into Europe for the purpose of work (Zlotnik 1995: 259). Domestic work has been one of the occupations that women migrating to Europe have undertaken, sometimes with very few other work opportunities available to them (Anderson 1997: 37). This may be due to the difficulties associated with entering Europe legally which results in many women working with an undocumented status (Zlotnik 1995: 266). Women's undocumented status and work within a private household may often result in low wages, excessive hours and an imbalance of power between the migrating woman and the woman of the household (Friese 1995: 197).

There are obvious advantages for 'employers' to have undocumented workers within their household as it enables them to avoid many issues that a contractual employment relationship entails. There is no necessity for formal legally enforceable contracts of employment which stipulate working hours, rights to holidays, pay and rest periods. This may lead to undocumented domestic workers being exploited and abused and also enables the employer to assert more control over the woman by threatening to report her to the authorities which would result in her deportation (Anderson 1997: 45). Those women that 'live-in' with their employer are exposed to further abuse and exploitation, as they are available within the household twenty-four hours a day, often without clear distinctions between work and private life (Anderson 1997: 38). Although migrant women have been reported to have some degree of free time, it often proved necessary for them to leave the house during that time to avoid being called upon to help within the household (Hess and Puckhaber 2004: 73).

The undocumented status of domestic workers impacts similarly upon children who are trafficked for this purpose. Their passports and documents are often confiscated by the woman of the household, and the threat of reporting their illegal status can be used as a method of controlling them (*Siliadin v France*, ((2006) 43 E.H.R.R. 16, paragraph 94). Child domestic workers' situation is further compounded by their immaturity and inexperience, and their isolation from networks of friends or other child domestic workers. Indeed, children may face more restrictive conditions than adult domestic workers. They are often 'hidden' away and the only opportunity to leave the house is under the direction and supervision of the woman of the household (*Siliadin v France* (2006) 43 E.H.R.R. 16: paragraph 44).

Migrating women who undertake domestic work often leave their children behind in their country of origin and send regular remittances home to their family (Zlotnik 1995: 264). The care of their own children is often passed onto either a female relative, or, alternatively, another female domestic worker (Zlotnik 1995: 263). This reveals a pattern of migration, whereby women in Europe employ migrant women to provide the necessary domestic labour, which is, in turn, facilitated by female family members or friends assuming the caring responsibilities of the migrant women in her country of origin (Mattingly 2001: 370).

Hochschild (2001: 131) suggested that the global care chain consists of varying lengths of 'chains' which involved 'a shift' of care from poorer to wealthier areas or countries and viewed these chains as usually involving women, sometimes both women and some men, and, very rarely, chains consisting of only men. Following Hochschild's focus on domestic care work and female migration, Yeates acknowledged and affirmed the legitimacy of the concept and suggested further development and broadening of the concept to include not only care workers within private households, but also care workers within institutionalized settings such as hospitals. She viewed the global care chain concept as 'a major innovation in the way the relationship between globalization, care and migration are analysed' (Yeates 2004: 81). However in both Hochschild's and Yeate's approach, one further link in the chain was not addressed; that of female children who have been trafficked for the purpose of domestic work. In this context, rather than the mother migrating in order to undertake domestic work to provide for her family, the child effectively takes her place allowing the mother to remain within the household with any remaining children. Within their own family homes, female children are often expected to care for younger siblings to enable their mother to migrate for work and, in doing so, the child forms part of the 'care chain'. However, when it is the girl herself who is sent to another household in another country she replaces her mother in the chain and provides benefits to her family, either directly through remuneration received by the parents or alternatively by reducing financial pressure on the family as they have one less child for which to provide. By broadening the global care chain concept in this way, the role of children who are forced into domestic work as a result of trafficking is acknowledged and the children who are trafficked for domestic work are viewed as a 'replacement link' in the global care chain.

In the approach taken by Hochschild, domestic care work relates to women migrating for the purpose of caring for another family's child. However domestic care work includes not only childcare, but other work within the household, such as cleaning, cooking, ironing and other household tasks that were traditionally seen as the responsibility of the woman of the household. Also Hochschild described domestic care work in terms of emotional care of the children. However, a distinction can be made between care in terms of emotional care and care as in physical labour. As Anderson stated, 'The labour of care is work that anyone can do, as opposed to care as emotion which is ultimately dependent on some genetic relationship. This construes paid domestic labour, then, as simply that: labour' (Anderson 2000: 119). Children who have been trafficked are often responsible for care of the children in the receiving household. This does not necessarily always require an emotional connection between the child domestic worker and the other children, but can exist as a purely physical role.

One of the main differences between migrant women undertaking domestic work and child domestic workers who have been trafficked is that women are paid and children are very often not. Indeed, this is one of the most alluring features of child domestic workers. Moreover, children are rarely in a position to leave and find alternative work and have limited grounds for demanding payment for their work. Due to their age, isolation, and fear of the authorities they are often completely dependent upon the adults (and particularly the woman) within the receiving household. This may also be an additional factor which appeals to the 'employer' as it allows them to assert much greater control over a child than they would over a migrant woman.

Gender, Children and the Legal Definition of Trafficking

The previous discussion has highlighted gender as an important variable influencing child trafficking (White 1999: 134). The culture in each particular country or community may have a bearing on how children are perceived and valued, particularly girls (Beevers 1997: 132). The existence of gender-based discrimination within cultures with girls sometimes being viewed as expendable or less valued than boys enhances girls' vulnerability to trafficking (UNICEF 2003: 9). All of these factors contribute to a disproportionate number of girls who are exploited in domestic work as a result of trafficking (Blagbrough 2008: 180).

Trafficking was first legally defined in Article 3 of the Protocol to Prevent, Suppress and Punish Trafficking in Persons, especially Women and Children, (the Trafficking Protocol, 2000 A//55/383 Annex II,) supplementing the United Nations Convention against Transnational Organized Crime (2000 A//55/383 Annex I). Article 3 (a) of the Trafficking Protocol states:

> Trafficking in persons shall mean the recruitment, transportation, transfer, harbouring, or receipt of persons, by means of threat or use of force or other forms of coercion, of abduction, of fraud, of deception, of the abuse of power or of a position of vulnerability or of the giving or receiving of payments or benefits to achieve the consent of a person having control over another person, for the purpose of exploitation. Exploitation shall include, at the minimum, the exploitation of the prostitution of others or other forms of sexual exploitation, forced labour or services, slavery or practices similar to slavery, servitude or removal of organs.

This definition can be seen in an identical form in Article 4(a) of the Council of Europe Convention on Action against Trafficking in Human Beings (2005 CETS No.197) (hereafter the Convention). The use of the identical definition within the Convention was seen as important as it then represents an international consensus regarding the definition of human trafficking (Explanatory Report note 72). The Convention differed from the Trafficking Protocol by extending the scope of human trafficking to include trafficking which is either national or transnational, whether linked to organized crime or not (Explanatory Report, note 36 and Article 2). The Convention also introduced the possibility of the establishment of criminal offences aimed specifically at those people who use the services of a trafficked individual with the knowledge that they have been trafficked (Article 19). The Convention has been ratified (as of 15 September 2008) by 18 of the 47 Member States of the Council of Europe with a further 22 having signed. The Convention entered into force on 1 February 2008. In contrast the Trafficking Protocol has been ratified by 146 States (as at 13 August 2008). The Trafficking Protocol's focus is transnational organized crime. The Convention extends the focus from a criminal response and provides for the first time in international law a human rights-centred approach to trafficking in human beings which focuses on the impact on individuals and appropriate responses to address the effects.

The particular aim of the Convention is to improve the protection of victims'[3] human rights and includes both gender equality and a children's rights approach (Council of Europe Convention Preamble), with the overall aim of extending the minimum standards agreed in other international instruments (Explanatory Report, note 51). It was seen as essential to include gender equality in the Convention as women were more likely to be exposed to practices which would qualify as torture or inhuman or degrading treatment (Explanatory Report note 54). The impetus for its inclusion derived from the Council of Europe Parliamentary Assembly Recommendation 1610 (2003) on migration connected with trafficking in women and prostitution. The Convention approaches gender equality not simply as a matter of non-discrimination (Article 3 of the Convention) but requires gender equality to be promoted through the support of specific policies for women (Explanatory Report note 54 and 55).

Similarly a children's rights approach requires State parties to take specific preventative measures to provide a 'protective environment' to render children less vulnerable to trafficking. The concept of a protective environment is promoted by UNICEF as a strategy for protecting children from harm and abuse (Article 5 of the Convention). This 'protective environment' is composed of three pillars: caregiver, community and governance. In order to make an environment a protective one for children UNICEF sees it as necessary for child protection to permeate each of these pillars. Trafficking for the purpose of domestic work raises issues that challenge this concept, however, due to the involvement of both the family (caregiver) and the community in the recruitment and transfer of the child. The fact that two of the three pillars (the caregiver and the community) are directly implicated in the trafficking process makes the task of prevention and legal implementation particularly problematic.

UNICEF aims to raise awareness within families, societies and governments in order for everyone to recognize and meet their responsibilities to enable children to live in a protective environment. This involves an understanding of the attitudes, traditions, customs, behaviour and practices of both caregivers and communities, supporting those that are protective and challenging those which are of harm to children (UNICEF 2008). Creating a protective environment also requires governmental commitment to fulfilling protection rights. A protective environment ensures that children are receiving an education, with laws in existence to provide sanctions for those who exploit children and an environment where children are safe and protected from harm and abuse.

By including a child-rights approach, with specific provisions relating solely to children, the Council of Europe Convention recognizes that there are particular vulnerabilities that children alone are subject to. One particular area where the

---

3 'Victim'is defined by the Convention as any natural person who is subject to trafficking in human beings as defined in Article 4 of the Convention.

Convention differs significantly to the Trafficking Protocol is the protection of and the assistance given to victims. The Convention requires the identification of victims and if there are reasonable grounds for believing that a person has been a victim of trafficking they will not be removed from the territory until the identification process is completed (Article 10(2)). Additionally, where a victim's age is unknown but it is believed that they are a child, there is a presumption that they are a child until their age is verified (Article 10(3)). This is important due to the special protection measures that apply if the victim is a child as contained within Article 10(4) of the Convention. These include the representation of the child by a legal guardian, organization or authority who will act in the best interests of the child. There is also a requirement that steps need to be taken to ascertain the child's identity and nationality, as well every effort made to locate the child's family when this is in the child's best interests.

Despite these measures, however, they are limited by virtue of the fact that they treat children as an homogenous group ('the victim') and fail to recognize the multiple characteristics that impact upon a child's experience. Specifically, the needs of both boys and girls are conflated and there is limited regard for specific vulnerabilities associated with different types of exploitation (which are also gendered).

Parental Complicity in Child Trafficking

The legal approach identified above fails to recognize the impact that parents, and particularly women, play in entrenching gender stereotypes in domestic work and trafficking. Issues of gender are visible throughout each stage of the trafficking process – that of recruitment, transfer and exploitation of female children – and women are taking an active role in each of these stages to varying degrees. Mothers may be influencing the number of girls sent to another household by reinforcing gender roles within the family and also by facilitating the child's entry into domestic work. By doing so, they are viewing this as the most appropriate form of work for girls and providing training for what they perceive to be the child's future life (Diduck 2006 and Blagbrough 2008). Although mothers intend that their daughters undertake these roles, they may not be conscious of the gendering impact of their actions. Women more generally are also potentially taking an active role in the trafficking of children for domestic work by accompanying and transferring the child from their home and country of origin into Europe. Alternatively women receiving the child into their homes are often responsible for the subsequent exploitation and control of the child (Anderson 2000: 23).

There are several possible motivations behind women, and, indeed, parents in general, consenting to their child being taken to live within another household: the possibility of the child having a better life is often a motivation for the parent(s) with the family hoping for a better standard of living, improved healthcare, possibly the removal of their child from a situation of conflict or danger and an opportunity for an education for their child. Parent(s) may often feel that they are acting in their child's best interests in these circumstances. In contrast, the motivation may be more of an economic one, with the parent(s) providing their consent with an understanding that money will be remitted to them on a regular basis in return for the work undertaken by their daughter. Alternatively the parent(s) may effectively 'sell' their child and receive payment in return for their consent (ECPAT 2004: 9). Parents may send their child away to alleviate the family's financial difficulties, using the remuneration received to support the other children remaining within the family, whilst at the same time providing, what they believe to be, a better life for their child (Surtees 2005–2006 and Shelley 2007: 128). The ease with which such arrangements become exploitative is illustrated by the following extract from Anderson (2000: 133):

> Roseline from Southern Nigeria was bought for £2 from her impoverished father, who was led to believe he would be paid that sum regularly every month to help feed his other five children. Roseline, he was told by the couple, was to stay as their guest and be taught domestic science. They brought her to Sheffield, where the husband worked as a doctor. She was not allowed out, had to sleep on the floor, and was made to kneel on the floor for two hours if she fell asleep before being allowed to go to bed. Her working day started at 5.30am and lasted 18 hours. She cleaned and washed for her employers and their five children. She was beaten and starved. On one occasion, in desperation, she wrote a note intended for the next-door neighbour offering sex for a sandwich.

By facilitating the trafficking of girls for the purpose of domestic work in this way, it is argued that women (and men) entrench stereotypes of 'female work'. The Council of Europe Convention on Action against Trafficking in Human Beings (CETS No. 197) explicitly recognizes that families can be at the root of trafficking (Council of Europe Convention Explanatory Report: paragraph 137). This point is further supported by Derby's research of child domestic servitude in Ghana. This work identified three distinct approaches to recruitment; that of formal, non-formal and informal recruiters. The informal recruiters include family members (Derby 2005: 1-2) with parents actively seeking 'employment' for their child in another household, regardless of the disruption this would cause to their education (Derby 2005: 2-3).

Women's Role in the Recruitment, Transfer and Exploitation

There is often a perception that trafficking involves men who are part of organized criminal groups. However, research has shown that women are also involved in trafficking in many different contexts (Kelly 2007: 75-77). Women play a significant role in some criminal groups involved in trafficking of human beings, illustrated by the fact that over 20 per cent of suspects in German human trafficking cases are women (as reported by the German Criminal Police (BKA)) (UN.GIFT

2008, 22). The role women play is also revealed by the International Organization for Migration's Counter-Trafficking Database which contains information based on projects in 78 countries that were aimed at assisting trafficking victims. This database reveals that 42 per cent of recruiters are women, with 6 per cent of recruitments involving both men and women together (UN.GIFT 2008, 12). Although this information does not relate exclusively to trafficked children, it does provide further evidence of women's active involvement in child trafficking.

In relation to the treatment of children following their reception in the host household, it is often the woman of the household who controls the child and instructs her in her duties (Blagbrough and Glynn 1999: 51). In this situation gender inequalities and traditional gender roles are further reinforced by women themselves. In employing young girls within the household context these women adopt and perpetuate a gendered view of domestic work (Anderson 1997: 40).

An example of women's control over child domestic workers was clearly seen in the case of *Siliadin v France* ((2006) 43 E.H.R.R. 16). A young girl, who was a minor on her arrival in France from Togo, was obliged to follow the woman's instructions regarding her working hours and conditions, working excessively long hours with little or no free time. This was not an isolated case of women controlling and exploiting children in their household, with similar cases being reported, for example by the Committee Against Modern Slavery in France, where children were reported to have suffered significant physical abuse at the hands of women (The decision of the Cour d'appel de Versailles, *De Souza*, 19 October 2006; and the decision of the Cour d'assises d'appel de Versailles, *Mensah*, 20 December 2006). Indeed, the exploitation and abuse suffered by children in this situation is also gendered; males within the household may inflict sexual abuse, while women tend to perpetrate other forms of physical abuse and may actively encourage other children within the household to participate (Anderson 1997: 46).

Consequences of Trafficking for Female Children

Girls are disadvantaged on several levels when trafficked for the purpose of domestic work in a household within Europe, and suffer emotional, physical and psychological effects. A child who is sent by her mother to undertake domestic work in order to provide financial support for her family is potentially deprived of direct contact with her family and is removed from kinship networks, as well as from her cultural, social and linguistic environment. The emotional care normally provided by parents is unlikely to be replaced by the woman in the receiving household (Anderson 2000: 23).

Returning to the global care chain theory, Hochschild described the existence of global links between the children of service-providers (the migrant women) and those of service-recipients (the receiving household). The children of the recipient household benefit at the expense of those left behind (Hochschild 2001: 132 and Newcombe 2004: 8). However the losses experienced by children are more direct when they themselves are trafficked into domestic work; their childhood is effectively sacrificed for the benefit of the service-recipients' needs. They are often deprived of the opportunity to experience the normal experiences of childhood such as social interaction with peers, rest and playtime, a right provided for in Article 31 United Nations Convention on the Rights of the Child (1989, A/55/25). Derby's research (2005), discussed above, indicates that parents perceive the benefits deriving from the domestic work arrangement as outweighing the potentially negative impact on the child's emotional, cultural, social and educational welfare.

Conclusion

This chapter has outlined the numerous methods of exploitation and control implied in trafficking. The gendered nature of trafficking is often recognized in terms of women and children as victims. However there is clearly another gendered side to this phenomenon. Women are reinforcing the gendered nature of trafficking for domestic work by perpetuating the stereotypical ideas of women's roles in the family and household. Domestic work is still very often viewed as 'female work' and this is reflected in the high number of girls being trafficked for this purpose. The gendering of roles by women themselves exacerbates the discrimination experienced by girls.

Although legal responses recognize that both gender and child's rights approaches are necessary, they are, to a certain degree insensitive to the gendered nature of child trafficking. Women's roles as recruiters and perpetrators of exploitation of the child are also not sufficiently acknowledged. The multi-dimensional gender issues of child trafficking mean that the law is ill-equipped as it stands to address these complexities. Culture and societal values also play a role in influencing the entry of girls into domestic work both in motivating the family to send a female child abroad, and in creating demand for female domestic workers in European family structures.

The concept of the global care chain exposes the effects of these global cultural factors. The global care chain has previously been considered as gendered purely from the perspective of migrant adult women. Children are obscured in this situation, as is the reality of the gendering impact of women's behaviour in creating demand for female child labour. Child domestic workers could be seen as part of the global care chain, effectively taking the place of the adult migrant woman (the mother) but with more limited opportunity to make any personal financial gain from the arrangement.

Perceptions and assumptions concerning trafficking for domestic work need to be challenged and the role that parents, and particularly women, play in such arrangements acknowledged. The distinction between private fostering, which truly provides children with better life opportunities than they would have had if they had remained within their own family, and the exploitative and abusive nature of child trafficking for the purposes of domestic labour is difficult for the law to unravel. This highlights the need for a multi-faceted approach, including education for families and communities as well as more effective legal provisions which recognize the complexity of child trafficking arrangements, and specifically the role that families can play in perpetuating such practices.

References

Anderson, B. (1997), 'Servants and Slaves: Europe's domestic workers', Race and Class 39: 37–49.

Anderson, B. (2000), Doing the Dirty Work? The Global Politics of Domestic Labour, (London: Zed Books).

Anti-Slavery International (2005), Compilation of Reports from the Conference of 'Trafficking of Human Beings and Migration: A Human Rights Approach'.

Beevers, K. (1997), 'Intercountry Adoption of Unaccompanied Refugee Children', Child and family Law Quarterly 9:2, 131–47.

Black, M. (2002), Child Domestic Workers: Finding a Voice, Anti-Slavery International http://www.antislavery.org/homepage/resources/AdvocacyHandbookEng.pdf.

Black, Maggie (2002a), 'Child Domestic Workers: Slaves, Foster Children or Under-Age Employees' in Fottrell, D. (ed.).

Blagbrough, J. (2008), 'Child Labour: A Modern Form of Slavery', Children and Society 22: 179–90.

Blagbrough, J. and Glynn, E. (1999), 'Child Domestic Workers: Characteristics of the Modern Slave and Approaches to Ending Such Exploitation', Childhood 6: 51.

Child Exploitation and Online Protection Centre (CEOP) (2007), on behalf of the Home Office and the Order and Immigration Agency, A Scoping Project on Child Trafficking in the UK, <http://www.ceop.gov.uk/pdfs/Child%20Trafficking%20Report%20June%202007.pdf>.

Committee Against Modern Slavery http://www.ccem-antislavery.org/.

Council of Europe Convention on Action against Trafficking in Human Beings, 2005, CETS No. 197.

Cullen, H. (2007), The Role of International Law in the Elimination of Child Labor, (The Netherlands: Martinus Nijhoff).

Derby, C. (2005), Rural Poverty and the Gendered Terrain of Household Responsibilities – The Role of Child Domestic Servitude in Ghana, Conference Paper/Unpublished Manuscript, American Sociological Association Conference, 12 August 2005.

Diduck, A. and O'Donovan, K, (ed.) (2006), Feminist Perspectives on Family Law (London: Routledge-Cavendish).

ECPAT UK (2001), What the Professionals Know: The trafficking of children into, and through, the UK for sexual purposes, <http://www.ecpat.org.uk/downloads/What_the_Professionals_Know_2001. pdf>.

ECPAT UK, (2004), Cause for Concern?: London Social Services and Child Trafficking <http://www.ecpat.org.uk/downloads/Cause_for_Concern_2004. pdf >.

Explanatory Report Council of Europe Convention on Action against Trafficking in Human Beings 2000, CETS 197.

Friese, M. (1995), 'East European Women As Domestics in Western Europe – New Social Inequality And Division of Labour Among Women', Journal of Area Studies 6: 194–202.

Hess, S. and Puckhaber, A. (2004), '"Big Sisters" are Better Domestic Servants?! Comments on the booming au pair business', Feminist Review 77: 65–78.

Hochschild, A.R. (2001), Global Care Chains and Emotional Surplus Value in Hutton, W. and Giddens. A (eds).

ILO (1990) International Standard Classification of Occupations Geneva, no. 9131.5-40.20.

ILO – IPEC, (2004), Helping Hands or Shackled Lives: Understanding Child Domestic Labour and Responses to it, <http://www.ilo.org/ipecinfo/product/viewProduct.do;?productId=348>.

Kelly, L., (2007), A conductive context: Trafficking of persons in Central Asia, in Lee, M. (ed.).

Mattingly, D.J. (2001), 'The Home and the World: Domestic Service and International Networks of Caring Labor', Annals of the Association of American Geographers, 91:2, 370–86.

Newcombe, E. (2004), 'Temporary migration to the UK as an 'Au Pair': Cultural exchange or reproductive labour?', Sussex Centre for Migration Research Working Paper no.21, COMPAS, University of Oxford.

Protocol to prevent, suppress and punish trafficking in persons, especially women and children, (the Trafficking Protocol) supplementing the United Nations Convention Against Transnational Organized Crime. 2000, U.N.Doc. A/RES/55/383 Annex I.

Shelley, L. (2007), Human trafficking as a form of transnational crime in Lee, M. (ed.).

Surtees, R. (2005–2006), 'Child Trafficking in South-eastern Europe: Different Forms of Trafficking and Alternative Interventions' Tulane Journal of International and Comparative Law 14: 445–502.

UN.GIFT, (2008) United Nations Office On Drugs and Crime, 'Human Trafficking: An Overview', <http://www.ungift.org/docs/ungift/pdf/knowledge/ebook. pdf>.

UNICEF (2008), 'Child Protection Strategy', E/ICEF/2008/5/Rev.1.

UNICEF (2005), 'End Child Exploitation, Child Labour Today', <http://www. unicef.org.uk/ publications/pdf/ECECHILD2_A4.pdf>.

UNICEF (2003), 'End Child Exploitation, Stop the Traffic!', <http://www.unicef.org.uk/store/details.aspx?id=8C96E395-7BEC-407B-95FB-AD3B34B98B7C>.

UNICEF, (1999), International Child Development Center, Innocenti Digest 5, Child Domestic Work http://www.unicef-irc.org/publications/pdf/digest5e.pdf

UNICEF, Child Protection from Violence, Exploitation and Abuse, <http://www.unicef.org/ protection/index_action.html>.

White, B. (1999), 'Defining the Intolerable: Child Work, Global Standards and Cultural Relativism', Childhood 6: 133–44.

Yeates, N. (2004), 'A Dialogue with "Global Care Chain" Analysis: Nurse Migration in the Irish Context', Feminist Review 77: 79–95.

Zlotnik, H. (1995), 'Migration and The Female: The Family Perspective', Asian and Pacific Migration journal, 4:2–3, 253–71.

PART 2

The Impact of Migration on Women's Careers

Chapter 4
Promoting Women? Lessons Learned from a Study of Mobility and Fixed-Term Work in Early Career Researchers

Elizabeth Oliver

The European Council meeting at Lisbon in 2000 set itself a goal to transform the European Union by 2010 into: 'the most competitive and dynamic knowledge-based economy in the world capable of sustainable economic growth with more and better jobs and greater social cohesion' (European Council 2000).

This target has intensified efforts to increase the volume of research and development carried out within the EU. The recruitment and retention of workers with science, engineering and technology (SET) skills has become key within UK and EU policy agendas, in line with this strategic transition. Kofman (2004: 657) criticizes narrow interpretations of knowledge workers and the skills required to sustain a knowledge economy because they focus on male dominated labour markets: '

> We … need to question the notion of the knowledge society, which privileges scientific and technological sectors as the driving forces of growth in the global economy. In this version particular transferable skills are privileged as the core of the new economy; they are embodied in specific elites in the First and Third World who are able to circulate, largely unhampered by borders.

This chapter explores the geographical mobility of women who seek to develop their careers within the context of the rather narrow 'version' of the global economy outlined above. It seeks to contribute to more nuanced understandings of the relationship between mobility and career progression within these male dominated 'elite', 'borderless' spheres. Scientists are highly mobile and mobility is seen as an important aspect of developing and sharing their knowledge (Mahroum 2000; Ackers 2005; Oliver 2007). The European Commission promotes 'greater mobility of researchers and the introduction of a European dimension to scientific careers' (CEC 2000: 8). The growing emphasis on the role of mobility in research and on the association between mobility and excellence serve to intensify this existing 'expectation of mobility' or 'mobility imperative' (Etzkowitz et al. 2000; Ackers 2003).

Key policy initiatives have sought to promote the recruitment and retention of women within academic science (Osborn et al. 2000; Peters et al. 2002). Although the dominant model of mobility and how it relates to scientific production and excellence has been slow to change, mobility schemes are beginning to recognize that researchers may be part of families and households. Career structures and policy agendas however fail to fully understand mobility itself as a resource that may be available to greater or lesser degrees across the life course.

This chapter looks into one aspect of mobility within the early (postdoctoral) stage of academic science careers: the role of turnover between fixed-term posts. The transition from (fixed-term) researcher to full member of academic staff is known to be a challenging aspect of career development in science (Hasluck et al. 2001; Allen-Collinson 2003; Bryson 2004). This stage also plays a key role in the loss of women from science (Xie and Shauman 2003; Bryson 2004). Moreover it is within this 'early career stage' that the majority of geographical moves are made (Van de Sande et al. 2005). Mobility perhaps has an increasing role to play in navigating the path to longer-term employment within universities.

Following a brief introduction to the study, the chapter begins by analyzing EU research and development policy and specifically, approaches to promoting mobility in science. The chapter then explores the experiences of women themselves, drawing on extracts from interviews with academic scientists. The aim is to identify factors that make the balance between work and family life problematic to the detriment of women's career progression.

The Study

This chapter is based on the findings of a cross national comparative research project entitled 'Mobility and Progression in Science Careers' or 'MOBISC'.[1] The research forms part of an ongoing programme of studies into various aspects of research careers within the UK and the EU including the career management of early stage researchers (Adams et al. 2005), salaries and stipends (Ackers et al. 2006) contractual status (Ackers and Oliver 2007) and the portability of researchers' pension rights. The MOBISC project was managed by the Centre for the Study of Law and Policy in Europe at the University of Leeds.[2] It involved collaboration with partners in Austria, Greece, Italy and Portugal as well as the UK's Women and Equality Unit (WEU).[3]

The MOBISC project examined mobility and work/life balance in the career progression of highly skilled women and men within sectors that demand high levels of international mobility. Previous research had shown that academic careers within the physical and life sciences entail an 'expectation of mobility' in order

1 Jan 2003–March 2004.

2 Now the European Law and Policy Research Group, University of Liverpool.

3 Now part of the Government Equalities Office.

to progress (Ackers 2003). The study therefore focused on these specific contexts. A socio-legal approach was adopted encompassing analysis of laws and policies at EU level and within the national contexts of each of the partner countries. This was presented together with analysis of qualitative interviews conducted with the recipients of the laws and policies, namely mobile scientists. In total 248 scientists were interviewed, around 50 respondents in each partner country.[4] In order to provide a more in-depth contextual analysis of some of the issues raised in relation to fixed-term work, and the development of policies 'on the ground', this chapter takes the approach of 'the UK in Europe'. A sub-sample comprising 114 respondents who have had an experience of working or studying within the UK was selected and further analyzed.[5]

Understanding the Policy Context

Since the launch of the European Research Area (ERA) in 2000 the 'ERA concept' has pervaded EU action developed under the 'Research and Technological Development' competency (CEC 2000). Two modes of action are available to EU institutions: promoting co-operation and the development of multi-annual framework programmes (FPs) which set research objectives and fund activities within a given period. Using the vision of the ERA as a principle vehicle, the European Commission has promoted co-operation in various areas identified as 'aspects of the ERA' and sought to bring these activities and the FPs together to form 'a cornerstone for a European knowledge society' (CEC 2007).

The Geographical Mobility of Researchers and the ERA

Promoting the mobility of researchers throughout the EU has always been a key element of research policy, the following sections explore recent developments.

---

4 The respondents were to be 'geographically mobile', 'EU nationals', and 'scientists'. Mobility referred to geographic mobility within the EU; respondents were targeted if they were from another EU country but living and working within one of the partner countries. A threshold of over one year spent in another country was applied to the definition of mobility. The stipulation that the respondents be EU nationals and move within the EU served to contain the members of the sample within a common legal status under the Free Movement Provisions of the EU. A very loose definition of 'science' was applied, around half the sample were to work in (poorly feminized) physical sciences and half in (highly feminized) life sciences. Throughout the sample an even distribution of respondents at various stages within their career and the life-course was aimed for. An even distribution of male and female respondents was sought; as was a fairly large proportion of respondents with children (of around a third).

5 50 interviews were conducted in the UK; 9 in Austria; 25 in Greece; 11 in Italy and 19 in Portugal.

A series of mobility grants known as Marie Curie actions, have been funded, developed and refined throughout the FPs. The central premise is that researchers will receive training by participating in projects carried out within host organizations in other EU countries (Van De Sande et al. 2005). Emphasis has shifted from facilitating the mobility of early career researchers (FP4 and FP5) towards encouraging mobility and networking throughout the career (FP6 and FP7). In tandem with these efforts the Commission has sought to further promote mobility through the ERA, calling for 'more abundant and more mobile human resources' (CEC 2000: 16). Mobility is to be harnessed as a way to bring a European dimension into national research practices and to encourage the creation of centres of excellence. To this end the Commission put together a mobility strategy for the ERA. It emphasizes the association between mobility and scientific excellence, and between mobility and successful research careers. It is acknowledged however that mobility should only be encouraged where it is beneficial. Moreover the definition of mobility is beginning to expand and develop (CEC 2001). The following sections introduce the incremental evolution of the mobility model.

Although geographical mobility continues to be valued, the definition of mobility has begun to expand to encompass a wider range of experiences. In 2005 the Commission set out the non-binding European Charter for Researchers (Commission Recommendation of 11 March 2005). Mobility is broadly defined encompassing: geographical, intersectoral, inter- and trans-disciplinary and virtual mobility as well as mobility between the public and private sector. Similarly within the Commission's 2007 ERA Green Paper, geographical mobility is presented as just one part of an open European labour market for researchers (CEC 2007). A multifaceted approach to international collaboration is also developing. The Green Paper promotes the creation of virtual research communities through information and communication technologies. Despite these developments, geographical mobility (in the form of a researcher moving to spend a fixed period of time in another country) is still favoured. For example when the Brussels European Council proposed the creation of a 'fifth freedom' – the free movement of knowledge – the cross-border mobility of researchers was emphasized above other forms of collaboration (European Council 2008). Geographical mobility thus remains the dominant mobility model of integration and exchange within the ERA. The following sections look at how the European Commission seeks to make this dominant mobility model more family friendly.

Promoting 'Mobility Equality' and Beyond, a More Family Friendly ERA?

EU institutions have developed a series of policies on human resources in science research encompassing efforts to increase the attractiveness of science to women. The Commission has called for 'gender lenses' to be applied to all aspects of research careers and has been keen to understand barriers to mobility faced by women researchers, promoting initiatives that support the mobility of women (CEC 2003a). However few attempts have been made to critique the dominant approach to mobility from a gender perspective.

The Commission Communication 'Women and Science' in 1999 (CEC 1999) stressed the importance of promoting the participation of women within EU financed initiatives. Information exchange and discussion of best practice was encouraged between the Member States. Mobility schemes were also evaluated to monitor the participation of women (Ackers 2003). Indeed some of the processes behind mobility and the constraints to mobility faced by scientists with family responsibilities began to be reported and incorporated into policy (Osborn et al. 2000). The Commission's mobility strategy called for a greater appreciation of family issues, stressing the need for adequate childcare facilities and flagging up the difficulties faced by dual career couples. The approach is primarily to encourage the participation of women in mobility schemes, calling for 'mobility equality for women scientists'. According to the Commission (CEC 2001: 8):

> … women researchers continue to face more serious obstacles to career progression than men do. Specific obstacles arising from the structures, procedures and criteria governing mobility schemes need to be addressed to ensure mobility equality for women scientists.

Aside from specific mobility policies the Commission has been keen to increase the attractiveness of research careers generally (CEC 2003a). On the recommendation of the Helsinki Group on Women in Science (Rees 2002) the Commission incorporated aspects of work-life balance into this policy. Within a staff document on women and science we can see a rather different approach to the 'mobility equality' strategy. The Commission called for a redefinition of career development and acknowledged mobility itself may make scientific careers unattractive to women who have family responsibilities (CEC 2005: 4):

> Scientists have the longest period of qualification coupled with highest levels of career insecurity and international mobility is a key element of their careers. Not surprisingly, significantly more women professors than male professors live alone and do not have children.

Responses to the Commission's ERA Green Paper also identified a pressure to be mobile as a key obstacle to the career progression of women in science. The European Platform for Women Scientists for example emphasized the specific barriers to mobility faced by women noting that mobility 'can force some researchers to choose between career and family life' (EWPS 2007: 1).

Within recent ERA developments, however, the promotion of better quality, more family friendly science careers appears to go hand in hand with promoting more geographical mobility. The title of the Communication on a European partnership for researchers 'Better Careers and More Mobility' somewhat demonstrates this tension (CEC 2008a). Moreover the recent Conclusions on 'Family-Friendly Scientific Careers' (Council of the European Union 2008b para. 4) appear to conflate mobility with enhanced employment conditions, calling on the Commission and on Member States to: 'identify and overcome remaining financial, administrative, cultural and mobility obstacles and to create more attractive and flexible working conditions in the scientific field, which will stimulate women's and men's interest in pursuing careers in all areas of science'.

It is clear that understandings of the barriers to mobility faced by women in science, particularly those with unpaid caring responsibilities, are beginning to inform policy making at EU level. Outside of monitoring and encouraging the uptake of mobility schemes by women, it is important that a more nuanced understanding of the impact of a growing expectation of mobility throughout the career trajectory informs the development of EU policy. As noted above, more complex forms of cross border collaboration and exchange are beginning to emerge, perhaps there is scope to better harness these developments to support a more family-friendly approach to promoting cross-border mobility. The following sections explore the role of mobility within the early career of researchers. This career stage has become a focus of policy initiatives that seek to promote better quality employment conditions and practices because of the high incidence of fixed-term employment and lack of clear career paths.

A Focus on Early Career Researchers

The employment status and career prospects of early career researchers is a key issue across the EU. The postdoctoral career stage is an important point of transition through which career progression is complex and challenging (Bryson 2004). Moreover this transition has been identified as an 'early barrier' to the career progression of women in science (Anderson and Connolly 2006: 4). As explored below, geographical mobility plays an important role in maintaining employment continuity between fixed-term posts and in navigating progression to a permanent academic post. The Commission (CEC 2008a: 8) sets out some of the issues: 'Young researchers are often employed on temporary short-term contracts to help carry out specific research projects. This restricts the chances of talented researchers making the transition to becoming independent researchers. This can encourage some to seek advancement elsewhere and delays the emergence of the next-generation of research leaders.'

The nature of academic science employment has been changing over recent decades and this is marked by an increasing diversity of experiences (Bryson and Barnes 2000; Enders 2000; Goode 2000). Research across the European Union has found that the distinction between, and adherence to staffing structures based on the traditional chair or departmental/college models has diminished (CEC 2003b). Enders (2000: 17) suggests that: 'this evolution of academic roles and careers has become more mixed-up for a variety of reasons and may well be at a critical turning point'.

Evidence from the Commission suggests a range of responses by the Member States (CEC 2003a). However the expansion of a group of academic employees, typically working on a fixed-term basis, that function outside of traditional career progression systems, seems common. Attention was drawn to this trend by EUROCADRES (2004: 3) who have stressed that: 'It is absolutely necessary to counteract the development in most European countries … of uncoordinated short-term and fixed-term research contracts'.

At the heart of the evolution of academic roles lies the nature and role of postdoctoral research posts. A diversity of 'atypical' posts and contract types have emerged within universities. However the continued adherence to linear career tracks and the dominance of the 'traditional' academic career models make the negotiation of career development through the postdoctoral phase more complex (Bagilhole and Goode 2001). The route to career progression remains narrow whilst the proportion of 'atypical' posts available have increased (Bryson 2004).

In the context of highly international labour markets, job to job migration is more likely to entail cross border mobility. Green predicted that as temporary and less secure forms of employment became more common, individuals would have to contemplate using geographical mobility as a means to maintain continuity in employment (Green 1997). This appears to be the case within some academic disciplines and employment contexts (Ackers 2004). In many situations mobility cannot be expressed as a 'choice' therefore, but as a direct result of the fixed-term nature of employment. This dichotomy in the nature of the expectation of mobility was captured by one of our respondents, Carla:

> … the type of mobility you are referring to I think is the higher of mobility. That people move around in order to go to a lab of excellence. But I think a lot of people move around due to the fact that they need to find a job … basically it's a question of how much a person wants to stay in their own country, and how much they are willing to learn, to move. [446 female]

EU and national initiatives recognize a need to reduce the proportion of fixed-term posts and to promote stability in the employment of postdoctoral researchers. Policy has commonly been developed as a response to a European Directive that sought to improve the quality of fixed-term work and to establish a framework to prevent abuse arising from the use of successive fixed-term contracts.

The Directive on Fixed-term Work and the Mobility of Early Career Researchers

Council Directive 99/70/EC Concerning the Framework Agreement on Fixed-Term Work Concluded by ETUC, UNICE and CEEP[6] (referred to here as 'the Directive') was developed as part of a number of instruments in the area of 'atypical work'. It was concluded on the 28 June 1999 and came into force on 10 July 1999 (Article 2). The legal basis for action can be found within the Title XI of the EC Treaty, which deals with 'Social Policy, Education, Vocational Training and Youth'.[7] The Commission Communication on the careers of researchers acknowledges that the future of fixed-term work within research is going to be shaped by the implementation of the Directive (CEC 2003a). The Commission (CEC 2003a: 19) considers that the legislation

> implies a major rethink of the structure and future of postdoctoral fellowships and contract research in the different European countries.

This section looks briefly at a key form of protection introduced by the Directive; measures to prevent abuse of successive fixed-term contracts. These measures have the potential to prevent the extension of fixed-term employment out into the career trajectory of individual researchers.

The definition of researchers varies amongst institutional and national contexts and this creates a level of uncertainty in the extent to which the Directive will apply in all situations. Assuming that postdoctoral researchers fall within the definition of fixed-term workers,[8] (this may not be the case where a stipend or studentship is the means of employment) the Directive entitles them to two key forms of protection: the principle of non-discrimination and measures to prevent abuse. The latter is contained in clause 5 and is explored below.

The Directive does not seek to regulate the use of fixed-term contracts per se but to limit the use of successive fixed-term contracts. The preamble to the Directive does not state that fixed-term contracts are inherently negative, it highlights the fact that at times they meet the needs of both employers and workers. In order to prevent abuse arising from the use of successive fixed-term employment contracts, clause 5(1) compels Member States, where there are no equivalent legal measures, to enact legislation. The aim is to prevent employers from using a string of fixed-

---

6 European Trade Union Confederation (ETUC), the Union of Industrial and Employers' Confederations of Europe (UNICE) and the European Centre of Enterprises with Public Participation and of Enterprises of General Economic Interest (CEEP).

7 For a detailed analysis of the instrument see Vigneau et al. (1999) and for commentary on the implementation of the Directive within various national contexts, see Baigi (1999).

8 Those who have an employment contract or relationship as defined in the law, collective agreement or employment practice in each Member State (cl 2 (1)).

term contracts to employ an individual in the long term. The Member States must determine under what circumstances fixed-term employment contracts or relationships shall be regarded as 'successive' and then determine when they shall be deemed to be permanent. A number options for the Member States to use are set out within the Directive.

The Directive does not require the regulation of the 'first', but of 'successive' fixed-term contracts. In the context of mobility and turnover within the postdoctoral phase this is a problem. The contracts taken up are likely to be with different employers; a series of 'first-time fixed-term' contracts (Bercusson and Bruun 1999). For example a researcher is likely to spend a year working within one institution and then move to another institution in another country to take up a further post. If the Member States interpret 'successive' as a series of fixed-term contracts with the *same* employer; it is unlikely that this aspect of the legislation will protect geographically mobile postdoctoral researchers in the same way as those who are employed longer term within one institution.

The legislation, as implemented in the UK, is beginning to have a welcome impact on the proportion of staff employed fixed-term within universities (Newman and Lipsett 2008). Institutions are having to rethink their use of fixed-term posts to employ research staff in the long term and the use of fixed-term contracts as a matter of course.[9] However, within UK and EU policy on researchers, the postdoctoral phase is promoted as 'transitional'. Researchers continue to be encouraged to move between short-term posts at least in the initial postdoctoral period. Roberts (2002: 148) describes the career path in the UK:

> The academic career expectation in SET [science, engineering and technology] is that a good postdoctoral researcher will fill a couple of postdoctoral positions (ideally in prestigious research groups, and preferably at least one outside the UK) and then take up a lectureship at a research-intensive university.

The emphasis is placed on encouraging the majority to move into other sectors, in order to develop longer-term employment security (Roberts 2002; CEC 2003a).

Moving Between Fixed-term Contracts: Identifying Life Course Issues

Fixed-term contracts facilitate mobility, allowing researchers to make short-term international moves that contribute to their training and development and to the transfer of knowledge (Enders 2005; Williams 2006). They also imply mobility allowing institutions to react flexibly to changes within funding systems (without

9 The UK's Concordat to Support the Career Development of Researchers states that 'Research posts should only be advertised as a fixed-term post where there is a recorded and justifiable reason.' (RCUK 2008: A. 3).

formally reconstructing the traditional career structures). As noted above, the traditional postdoctoral career phase where researchers commonly work on fixed-term contracts, extends well into the career trajectory and importantly, the life course of science researchers. The combination of contractual insecurity and an expectation of mobility, pose key challenges to managing developments in the life course such as co-habiting, marriage and having children. The following sections seek to explore some of these issues.

Within this study a subgroup of 'repeat movers' can be identified within those respondents who were employed fixed-term at the time of the interview. A total of 27 respondents (11 women and 18 men) had made repeat international moves and were employed on a fixed-term contract. The majority of these (21 respondents) had held at least one fixed-term post before their current contract. It is noteworthy that twice as many men than women respondents reported making repeat international moves between fixed-term posts.

A key issue for women researchers is the interplay of the life course with mobility and future career progression. Although such developments as parenting and partnering do not inherently stop researchers from moving altogether, they add complexity to career and mobility decisions and obstruct researchers from simply taking opportunities as they arise (Ackers 2003). Hardill and Watson (2004: 21) suggest that

> relationships formed around family and co-habitation/marriage imply a large element of 'common interests' in order to override individual competitiveness and demands for mobility when decisions concerning the allocation of domestic responsibilities have to be made. Occasionally therefore one or more partners may be expected to sacrifice (give a lower priority to) their own particular career interests to invest more resources in the collective project called 'family'.

This study found that women scientists with partners and children were keen to use geographical mobility to develop their careers. However the matter of negotiating moves with partners and children had an impact on planning moves in the future. Some women respondents discussed limitations to the 'footlooseness' with which they approach mobility. They were willing to orchestrate a move for themselves and their family but only if the new post was of high enough quality and entailed clear benefits for their career. Simply being mobile for the sake of it was not an option.

Putting Life on Hold?

Insecurity and an inability to plan in the long term are key consequences for the individual of fixed-term employment. This section looks into the impact of contractual insecurity and geographical mobility on planning ahead. The Academic Research Careers in Scotland survey found that insecurity was manifest in two ways: firstly, the lack of short-term security when future funding remained uncertain; and secondly, the lack of long-term security, in terms of being able to build progression into a career and plan for long-term commitments (such as buying a house) (Hasluck et al. 2001). This study confirms these findings, many respondents discussed an inability to plan ahead. Bianca explains why her permanent contract was important to her: 'You can't buy a house, you don't know … [the permanent position] really gave me huge peace of mind in terms of I feel secure, I feel much more secure. I feel I can sort of plan my life a bit more'. [426 female]

Successive fixed-term posts in different locations led to practical problems with, as many respondents term it, 'settling down'. This is not entirely associated with having a partner or children, but also with building a 'life' for example by having a home and building close friendships. Anke is from the Netherlands, she is working in Greece at the moment and has started applying for her next job, she talks about future plans: 'I would like to go back to Holland now. To settle down. It would be nice to have a house, to stay for longer and buy some furniture and not to start all over again making new friends, learning new language, getting to know another country.' [218 female]

Some respondents discussed delaying building longer term relationships or relationship breakdown. Several quantitative studies have highlighted the profusion of dual science career partnerships particularly amongst women scientists (McNeil and Share 1999; Von Ruschkowski 2003). In the context of both partners pursuing scientific careers and perhaps conflicting mobility imperatives, building and maintaining longer term relationships can be problematic. Some researchers attribute relationship breakdowns to the need to remain mobile. Eleni is a Greek researcher who has made several international moves within her career. She discusses mobility having an impact upon her relationships: '… the close relationships were affected since there was constant mobility. So they were broken. Both relationships in Britain and the US were with people that had a similar profile and they could not follow my choices. So there was no room for negotiating.' [248 female]

A further response to feelings of insecurity is to delay having children. In this context respondents commonly discussed their contractual status and not knowing where they will move to next. Linda is over thirty years old, her contractual status and repeat moves have contributed to her decision to delay having children: 'I made the decision we would postpone having children because we have not been settled in a place like having first in Scotland a two years contract and then one in Spain and back here and we weren't sure for how long so we wait and see. [007 female]

Some couples manage the mobility imperative by spending periods of time living in separate countries, delaying having children is common here. Aurélie is French, she met her British partner some time ago. They work in the same research area and have both worked in different countries as postdoctoral researchers. Aurélie explains that even though she and her partner now cohabit, they don't want to have children straight away and the primary reason is that they haven't lived together for very long:

> 'No we don't have children, not yet..with this postdoctoral situation, I was in the US for two years, then I came back for two and a half years and all that time we were not actually living together ... it's only two years ago that I moved here and we've been a normal couple so you can't just rush and have children, even if you are 30 years old.' [049 female]

Although most of the respondents within this study were very passionate about their research, the difficulty of maintaining employment and the risk of not achieving a permanent post in the end, lead some researchers to consider a change of career. Some respondents felt that by developing their career they had to sacrifice important parts of their personal lives. Katelijn explains why she thinks that postdoctoral positions are difficult for women to take up: 'I mean if you have a happy family life it doesn't really permit you to take these kinds of decisions and it basically means the end of your science career in the Netherlands.' [064 female]

Nevertheless some respondents engage in partnering and parenting throughout the postdoctoral phase the sections below use three case studies to identify tensions and to assess the implications for women scientists.

Balancing Repeat Mobility with Family Life

This section draws from the stories of three women interviewed in the course of this study. These examples are used to explore the tension between a demand for repeated mobility and the management of households and families. The first section raises issues associated with partnering where both partners are scientists and seek to be mobile. Then the impact of motherhood in the context of dual science career couples will be explored through the two remaining case studies.

As discussed above a high incidence of dual career couples is found within academic science, and the likelihood that women will be part of dual science career couples is higher than men (McNeil and Sher 1999; Von Ruschkowski 2003; Ackers 2004). The difficulty of securing jobs for two professionals within one location has been acknowledged by the Commission, it should not be underestimated. Research into the role of professional women within dual career mobility decision-making have tended to focus on the role of the 'tied' partner in either facilitating or inhibiting the migration of the 'leader' (cf. Ackers 2004). Throughout the sample, researchers discuss a variety of responses to career planning and the development of relationships. There is not a simple link between gender and a tendency to become a 'tied' mover or stayer. Both male and female researchers discuss the tensions of managing mobility and partnering. The data reveals a spectrum of scenarios within which the respondents discuss managing their mobility and their personal and family lives. However as mobility decisions begin to be taken as part of a household there starts to be evidence of a propensity for female career aspirations to take a secondary role and for women to be less free to take mobility decisions purely on the basis of their career.

Katelijn is a researcher from the Netherlands, she is 32 years old. Following her PhD Katelijn moved to take up a postdoctoral position in the UK. She explained that it is important for scientific researchers to be mobile, but acknowledged that deciding to move may be difficult, particularly for women. Katelijn and her partner decided that she would only move if they could both move together. Katelijn moved to London and her partner moved with her, leaving his permanent job in information technology. He suffered a long period of unemployment and was considering moving back to the Netherlands, when he eventually found a post, less senior than his previous position. Katelijn describes not wanting to make another international move because of the difficulties that her partner faced: 'I really enjoy my work, I really enjoy the scientific environment here but my partner was getting so unhappy with being unemployed and not being able to find a job … and that became very much why we are never going to do it this way again.'

Katelijn explains that it would be difficult for her to continue to work in research if she doesn't secure a permanent contract soon: 'I definitely would like to stay in science. I do hope to be able to get a permanent position after this but I'm not really keen on doing post-docs one after the other, I would like some stability you know in life and not a year planning ahead … I would hope to get a permanent position somewhere in the next five years. If that's not going to work then that would worry me, that would make it quite hard for me to carry on.'

Katelijn's example challenges the traditional 'trailing wife' assumption but illustrates how negotiating dual career moves can impact on moving again in the future and can perhaps cause women to re-evaluate their career plans.

EU cross-national studies show that the context of migration poses specific challenges to balancing participation in the paid labour market with the provision of unpaid caring work (Ackers and Stalford 2004; Wall and São José 2004). Within this study childcare was a key factor shaping migration decisions. Moreover female respondents discussed taking responsibility for organizing childcare when they move, far more frequently than male respondents. Whilst migration decisions cannot be attributed purely to economic factors, Ackers suggests that a 'multiplier' effect can occur where economic logic 'kicks in' within household decision-making on migration and having children (Ackers 2004). Here small decisions that favour the male partner can have a much greater impact on the female in the longer term. This is particularly so within science careers where it is very difficult to re-enter the labour market after a career break (DTI 2002). Ackers and Stalford emphasize the extent to which the management of family and migration is ongoing, context dependent and likely to change over time. They maintain that: 'those who migrate with children consider a complex myriad of family-led factors that shift in prominence over the life course, demanding constant re-negotiation and re-evaluation, with the initial migration constituting just one stage in the process' (Ackers and Stalford 2007: 321).

The following case study of Liana indicates some of the tensions of managing childcare within a dual career situation. One of the strategies used by Liana and her partner to manage conflicting career and mobility demands was to separate the family unit. While respondents within this study were commonly reluctant to live in separate countries to their children, negotiating periods of separation is becoming an increasingly common means to balance professional demands for mobility (Ackers and Stalford 2007). Liana is 38 years old, she has a partner and two children (four and eight years old). She moved from Spain to the UK for her doctoral training, there she met her Portuguese partner who was also a doctoral candidate. When Liana finished her PhD she moved back to Spain as a fixed-term postdoctoral researcher taking their baby son with her, Liana's partner returned to his permanent job in Portugal. 'At the time, my son wasn't one year old yet. So, in Spain, he was always at home with [the childminder] I would go to work … things were well organized. I think it was more about missing my husband … It was very hard to continue like that, for me and for him, especially when there's such a small child and when you miss someone so much'.

After three years Liana decided to move to join her partner in Portugal, she explained that it didn't make sense for her partner to move to join her in Spain: 'In a way, he would be risking everything. So, we spent three years thinking, ok, someone has to give up things and, I don't know, I suppose it was easier for me'

Liana succeeded in gaining a fellowship and continued her research in Portugal. She had just received news that her present contract would renewed. Liana told us that on several occasions she felt like she was being forced to reconsider her career. She explains:

> The past two years were very hard because you have invested so much in a career and then you think you are not going to make it and you will have to give up and do something else.
>
> Interviewer: 'Were you ready to quit?'
> 'No, but I was being forced to!' (laughs)..

Where women researchers build households and have children prior to securing a permanent post, limitations to mobility may result in the researcher having to leave academic science. As discussed above it becomes more difficult for women with partners and children to respond to the most advantageous options by using mobility. In Liana's case a desire to maintain the cohabitation of the family unit when her children were young triggered her move to Portugal. Ackers and Stalford highlight the importance of education and the welfare of older children as factors in the migration decisions of parents, they note that such concerns are likely to change over the life course of the child (Ackers and Stalford 2007).

Kaisa is from Finland, she had made several international career moves and then moved to Italy because her partner had secured a permanent job there. Her fixed-term contract is coming to an end and she is facing difficulties finding another post in Italy. She considered several positions in different countries but she does not want to make her children move to another school particularly in a country where they don't speak the language. Here the issue of children's education and social wellbeing forms an important aspect of Kaisa's decision not to move. Kaisa considered commuting to a post in Ireland as a way to maintain employment and to keep the family unit in Italy. She applied for a post and was offered an interview. Kaisa thought she had a good chance of getting the job, and was about to go to the interview when she changed her mind, she explained that it was too complicated to move away from her children.

> … the kids didn't like it. They didn't want me to go there. They say, 'No, no, mum, you mustn't go to Ireland, it's too far away'. So then I decided that I will not go to this interview, but I think that I would have got this job [430 female]

Kaisa does not feel that she will get a permanent job in physics in Italy: 'I still don't have a permanent position here, and I think it's late for me to do something else, and the education is wasted. So it's really a shame.' [430 female]

Sonnert and Holton (1995) found that in the US a key issue for women in science was that the years of raising a family coincide with a career phase in which researchers are expected to establish themselves. Etzkowitz and Kemelgor (2001) also note that across Europe and the US the coincidence of childbearing and rearing years with vital stages of entry to the career continues to be a barrier for women scientists.

The issues discussed above highlight the complexity of managing mobility between fixed-term posts in the context of building households and families. As migration decisions are made at the household level a variety of factors can lead to the woman's career development taking a secondary role. Many of the researchers who discuss balancing mobility with partnering and or parenting are dedicated to their science and to their research careers. However where access to continued employment and longer-term career development entails geographic mobility, potent barriers are erected. This tension undermines the attractiveness of science careers and raises questions as to the efficiency of a mobility and career 'model' that appears to perpetuate the movement of researchers on fixed-term contracts. Moreover the appropriateness of the European Commission's focus on promoting 'mobility' equality for women within this model is also questionable.

Conclusion

The ERA is a key instrument in the development of a 'European Knowledge Society'. Although the governance of the ERA is distinctly light touch and co-operation is on a non-coercive basis, the concept has maintained high level and strategic value. Throughout the ERA agenda the geographic mobility of researchers is championed as a key way to optimize results and to build an EU dimension to science research. Through the FPs the EU has funded a range of training and networking activities with the geographic mobility of researchers at their core. The Commission has sought to promote the value of mobility within the broader agenda of developing an open and attractive research labour market. In this context geographic mobility continues to be a prime concern although other transitions and forms of connectivity are to be facilitated. Greater attention is also being paid to the employment and working conditions of fixed-term academic research staff, however little attention is given to the negative aspects of mobility between fixed-term posts.

Over the years more emphasis has been placed on understanding the obstacles to mobility faced by scientists with partners and children, and specifically the gendered impact of these. The approach of EU institutions has been to promote the 'mobility equality' of women by addressing the terms and conditions of EU funded mobility grants and schemes. Through other measures EU policy seeks to promote the family friendliness of research careers in a broader sense. Here enhanced mobility is often equated with better quality posts. There is scope for the Commission to harness this family friendly agenda and apply it to the promotion of mobility in a more nuanced way, for example by critiquing current mobility models and promoting forms of internationalization that better support the balance of work with family life.

A key area of policy formation is that of the employment and career development of postdoctoral research staff. There appears to be a trend across the EU towards an increase in the proportion of fixed-term research positions and a blurring of routes to further career progression. Within this context mobility, often internationally, between fixed-term posts is a key means of maintaining employment and competing for a permanent post. Mobility could be considered crucial to making the transition from postdoctoral researcher to permanent member of academic staff. This transition has been found to be challenging and a critical point in the loss of women from science. Policies devised to promote stability in the employment of researchers have followed the enactment of a Directive on fixed-term work. However the postdoctoral phase continues to be promoted as transitional and mobility remains a valued aspect of this transition. There is a danger that researchers moving between a series of first time fixed-term posts could escape protection from the abuse of successive fixed-term contracts. As these postdoctoral years are likely to correspond to key household building and child rearing years there is the potential for mobility and fixed-term employment to have an impact on the extent to which women progress to the next level.

Respondents within this study in general value mobility as a useful way to learn scientific techniques and to disseminate findings. However repeat movers found mobility between fixed-term posts to be difficult to balance with developments in their private and family life such as investing in property, cohabiting and having children. Some respondents attribute relationship breakdown to repeat moves, particularly where both partners are managing an expectation of mobility. A common response was to postpone decisions and developments in the life course until a permanent post was secured and this trend was particularly strong in relation to the decision to have children. Some respondents felt that by investing in their career they were sacrificing important aspects of their personal life, this impacted on the attractiveness of academic science careers, causing some to seek other options.

For those women who were engaged in balancing career building with family commitments throughout the postdoctoral phase a number of challenges were faced. Making mobility decisions as a household limits the extent to which both partners can focus purely on career goals. A key issue for women is the risk that their career could take second place within household decision-making. Within this study a range of scenarios can be identified. Those respondents who had the support of a partner who followed them were more likely to be men and those respondents who followed their partner more likely to be women. However between those extremes a range of combinations of following, leading, living separately and commuting were undertaken by women and men. Where dual career couples combine geographic mobility with child rearing a variety of factors can act to the detriment of the women's career development, particularly where the male partner secures a permanent post first. These factors are likely to shift according to the life course of the child his or her self. In some contexts families negotiate periods of separation as a means to balance both partners' continued mobility. Concerns around the education and welfare of children however can have an impact on the extent to which women in particular continue to be mobile.

Although academic career tracks differ between the Member States the postdoctoral phase appears to be a key and challenging transition. Where traditional career paths have become blurred this phase appears to extend out into the career trajectory and importantly the life course of early career researchers. In some cases mobility is an important way to maintain employment and to compete for a permanent post. As the case studies explored earlier show, being unable to move geographically within the postdoctoral phase can cause women scientists to feel forced to consider other career options. The Commission (CEC 2005: 4) seeks to send out a signal that: 'It is feasible, and normal, both for women and men scientists, to combine family and work, children and career'.

In order to realize this goal the Commission must address more explicitly the tensions associated with geographical mobility between fixed-term posts in the postdoctoral career phase. Within this context it may be more appropriate to shift emphasis from understanding barriers to mobility within the careers of women scientists to understanding mobility itself as a powerful barrier to career progression. Taking this approach is not at tension with increasing internationalization and developing an EU dimension to research careers although it does require that policy makers embrace the emerging complex and more diverse approaches to promoting mobility.

References

Ackers, H.L. (2003), *The Participation of Women Researchers in the TMR Marie Curie Fellowships*. (Brussels: European Commission Directorate General for Research).

Ackers, H.L. (2004), 'Managing Relationships in Peripatetic Careers: Scientific Mobility in the European Union', *Women's Studies International Forum* 27:3, 189–201.

Ackers, H.L. (2005), 'Moving People and Knowledge: Scientific Mobility in the European Union', *International Migration* 43:5, 9–131.

Ackers, H.L. and Gill, B. (2005), 'Attracting and Retaining 'Early Career' Researchers in English Higher Education Institutions' *Innovation the European Journal of Social Science Research* 18:3, 277–301.

Ackers, H.L., Gill, B. et al. (2006), Assessing the Impact of the Roberts' Review Enhanced Stipends and Salaries on Postgraduate and Postdoctoral Positions. (Swindon: RCUK).

Ackers, H.L. and Oliver, E.A. (2007), 'From Flexicurity to Flexsecquality? The Impact of the Fixed-term Contract Provisions on Employment in Science Research', *International Studies of Management and Organization* 37:1, 53–79.

Ackers, H.L. and Stalford, H. (2004), A Community for Children? Children Citizenship and Internal Migration in the EU. (Aldershot: Ashgate).

Ackers, H.L. and Stalford, H. (2007), 'Managing Multiple Life Courses: The Influence of Children on Migration Processes in the European Union', in Clarke, K. et al. (eds) *Social Policy Review 19* (Bristol: The Policy Press) 317–38.

Adams, J., Mount, D. et al. (2005), Researchers in Higher Education Institutions: Scoping Study of Career Development and Human Resource Management R&D Reports, (Bristol: HEFCE).

Allen-Collinson, J. (2003), 'Working at a Marginal 'Career': the Case of UK Social Science Contract Researchers', *The Sociological Review* 51:3, 405–22.

Anderson, J. and Connolly, S. (2006), 'Equal Measures: Investigating University Science Pay and Opportunities for Success', *Research Briefing* (Bradford: UK Resource Centre for Women in Science, Engineering and Technology).

Bagilhole, B. and Goode, J. (2001), 'The Contradiction of the Myth of Individual Merit, and the Reality of a Patriarchal Support System in Academic Careers: A Feminist Investigation', *The European Journal of Women's Studies* 8:2, 161–80.

Bercusson, B. and Bruun, N. (1999), 'The Agreement on Fixed-Term Work – A First Analysis' in Vigneau, C. et al. (eds) *Fixed Term Work in the EU* (Stockholm: National Institute for Working Life), 51–131.

Bryson, C. (2004), 'The Consequences for Women in the Academic Profession of the Widespread Use of Fixed Term Contracts', *Gender, Work and Organization* 11:2, 187–206.

Bryson, C. and Barnes, N. (2000), 'Working in Higher Education in the United Kingdom' in Tight, M. (ed.) Academic Work and Life: What it is to be an Academic, and How This is Changing (Amsterdam, London: Jai.), 147–241.

CEC (1999), 'Women and Science Mobilizing Women to Enrich European Research', *Communication from the Commission,* COM(1999) 76 final.

CEC (2000), 'The Economic and Social Committee and the Committee of the Regions, Towards a European Research Area', *Communication from the Commission,* COM(2000) 6.

CEC (2001), 'A Mobility Strategy for the European Research Area', *Communication from the Commission,* COM(2001) 331 final.

CEC (2003a), 'Researchers in the European Research Area: One Profession, Multiple Careers', *Communication from the Commission,* COM(2003) 436 final.

CEC (2003b), 'The Role of the Universities in the Europe of Knowledge', *Communication from the Commission,* COM(2003) 58 final.

CEC (2005), 'Women and Science: Excellence and Innovation – Gender Equality in Science', *Commission Staff Working Document*, SEC(2005) 370.

CEC (2007), Green Paper The European Research Area: New Perspectives, COM(2007) 161 final.

CEC (2008a), 'Better Careers and More Mobility: A European Partnership for Researchers', *Communication from the Commission,* COM(2008) 317 final.

CEC (2008b), Marie Curie Actions in Brief: A Pocket Guide. (Brussels: European Commission) Chancellor of the Duchy of Lancaster (1993), Realising our Potential; A Strategy for Science Engineering and Technology. (London: HMSO).

Cooke, P. (2001), 'Biotechnology Clusters in the UK: Lessons from Localization in The Commercialization of Science', *Small Business Economics* 17:1–2, 43–60.

Council of the European Union (2007), 'Outcome of the Proceedings of the Council (Competitiveness) on 23 November 2007' *Council Conclusions on the Future of Science and Technology in Europe*, 14693/07, Brussels, 29 November 2007.

Council of the European Union (2008a), 'Towards Full Realization of the ERA' *Council Conclusions on the Launch of the 'Ljubljana Process'* 9076/08, Brussels, 16 May 2008.

Council of the European Union (2008b), '2871st Competitiveness (Internal Market, Industry and Research) Council Meeting' *Council Conclusions on Family-Friendly Scientific Careers Towards an Integrated Model*, 10021/08, Brussels, 29 and 30 May 2008.

de Elera, A. (2006), 'The European Research Area: On the Way Towards a European Scientific Community?' *European Law Journal* 12:5, 559–74.

Dess, G.G. and Shaw, J.D. (2001), 'Voluntary Turnover, Social Capital, and Organizational Performance', *The Academy of Management Review* 26:3, 446–56.

DTI (2002), Maximizing Returns to Science, Engineering and Technology Careers (London: DTI).

Enders, J. (2000), Academic Staff in Europe: Changing Employment and Working Conditions. *Women in European Universities Research and Training Network Conference.* Innsbruck, October 2000.

Enders, J. (2005), 'Border Crossings: Research Training, Knowledge Dissemination and the Transformation of Academic Work', *Higher Education* 49: 1–2, 119–33.

EPWSW (2007), 'EPWS Position Paper Public Consultation on the Green Paper 'European Research Area: New Perspectives' (published online 16 August 2007), <http://www.epws.org/index.php? option=comdocman&task=doc_view&gid=108> accessed 17 June 2008.

Etzkowitz, H., Kemelgor, C. et al. (2000), *Athena Unbound, The Advancement of Women in Science and Technology.* (Cambridge: Cambridge University Press).

Etzkowitz, H. and C. Kemelgor (2001), *'Gender Inequality in Science: A Universal Condition?'* Minerva 39: 2, 153–74.

EUROCADRES (2004), 'EUROCADRES Proposals for European Researchers Brussels', (published online 2004), <http://www.eurocadres.org/en/p_ms_in_europe/researchers> accessed 21 April, 2007.

European Council (2000), 'Presidency Conclusions', *Lisbon European Summit,* 23 and 24 March 2000 DOC/00/8 of 24/03/2000.

European Council (2003), 'Presidency Conclusions', *Brussels European Summit,* 20 and 21 March 2003, 8410/03.

European Council (2008), 'Presidency Conclusions', *Brussels European Summit,* 13 and 14 March 2008, 7652/1/08.

EWPS (2007), Position Paper, *Public Consultation on the Green Paper 'European Research Area: New Perspectives'*, 16 August 2007. Available at <http://www.epws.org/index.php?option=com_ dosman&task=doc_view&gid=108>

Goode, J. (2000), 'Is the Position of Women in Higher Education Changing?' in Tight, M. (ed.) *Academic work and life: what it is to be an academic and how this is changing.* (Amsterdam; London: JAI), 243–84.

Green, A.E. (1997), 'A Question of Compromise? Case Study Evidence on the Location and Mobility Strategies of Dual Career Households', Regional Studies 31:7, 641–57.

Hardill, I. and Watson, R. (2004), 'Career Priorities within Dual Career Households: An Analysis of the Impact of Child Rearing Upon Gender Participation Rates and Earnings', *Industrial Relations Journal* 35:1, 19–37.

Hasluck, C., Pitcher, J. and Simm, C. (2001), *Academic Research Careers in Scotland: A Longitudinal Study of Academic Contract Research Staff, Their Jobs and Career Patterns* (Edinburgh: Scottish Higher Education Funding Council).

HESA (2006), *HESA Staff Record 2004/05. (Cheltenham: HESA).*

King, R. (2002), 'Towards a New Map of European Migration', *International Journal of Population Geography* 8:2, 89–106.

Kofman, E. (2004), 'Gendered Global Migrations: Diversity and Stratification', *International Feminist Journal of Politics*, 6:4, 643–65.

Mahroum, S. (2000), 'Highly Skilled Globetrotters: Mapping the International Migration of Human Capital', *R&D Management* 30:1, 23–31.

McNeil, L. and Sher, M. (1999), 'Dual-Science-Career Couples Survey Results.' *Dual-Science-Career Couples*, <http://www.physics.wm.edu/dualcareer.html>, accessed 17 June 2008.

Metcalf, J., Rolfe, H.et al. (2005), *Recruitment and Retention of Academic Staff in Higher Education.* (London: National Institute of Economic and Social Research).

Musselin, C. (2004), 'Towards a European Academic Labour Market? Some Lessons Drawn from Empirical Studies on Academic Mobility', *Higher Education* 48:1, 55–78.

Newman, M. and Lipsett, A. (2008), 'Research Joy Over Rise in Job Security', *Times Higher* Education 1784, 1.

Oliver, E.A. and Ackers, H.L. (2005), 'Fixed Term Positions in the Academic Career Trajectory' *CSLPE Working Paper.* (Leeds: Centre for the Study of Law and Policy in Europe, University of Leeds).

Oliver, E.A. (2007), Gender Equality and Career Progression in Science: Managing Work and Family Life on Fixed Term Contracts. Thesis, (PhD). University of Leeds.

Osborn, M., Rees, T. et al. (2000), ETAN Report on Women and Science: Science Policies in The European Union: Promoting Excellence through Mainstreaming Gender Equality (Brussels: European Commission Research Directorate-General).

Peters, J., Lane, N. et al. (2002), Set Fair: A Report on Women in Science, Engineering and Technology from The Baroness Greenfield to The Secretary of State for Trade and Industry (London, Department of Trade and Industry).

RCUK (2008), The Concordat to Support the Career Development of Researchers. An Agreement between the Funders and Employers of Researchers in the UK (Swindon: RCUK).

Rees, T. (2002), The Helsinki Group on Women and Science: National Policies on Women and Science in Europe (Brussels: European Commission DG Research).

Roberts, G. (2002), SET for Success – The Supply of People with Science, Technology, Engineering and Mathematics Skills. (London: HM Treasury).

Sastry, T. (2005), Migration of Academic Staff to and from the UK: an Analysis of the HESA Data. (Oxford: Higher Education Policy Institute).

Sonnert, G. and Holton, G. (1995), *Who Succeeds in Science? The Gender Dimension.* (New Brunswick: Rutgers University Press).

Van de Sande, D., Ackers, H.L. et al. (2005), Impact Assessment of the Marie Curie fellowships under the 4th and 5th Framework Programmes of Research

and Technological Development of the EU (1994–2002) (Brussels: European Commission DG Research).
Vigneau, C., Ahlberg, K. et al. (1999), *Fixed Term Work in the EU* (Stockholm: National Institute for Working Life).
Von-Ruschkowski, E. (2003), 'Raising Awareness' *Science Careers*, (published online 7 March 2003), <http://sciencecareers.sciencemag.org/career_development/previous_issues/articles/2240/raising_awareness>, accessed 17 June 2008.
Wall, K. and São José, J. (2004), 'Managing Work and Care: A Difficult Challenge for Immigrant Families', *Social Policy and Administration* 38:6, 557–64.
Williams, A. (2006), 'Lost In Translation? International Migration, Learning and Knowledge', *Progress in Human Geography* 30: 5, 588–607.
Xie, Y. and Shauman, K.A. (2003), *Women in Science, Career Prospects and Outcomes*. (London: Harvard University Press).

Official Documents

Commission Recommendation of 11 March 2005 on the European Charter for Researchers and on a Code of Conduct for the Recruitment of Researchers, OJ L 075, 22/03/2005: 67–77.
Council Directive 1999/70/EC of 28 June 1999 concerning the Framework Agreement on Fixed-Term Work concluded by ETUC, UNICE and CEEP: OJ L 175, 10/07/1999: 0043 – 0048.
Council Directive 2005/71/EC of 12 October 2005 on a Specific Procedure for Admitting Third-Country Nationals for the Purposes of Scientific Research: OJ L 289, 3/11/ 2005: 15–22.

Chapter 5
Situating Women in the Brain Drain Discourse: Discursive Challenges and Opportunities

Parvati Raghuram

In July 2007, the Institute for the Study of Labour, Bonn (IZA) published a paper on the gender dimensions of the brain drain analysing how men and women are differentially represented in highly skilled migration to Organization for Economic Co-operation (OECD) countries (Dumont et al. 2007). The report began by claiming that gender has been frequently neglected as an analytical axis in discussions of brain drain. They argue that this is despite the fact that although overall higher proportions of male than female migrants possess tertiary educational qualifications, the difference between the levels of qualifications amongst recent migrant flows is relatively small. In Australia, the proportion of women and men who would be recognized as highly skilled migrants is almost gender-balanced. In the United States in 2000, one of the main destination countries of foreign human capital, just over a quarter of all immigrants held tertiary degrees and the difference between men and women with such degrees was just one percentage point (p. 9). According to Dumont et al.'s (2007) calculations highly skilled women migrants actually outnumber skilled migrant men in several European countries such as the UK, Sweden, Germany, France, Switzerland and Italy. This raises the sceptre of brain drain and the extent to which such migration is leading to a loss of human capital amongst countries of the global South.

The concerns of the authors of this report are partially correct. Although there is some literature on gender and the brain drain this work has, on the whole, been sparse (although see for instance, Dodson 2002). This chapter will address this lacuna through an exploration of how this invisibility is produced in the context of female health workers in two relevant literatures – the analysis of female migration and that of brain drain. Analysis of female migration from the global South to the North often adopts a feminizing optic so that women who do not experience migration as inherently feminizing are often ignored. On the other hand existing discourses around immigration and labour market participation of migrants in sectors such as medicine are usually framed as brain drain and are often presented as gender-neutral or explicitly focus on the experiences of male migrants. However, gender relations, gendered hierarchies and career issues that face such migrant women may be significantly different from those affecting other women migrants.

The second section explores some characteristics of the literature on female migration, especially as it pertains to migrant women moving from the Global South to the North. The third section looks at the literature on brain drain to understand how and why questions of gender are often obscured. The discussion then moves on to look at why it is important to insert women into such narratives and considers some of the conceptual implications arising from this.

It is worth stating at the outset that there is some literature on gender and knowledge migration within Europe. For instance, Louise Ackers has, in a series of interventions, highlighted the limits to gendered mobility amongst highly skilled scientists and other academics (2004; see also Oliver this collection). Eastern Europe, in particular, has come to be seen as a place of exit for skilled migrants but there is much less knowledge about migrant women from the global South who move to OECD countries. One exception is Docquier et al.'s study (2007) which suggests that women's brain drain migration is much higher from countries where women have less access to education. However, this is not to say that there is no interest in the forms of brain drain migration that are highly gendered. Specifically, the migration of nurses (usually women) has come to be seen as one of the most significant elements of brain drain but in such analyses migrants are not seen as women; their femininity is often submerged. Finally, it is interesting that Europe has taken a lead in debating issues of gender and brain drain migration (Docquier et al. 2007; Dumont et al. 2007). In the 1970s many of the anxieties around brain drain posited Europe alongside countries of the global South as places from which people left to work in well-funded institutions in the US. As the analytical focus on brain drain has resurfaced Europe has been repositioned as a place of destination, not just of exit.

Migration Literatures and the Feminizing Optic

Interest in international labour migration of women is not a new phenomenon, yet it is only recently that such migration has been the topic of sustained interest from researchers (Castles and Miller 1998). It is the great increase in such migration over the past decade, particularly those moving to take up jobs as domestic workers, as sex workers and as nurses that has excited particular academic interest (Ehrenreich and Hochschild 2000; UNIFEM 2002). Feminist researchers trying to get to grips with the conditions that stimulate such migration have examined the ways in which pressures both in the source and the destination countries have led to a growth in female labour migration (Lan 2003; Parreñas 2001). They argue that these pressures are alive at a number of levels, from the individual to the familial, the national through to the international, and the pressures at all of these levels overlap and intersect to trigger migration (Sassen 2003).

While the focus on international female labour migration is a relatively new occurrence, that on women moving as family migrants has a much longer history (Phizacklea 1983). In both debates, it is their gender roles that condition women's entry into a country and thus into debates on migration. For instance, gender appears to be a guiding principle in determining the nature of work (domestic work, nursing), and the terms of incorporation into both the labour market and the destination country. It also influences women's mode of entry in the family labour migration literature as trailing wives of the principal migrant. Femininities thus write the conditions in which migration occurs. It appears then that such femininities are necessary for women's migration to be considered seriously. Women, who enter male-dominated sectors of the labour market, therefore, rarely receive attention, especially within the European context (Raghuram 2008; and for the US context see Radhakrishnan 2008).

A Gender-Neutral Brain Drain

Although there has been a history of international migration of skilled people from 'East to West', from 'South to North' and from the colonies and newly independent states to the imperial centres, the proportion of such migrants in overall population movements remains small. Arguably, the impact of skilled migration has, however, been greater than that warranted by the number of migrants, a proposition which has fuelled a significant amount of research for many years (Salt 1992; Iredale 2000; Ouaked 2002). The analysis of the effects of such migration has been conceptualized under the rubric of brain drain (Kupfer et al. 2004). It has been argued elsewhere (Raghuram 2000) that there are two primary theoretical lenses through which this migration is being understood – modernization and globalization. Although there are overlaps in these forms of analysis, some distinctive elements too can be uncovered.

Much of the research carried out more recently on skilled migration conceptualizes migrants as agents of globalization. However, debates on such migration predate the emergence of the globalization thesis. For instance, through the 1960s and 1970s, skilled migration was understood and analysed as 'brain drain' migration (see for instance, Bhagwati 1978). These debates focused on the impact of highly skilled mobility, particularly the movement of scientific personnel, researchers and doctors from the global South countries to the North, and from the UK to the US (Mejía 1978). In the former instance, it was the impact on development of 'Third World' countries that was of interest, where development was viewed through the modernization lens.[1] The questions that were asked

1 This is partly a reflection of the period when some of the analysis took place, i.e. the 1960s and 1970s when the modernization paradigm was particularly influential in the development literature. Brain drain has once again come back into focus and this time the interest is less likely to wane (Bach 2004).

concerned the effects of skilled emigration or 'brain drain' on source countries, of 'brain gain' on destination countries, and of 'brain waste', or in other words, the loss of human capital due to the lack of recognition and utilization of skills, for both the individual and the destination and source countries. Some positive effects of such migration such as 'transfer or knowledge' and the flow of remittances too have also come to be recognized (Docquier and Rapoport 2004; Lethbridge 2004; Levy 2003).

In the 'globalization thesis' the movement of skilled people is tied to the rapid growth in the movement of goods, services, information and capital. Studies focusing on the migration of skilled personnel employed in transnational financial corporations and the IT sector have dominated this literature (Koser and Salt 1997; Xiang 2001). These studies are theoretically and analytically linked to the large and growing literature on globalization. Skilled migration involves the movement of people as actors facilitating and regulating flows of money and goods in an increasingly interdependent world (Beaverstock 1994, 1996). It is argued that such movement is not simply unidirectional but multilateral often involving moving back to the source country, frequently as employees of firms in the original destination country (Saxenian 2000) leading migration researchers to claim that brain drain was being replaced by brain circulation (Gwynne 1999). Brain circulation unlike brain drain offers some advantages to source countries in terms of returns to human capital.

The discourse of brain circulation has been useful for understanding the experiences of migrant IT professionals and of scientists (Saxenian 2000) but has rarely been applied to understanding the experiences of professionals in some of the 'traditional sectors' of the brain drain literature, i.e. medicine and nursing. Firstly, although the conditions of recruitment of migrant medical workforce have led to the circulation of migrants, the temporariness of this form of migration is different from that experienced by IT workers and scientists. Systemic knowledges play a greater part in medical migration so that complete and frequent transference between different health systems cannot be achieved at the same frequency as in the case of, say, IT workers. Secondly, both the state and professional bodies have large investments in enabling and regulating the movement of health workers, unlike in the IT sector, so that mobility itself takes much longer to organize and arrange. As a result, the extent and nature of mobility of medical professionals is different to that of IT workers. Finally, its effects are also much more asymmetrical (Pang, Langsang and Haines 2003; Marchal and Kegels 2003). The negative effects of the migration of nurses and doctors not only on the skills base of the source country but also on the provision of health care in the source country (Kingma 2006), alongside the fact that much of the movement of professionals is from the South to the North has meant that such migration raises important ethical questions (Friedman 2004; Chikanda 2004). The ethics of migration are conceptualized within the terms of redistributive justice – it is argued that the erosion of human capital has a direct impact on the provision of welfare and knowledge and can be measured in terms of falling health indicators (Stillwell and Adams 2004). Thus, health workers' migration can lead to the loss of health know-how, and thus, to poorer health, and even higher mortality rates. Moreover, the cost of training such professionals is being borne by the poorer countries to the advantage of the richer ones so that the need for policy to arrest this process has become pressing. Intervention to promote a more ethical policy is largely being taken up by the destination state both through its immigration and its labour market policies (Stillwell et al. 2004). In the UK, for instance, the instrument that is being used to achieve this is guidelines on ethical recruitment, which enforces bans on recruitment from some countries (Department of Health 2001; Willetts and Martineau 2004).[2]

The ethical issues that surround the migration of skilled professionals in some professions have meant that brain drain continues to be a preferred model for understanding their mobility. It is also widely adopted by policy makers (Buchan and Dovlo 2004) and therefore the contours of this debate, its markers, absences and presences are significant in understanding how migration of skilled persons is analysed. In particular, we need to broaden the frame in which we understand brain drain and to be reflexive about the co-ordinates that surround this debate. These are the issues to which I turn next.

Scalar Emphases

The brain drain discourse is marked by a focus on certain scales, in particular, an overwhelming focus on the nation state. This is the scale at which optimum migration, ethical policy and notions of development are mobilized. The term brain drain is employed in order to take account of the effects of migration on source states and policies are formulated in order to understand how to limit or overcome these negative effects. Policy measures including limiting migration from countries where the effects of migration are most likely to be detrimental to the nation's health, by encouraging or enforcing return, or by building in linkages between source and destination countries so that the source countries are somewhat recompensed for the losses that they bear. Newer initiatives are attempting to stem brain drain through diaspora programmes that link migrants with those left behind and facilitate flows of knowledge and resources (Meyer and Brown 1999). In most of these programmes state policies become the primary route to achieving these aims, either through direct regulation or preferential funding for particular programmes. These policies are largely instituted by the destination state, albeit very often at the instigation of source states.[3] For example, the South African government has exerted pressure on the UK government to limit recruitment of health professionals from South Africa. As such both the data sources on which

2 However the guidelines are a voluntary code of conduct.

3 Multilateral attempts include the UNDP's Transfer of Knowledge through Expatriate Networks (TOKTEN) programme.

brain drain discourses draw and the policy initiatives that are adopted operate primarily at the level of the nation state (Ray et al. 2006; Stark 2004).

While the primary agent in such analysis is the state, it is the individual migrant who is acted upon. Policy interventions implemented at a national level aim to alter the individual's migration decisions – to encourage them to stay behind in their home country, or to return to it after a period abroad. Towards this, the brain drain discourse also attempts to come to terms with the individual's aspirations for movement and their personal motivations for migration. Thus, the brain drain migrant, more than any other, is an autonomous rational individual – after all 'the brain' is what marks brain drain migration. Underpinned by enlightenment notions of the individual – of the bounded, autonomous self, moving freely and rationally within the world – brain drain migrants are conceptualized as both unencumbered and disembodied. The decision to move becomes an exercise in rational discrimination. The literature also presumes an aspirational individual, one who charts out their course, and has particular stakes in the 'modern', particularly as understood in the context of occupational mobility (Attafi 1994; Kuska and Gyarfasova 1997). Thus, the brain drain analysis of the mobility of the highly skilled attempts to recognize migrants' agency, and their ability to use migration to overcome structural impediments to personal development (Vizi 1993).

The brain drain migrant is also seen as making these decisions within the context of the labour market. The labour market presents one of the meso-levels of analysis that Findlay and Li (1998) urge us to adopt in understanding professional migration. Brain drain migration is inevitably influenced by the structures of the labour market – its opportunity structures and the career progression and blockages that ensue.

Although the level of the nation state is still significant in regulating migration the globalizing imperative is catching up here too. Perhaps, the most significant mode in which this is occurring is through the World Trade Organization's General Agreement on Trade in Services, an agreement, which was negotiated by member states in 1995 (Shifrin 2002) to liberalize service delivery globally. As Wade (2003) conclusively argues, this has particular implications for the flow of capital investment from the First World to the Third, and the circulation of service deliverers including doctors with detrimental effects for the poor. The possibilities offered by multilateral organizations such as the United Nations in helping to set up return flow of investments and knowledge to the Third World are increasingly being recognized. Moreover, organizations like the WHO and the ILO (Wickramasekara 2003) have been increasingly involved in correcting the distributional imbalances in health that are seen as part of the brain drain.

Gender Biases

This scalar emphasis misses many things but also contains significant gender biases. For instance, brain drain migration, unlike brain circulation migration of workers employed primarily in the private sector, is much more likely to be influenced by regulating bodies and by professional organizations. These organizations implicitly shape migration through their ability to award internationally accredited professional qualifications. In the case of doctors it is the qualifications awarded by the Royal Colleges in the various medical specialities that may influence migration because of their 'long reach' (Aluwihare 2002). Their imperial legacy means that they have both credibility and transferability across different parts of the old empire. Their link to a very recent powerful empire also means that this reach overstretches beyond the geographical boundaries of the old empire – it has a wider currency and facilitates and smoothes out professional mobility as well as geographical mobility. Thus, doctors who have a qualification from the Royal Colleges are usually offered a higher wage in parts of the Commonwealth and also in some of the Gulf countries. Focusing on the nation state does not take account of the social and historical formation of international labour markets and the ways in which nationally embedded regulators gain international power because of historical forces. To recognize the constitutive role that organizations such as the Royal Colleges play in maintaining practices and structures that shape the nature of work in this sector is therefore essential. It tells us something of the hierarchies, the power relations and, therefore, the aspirations and the notions of career and success that shape brain drain migration.

These are often gendered hierarchies, as the professional organizations that shape what constitutes a medical career remain male-dominated. Women continue to be under-represented in the higher levels of administration on academic boards and grant awarding bodies (Royal College of Physicians 2001). Working practices, benchmarks of achievement and, therefore, ideas of success are set by such institutions and will influence how work is experienced The hierarchical and patriarchal nature of professional organizations also holds true in the home countries. Hence, women's mobility will also be shaped by the nature of the profession and the different gender norms that are adopted in the source and destination countries.

The primary geographic scales at which we analyse brain drain also limits the possibilities for understanding the role of women in 'brain drain' migration. In its focus on the nation state, the literature does not recognize the different relationships that men and women may have with the state (Yuval-Davis 1997). Secondly, cultures of work splinter across a range of vectors that are internal to the nation state – along lines of religion, class and region amongst others (Wibulpolprasert and Pachanee 2008). Some of these differences may be more important for women than men, as women's participation in the workforce is more likely to be regulated by social mores occurring at the interstices of these differences. For example, a study of Pakistani nurses found that non-Muslim women and Ismaili women were more likely to take up nursing than Non-Ismaili or Muslim women (French, Watters and Matthews 1994). Similarly Sheba George's study shows us that Malayali Christian women are over-represented among Indian nurses (2000) while gynaecology and obstetrics are female dominated in some countries such as India but not across the globe, leading to marked shifts in the gendering of such subspecialties in countries of destination too (Rajesh and Nagrani 2003). It is unclear whether such differences are also seen amongst another category of brain drain migrants – doctors – but it does point to the need to look more closely at the way in which work is socially constructed within the nation – in different regions. The complex intersections of gender and class will influence who migrates and which source communities are most likely to be affected by migration.

As a result the national scale is inadequate for understanding how 'brain drain' migration occurs or is experienced.[4] It presumes a continuity of interests within individual nation states – both source and destination – which cannot be empirically validated. The interests of national governments and the professional bodies are also not necessarily co-terminus. In the UK the national government's attempt to deliver health services and expand the numbers entering the labour market can often run counter to the wishes of regulatory bodies to maintain standards. The ability of such bodies to provide accreditation and to broker entry into work and, thus, the size of the labour market, and the conditions under which such labour is performed can mean that their interests conflict with those of the Department of Health. These conflicts also affect the relationship between labour unions such as the British Medical Association and the Department of Health. Moreover, the Ministries of Health, Finance and Foreign Affairs or International Development themselves have conflicting views and investments in the migration of health workers (Stillwell and Adams 2004). These departments and organizations also adopt different attitudes and have different investments in women's work and their participation in the labour market so that some may see migrant women as having no specific interests because of their gender, while others may see them primarily as gendered bodies or as targets of welfare. Similarly, in source countries too, the rhetoric of limiting brain drain migration expressed by national governments may not find sympathy everywhere. As health services are often provided within national formations, and the capacity of the state to employ doctors is crucial for doctors seeking employment, the impact of structural adjustment and the shrinking welfare state can mean that it is not necessarily in the interest of doctors to keep their colleagues in their home country. For instance, in the context of limited state capacity, small health services and therefore few jobs, it may not be in the interests of those within the profession to stop brain drain migration (Chikanda 2004). Migration of a few can reduce the competition for scarce jobs so that some doctors may well seek to encourage the migration of others while paying lip service to the state's rhetoric of controlling migration.

As the controls over migration are not merely enforced through the state but are also influenced by discourses circulating within the professional communities the importance of such processes cannot be underestimated. Increasingly, scientific activity is analysed as being embedded within the processes and practices of

4 Findlay and Li (1998) suggest that a migration channels approach focuses on the meso scale and is more appropriate for those who migrate professionally. However, there has been little work exploring how these processes are figured in professional migration.

scientific communities. The sociology of science and technology has allowed us to understand the collective nature of knowledge creation and the role of scientific communities in these processes (Meyer and Brown 1999). It has made us recognize the importance of thinking about groups such as doctors and nurses not only as people who share technical knowledge but also as part of socio-cognitive communities. Such communities have a range of collective knowledge and practices that are highly specialized and influence what it means to be a member of that profession.

Within this landscape of work we will undoubtedly see gendered hierarchies at play as skills are embodied in gendered human beings who move through gender-selective and gender-discriminatory labour markets, both in the source countries and in countries of destination. Women and men do not have equal access to skills, and even those with equal or equivalent skills have differential access to jobs, to promotion, to wages and to human capital development, so that women face career blocks in ways that men do not. They may find it more difficult than men to gain access to the labour market or to find employment that is commensurate with their skills. These gendered inequalities in both entry to the labour market and progression within it shapes the experience of female brain drain migrants. Moreover, these processes may also vary between feminized sectors and male-dominated sectors of the labour market. Thus the experience of gender selectivity and discrimination will be distinctive for nurses and doctors, for instance.

The family and or the household is another level at which gender differences are played out, and these differences influence both men and women's ability and inclination to migrate. The brain drain literature has still not fully engaged with the large and expanding literature on households as locales where decisions about migration are taken (Bailey and Boyle 2004). Feminists, in particular have argued that both gender and generation affect the ability of individuals to influence decisions, and to make them (Kofman et al. 2000; Oliver, this collection). Men and women do not have equal ability to decide to move, and migration decisions are products of unequal bargaining between different members of a household. The micro-level, functionalist analysis of decision-making precludes an understanding of these complex bargaining processes, which occur at a different scale. Thus, although Zweig (1997) in his research on Chinese emigrants to the US notes that the presence of wives abroad greatly increased the desire of migrants to stay abroad, he does not explore the way in which family migration influences the desire to return among skilled migrants.

Moreover, brain drain migration of women can be obscured because family migrants are not seen to participate in the labour market so that professional women who may often enter as family migrants rather than primary labour migrants are simply not counted as brain drain migrants. This is particularly important in some sectors such as medicine because medical professionals often marry other medical professionals and men are more likely than women to be lead migrants (but see

Raghuram 2004).[5] Moreover, as skilled migrants they quickly accrue the resources to bring their families along so that the migration of doctors is often family migration. Women doctors who enter through the family reunification route and not on work permits can simply disappear from the analysis. On the other hand, basing brain drain studies on numbers of doctors who enter the medical labour market too, fails to take account of female migrants who may be unable to join the labour market after migration because they have little ability to garner resources to re-qualify or work in the new country. Re-qualification may depend on migrant women getting the time to study and money to attend courses and pay tuition fees for qualifying exams. This will involve negotiating childcare and household responsibilities with a partner – who is also adjusting to a changed labour market, and may also be studying for examinations, either for re-qualifying or obtaining further qualifications (Raghuram 2004). Women find this harder to achieve as they often continue to bear the responsibilities for social reproduction of the family in the post-migration scenario.

The autonomous individual of the brain drain literature too needs further attention. The notion of the autonomous self is central to modernity and to the brain drain literature. Yet such autonomy is difficult for women to achieve. In many societies ideologies of caring and having children can themselves be an accomplishment of gender for women (Aranda 2003: 616). Nurturing and reproductive labour are, by definition, about co-dependence (Hollway 2006) so that women find it difficult to ever achieve autonomy. The autonomous subject of the brain drain is therefore imagined as having the characteristics of a masculine subject.

Moreover, this autonomous subject is one who is to be acted upon, a subject to be manipulated through national policy because the analysis of brain drain migration, more than most other migration analysis, carries with it ethical and political stances and a policy imperative. It is, therefore, more crucial for such analysis to take better account of people's subjectivities and the riven and shifting nature of the subject. The ambiguities and the ambivalences that brain drain migrants experience, their mixed emotions, have to be grasped if their motivations for migration are to be properly recognized. To consider migrant decision-making as migration strategies implies an instrumentality and pre-thinking that sits comfortably with the modern scientific notion of a medical migrant but fails to capture the complexity of migration decisions – the impulsive, the chaotic, the contingent, the conditional, the coercive. Brain waste too does not fully encapsulate the toil and the struggle that surrounds mobility, the failed aspirations and expectations, and particularly the re-routing of these aspirations to the next

5 For instance, doctors who were part of 'medical couples' were seen to alter their jobs and thus, their immigration status in order to maximize their career. What was also clear was that very often women doctors were able to become lead migrants because they were in specialties that had labour shortages (Raghuram, 2004).

generation (McLaren and Dyck 2004). It misses not only the cultural but also the emotional elements that make up the subject of brain drain migration.

In sum, there are many different ways in which the analysis of brain drain migration adopts scalar levels that are inappropriate or insensitive to the characteristics of female migration. In this context it is easy then to overlook female brain drain migrants.

Functionalism and its Gender Limits

The brain drain literature is also marked by a functionalism where the brain drain migrant is largely seen to be an economic actor. This economism leads to a focus on the labour market as the primary unit that influences migration decisions. Moreover, the individual who moves through these labour markets is usually considered to be ungendered. They often masquerade as dependent on human capital. This validation of a meritocratic version of knowledge is, according to Boyer (2006), a part of professional knowledge more generally. He argues in the context of East European journalists that professional discourse 'appears to dissolve or to subsume modes of knowing that are not oriented to epistemic priorities of professionalism' (p. 178) so that the role that other forms of social distinction play in producing professionals is often obscured. Hence the discourse on brain drain fails to recognize the complex and differentiated nature of gendered disadvantages in labour markets around the globe. In the context of migration, a complex interplay of social and cultural positionings, such as ethnicity, gender and age (Hawthorne 1997) operate to structure labour market disadvantages. For instance, the utilization of migrants' skills in the destination country could be influenced by the intersection of racism and sexism and by ethnocide gender stereotyping (Ip 1993; Man 1995).

Economic functionalism also misses the multi-dimensionality of the migration process, the intersecting, messy 'chanciness' and the chaotic nature of some migration decisions. The purposive rationality that is often characteristic of brain drain can be limiting. Rather, migration decisions are often multi-layered and relational, especially for women whose migration decision-making may have many axes and values. As Carling (2001: 17) argues, migration is not simply a demographic event, a move from A to B, but a parcel of expected actions and consequences. A person's wish to migrate will often be based on ideas about a culturally defined 'emigration project', but if they do migrate, their own particular experience is likely to diverge from this ideal. Hagerstrand (1996: 653) refers to such projects as 'ready-made blueprints, preserved in the store-house of culture' (Carling 2001: 17).

In sum, like other modernization theses, the analysis of brain drain has been economically driven and has privileged mobility in the context of the labour market. It has largely neglected the social and cultural characteristics of brain drain, including gender, as it is professedly gender-neutral. Even where other factors influencing decision-making are considered, such as political conditions and educational opportunities for children (Cheng and Yang 1998), gender differences in the experience of 'political conditions', of social and cultural conditions and the possibility of attaining skills are not adequately taken into account. Gender differences in human capital development, in the aspirations people have, and of their ability to achieve these aspirations, too are ignored. The terms of the brain drain debate have, therefore, led to a relative neglect of the presence of women in accounts of this form of skilled migration. The following section explores three specific issues that may be opened up through the interrogation of gender in sectors that are usually treated in terms of brain drain: the contrasting experiences of migrant men and migrant women in a given employment sector; the differences between the experiences of migrant and non-migrant women; and finally the differences between the experiences of migrant women in different sectors of the economy.

Taking Gender Seriously

As suggested earlier, analysis of female migration has often failed to address the presence of women in sectors usually seen to be part of brain drain migration. The feminizing optic in most discussions of female migration have meant that the experiences of women who occupy male dominated sectors of the labour market are rarely discussed. On the other hand, although there is a large literature on female migration in some aspects of brain drain literature such as nursing, migrants are, in this instance, rarely analysed as women (as stated above). Rather, the analytical emphasis seems to veer towards the national scale. In this section I want to explore three specific issues that have rarely been addressed because of the dominance of these conceptual approaches but which would add richness to any understanding of migration from the global South to the North. As suggested earlier, the importance of Europe as a destination (rather than sending) area has meant that this analysis is especially timely. I also want to argue that taking gender seriously within the work places that brain drain migrants inhabit can lead to new questions being asked.

First, there is little research that addresses the ways in which migrants have to negotiate the *gender differentials in work experience and in rewards obtained* that already exist in destination countries. The labour markets that migrant women enter are often gender coded in their own specific ways. Thus, there is a growing literature on gender differentials in employment and opportunities amongst those with similar qualifications and educational opportunities (Purcell 2002). What happens to migrant women who enter these parts of the labour market? For instance, Purcell (2002) points out that both men and women have higher earnings in the male-dominated sectors. However, even within these male-dominated sectors there is a gendering of tasks and differences in the extent to which women reach the higher echelons of Human Resources Management and other managerial posts (Purcell 2002). Women usually earn less than men do in similar posts. They also appear to be more likely to work in smaller rather than larger organizations and in the voluntary or public sectors rather than in the private sector. This sectoral difference intersects with occupational differences to map onto pay differentials and job security. For instance, women working for smaller organizations seem to be disadvantaged compared to those in larger organizations.

How do these patterns map on to the experiences of migrant women? And does migration alter these patterns of inequality? A contextualized analysis of mobility, sectoral employment and occupations is largely limited to migrant nurses but such an analysis can be illustrative of the limits of transposing wider results on women's occupational experiences to that of migrant women. It can also highlight the ways in which the 'migration penalty'[6] alters the relative benefits and costs of particular organizational contexts.

The nursing sector (one marked by relatively high levels of gender concentration) in the UK offers one site to explore these issues. In the UK, the wage differentials between private hospitals and the government-owned and run National Health Service may be small for non-migrant workers but amongst migrants they may mask deeper forms of inequality. The private care sector is becoming increasingly dependent on migrant nurses who undertake 'adaptation courses'[7] in care homes and then become trapped in the sector. For migrant nurses then, public sector employment is a mark that their qualifications and experience have been recognized. Hence, it is the public sector that offers higher wages and greater job security than the private sector. However, there is little analysis of how the experiences of female nurse migrants compares with those of male nurse migrants as there is very little acknowledgement of the presence of the latter (but see Winkelmann-Gleed 2006). It appears that the normative gender assumptions preclude any detailed analysis of the experience of male migrants, let alone a comparison between male and female migrant nurses' experiences.

Analyses of the complexities of these intersections between gender, organizations and the workplace have been much more limited outside the nursing sector. The focus on female migrants employed in informal, casualized sectors such as domestic work and sex work means that questions around gender differentials in the workplace are rarely asked. Moreover, there is little work that attempts to

6 The term migration penalty, adapted from the term 'ethnic penalty' suggests the forms of disadvantage that result from the migration process. This is not to suggest that migrants are all or only penalized but to suggest that there are considerable losses (as well as some gains) in migrating and that they are constituted through a complex intercalation of social formations and migratory processes.

7 An adaptation programme is a programme of supervized practice designed for nurses trained outside the EEA who want to become registered on UK's Nursing and Midwifery Council (NMC) professional register. It assists internationally qualified nurses to gain the requisite supervisory experience to establish themselves within the UK health care service.

compare the gendered experiences and rewards of work in the same sector among migrant and non-migrant populations.

Second, there is also very little on how female migrants negotiate *gender relations* in a formalized workplace. In much of the literature on female migrants gender relations are interrogated primarily through the familial lens. This has been made easy because for many migrant women from the global South, the household is the setting for providing waged labour. As domestic workers and even as sex workers, it is familial relations that are brought under the spotlight. Feminist interest in domestic work, for instance, has focused on the challenges that an occupation where women employ other women poses for the sisterhood of women, and hence on the classed and racialized differences among women (Anderson 2000). The inadequacies of men's contributions to household work in the employing households, it was argued, necessitated the employment of other women so that employment of domestic workers becomes a conservative alternative to challenging patriarchal norms (Gregson and Lowe 1994). More recently, as domestic work arrangements have been stretched across space through the conceptualization of care chains, men's failure to contribute to the households that migrant workers leave behind too have been highlighted (Hochschild 2000; Yeates 2004).

In the brain drain sectors, the family does not occupy centre stage as the broker of gender relations, nor the household become the all-important site where such working relations are played out. For instance, nursing demands women to negotiate gendered hierarchies in hospital settings. This requires a range of technical skills that imply negotiating specific hierarchies (George 2000). The definition of some of these skills and the recognition and rewards for performing such skills are likely to vary between countries of destination and countries where the nursing skills were acquired. But it also requires migrants to draw upon caring and nurturing skills which are often very feminized, which too may have place-specific manifestations The forms of femininities that are called upon and how they are mobilized by nurses in different settings, are likely to vary but how they impact on work are rarely addressed. To summarize, a focus on feminized sectors has also gone hand-in-hand with very specific ways of addressing gender relations as they influence migrants. Most work focuses on gender relations as they are played out within the household (Hondagneu-Sotelo 2005). They leave unasked a range of questions about migrant women's experience of work.

Finally, by thinking about gender issues as they pertain to brain drain, one may also be able to insert women into discourses around the brain. On the whole, discussions of brain drain take the skills involved in developing the brain drain for granted and focus instead on the losses to national repositories of brains due to mobility. However, men and women also seek to be mobile because of their desire to further their knowledge and thus their careers. Inserting gender issues into discourses of brain drain challenges the exclusivity of discourses of career satisfaction, aspirations and promotion to male migrants (as in much of the skilled literature), a ground that they increasingly share with non-migrant women.

In much of the existing literature on migrant women, their participation in the labour market is underwritten by the need to survive some combination of global inequities (Sassen 2003), troubled gendered/political regimes, or conflictual families. Women's mobility seems to be driven by economic imperatives rather than the language of career or individual aspirations, or their aspirations appear to be embedded within familial objectives. Women may move in order to benefit the families they leave behind or bring with them, or in order to escape from difficult or exploitative familial situations. There is little space for women who want to improve their skills or better their career through migration, especially if they have arrived from the global South (although in the European context see Oliver, this collection). Yet, narratives of work appear to be becoming increasingly recognized and validated for non-migrant women in the global North (McDowell 2001) and human capital enhancement has remained the prerogative of male migrants (DTI and Home Office 2002). However, migration may also be one route into circumventing career blockages in the home country. This is exemplified by Ono and Piper's (2004) study of Japanese women who move to the US to study in order to break out of the cycle of disadvantage caused by gender discriminatory practices within education which then translate into gender discrimination in employment. It appears then that migrant women too may have career aspirations and that their movements may not be driven by survival but because work is increasingly central to women's identities in the middle classes around the world. But there are very few accounts of the immigration of women which charts such a story. By suggesting that migrant women may invest in work per se and not just see work as a route to survival (Sassen 2003), we can expand the scope within which female migrant identities may be understood and ensure that narratives of economic survival and of familial hardship do not constrain our analysis of female migration.

Conclusion

Although it is clear that women migrate through a variety of routes and in a range of roles, in most instances, migrant women's narratives are ultimately mediated through their feminine roles, especially as they relate to women's movement from the global South to the North. Both in narratives of labour migration and in family reunification, female migrants who move are rarely recognized as part of brain drain unless they operate within feminized sectors of the labour market such as nursing. As European countries have become important destination countries for such migrants, these issues have become pressing for European academics (Docquier et al. 2007; Dumont et al. 2007).

On the other hand, the analysis of skilled migrants from the South to the North has often been seen under the rubric of brain drain migration, especially as they relate to the health sectors. This analysis has remained largely gender-neutral. However, nursing and medicine are both sectors where women migrants are present and, in some instances, dominate. As a result, both the state, through its immigration policies, and professional organizations through their systems of accreditation of skills, act as gatekeepers to the participation of migrants in the welfare sectors of the labour market. This affects women disproportionately as a larger percentage of skilled women (than men) who migrate are entering such sectors. These are the brain drain sectors within which women find jobs so that the gender relations and gendered rewards as they pertain to these sectors need particular scrutiny, both in the context of source and of destination countries.

This chapter, therefore, argues for the need to reconfigure the modes of analysis adopted both in understanding female migration and in thinking about brain drain to recognize the gendered subjectivities that are part of the 'brain drain' flows. It suggests that the analysis of brain drain migration should move away from gender neutrality because the terms of participation of migrants in labour markets, both in source and in destination countries, are deeply gendered. They carry with them traces of social formations such as class as it intersects with gender, but this fertile intersection has been largely ignored in migration research.

Recognizing the importance of brain in the mobility of women also inserts such women into discussions of work and the identificatory spaces that work provides for women worldwide. Moreover, inserting migrant women's desires within the framework of career makes room for moving beyond both the household and the nation state, and instead situating it within the labour market.

Ultimately it could also lead to interrogating the logic of 'brain drain', and to questioning the spatial ontologies that are being mobilized in current thinking around the brain drain. It can lead to the adoption of a quizzical approach to discussions of brain drain and the contours of this debate as it is currently configured. This has to be an important element for migration researchers globally because the policy focus on such migration is likely to be sustained in future years (Bach 2004).

References

Ackers, L. (2004), 'Managing relationships in peripatetic careers: Scientific mobility in the European Union', *Women's Studies International Forum* 27: 3, 189–201.

Agrawal, A. (2006), (ed.) *Migrant women and work.* (New Delhi: Sage).

Aluwihare, A. (2002), 'The long arm of the RCS', *The Bulletin of the Royal College of Surgeons of England* 84:8, 288.

Anderson B. (2000), *Doing the Dirty Work? The Global Politics of Domestic Labour*. (London: Zed).

Aranda. E. (2003), 'Global Care Work and Gendered Constraints: The Case of Puerto Rican Transmigrants', *Gender and Society* 17:4, 609–26.

Attafi, A. (1994), 'The Brain-Drain – Theoretical Framework and Hypotheses', *Canadian Journal of Development Studies* 15:1, 89–99.

Bach, S. (2004), 'Migration pattern of physicians and nurses: still the same old story?', *Bulletin of the World Health Organization* 82:8, 624–5.
Bailey, A.J. and Boyle, P. (2004), 'Family Migration and the New Europe', *Journal of Ethnic and Migration Studies* 30:2, 229–413.
Beaverstock, J. (1994), 'Rethinking Skilled International Labor Migration: World Cities and Banking Organizations', *Geoforum* 25:323–38.
Beaverstock, J. (1996), 'Lending Jobs to Global Cities: Skilled International Labor Migration, Investment Banking and the City of London', *Urban Studies* 33:1377–94.
Boyd, M. and Grieco, E., (2003), 'Women and Migration: Incorporating Gender into International Migration Theory'. *Migration Information Source*, <http://www.migrationinformation.org/Feature/ display. cfm?id=106>, accessed 5 June 2006.
Buchan, J. and Dovlo, D. (2004), *International Recruitment of Health Workers to the UK: A Report for DfID* available at: http://www.dfidhealthrc.org/shared/publications/reports/int_rec/int-rec-main.pdf (accessed online 13 December 2005).
Carling, J. (2001), 'Migration in the age of involuntary immobility: theoretical reflections and Cape Verdean experiences', *Journal of Ethnic and Migration Studies* 28:1, 5–42.
Castles, S. and Miller, M. (1998), *The Age of Migration.* (London: Macmillan).
Cheng, L. and Yang, P. (1998), 'Global Interaction, Global Inequality and Migration of the Highly Trained in the United States', *International Migration Review* 32: 626–53.
Chikanda, A. (2004), 'Skilled health professionals' migration and its impact on health delivery in Zimbabwe', *COMPAS Working Paper, No. 4*, WP-04-04.
Department of Trade and Industry and the Home Office. (2002), *Knowledge Migrants: The Motivations and Experiences of Professionals in the UK.* (DTI and the Home Office: London).
Department of Health (2001), *Code of practice for NHS employers involved in the international recruitment of NHS professionals.* (London: Department of Health).
Docquier, F., Lowell, L. and Marfouk, A. (2007), A gendered assessment of the brain drain, *IZA Discussion Paper No. 3235*. (Forschungsinstitut zur Zukunft der Arbeit/Institute for the Study of Labour, Bonn: IZA).
Docquier, F. and Rapoport, H. (2004), *Skilled migration: the perspective of developing countries*. (Washington: World Bank).
Dodson, B. (2002), 'Women in the brain drain: gender and skilled migration from South Africa', in McDonald and Crush (eds).
Dumont, J.C., Martin, J.P. and Spielvogel, G. (2007), 'Women on the Move: The Neglected Gender Dimension of the Brain Drain', *IZA Discussion Paper No. 2920*. (Forschungsinstitut zur Zukunft der Arbeit/Institute for the Study of Labor, Bonn: IZA).

Ehrenreich, B. and Hochschild, A. (eds) (2003), *Global Woman: Nannies, Maids and Sex Workers in the New Economy.* (New York: Metropolitan Books).

Findlay, A. and Li, F.L.N. (1998), 'A migration channels approach to the study of professionals moving to and from Hong Kong', *International Migration Review* 32:3, 682–703.

French, S.E., Watters, D. and Matthews, D.R. (1994), 'Nursing as a career choice for women in Pakistan, *Journal of Advanced Nursing*, 19:1, 140–151.

Friedman, E. (2004), *An action plan to prevent brain drain: building equitable health systems in Africa* (Boston: MA Physicians for Human Rights).

George S. (2000), '"Dirty nurses" and "men who play": Gender and class in transnational migration.' In. *Global Ethnography: Forces, Connections and Imaginations*. Burawoy M. et al. (eds), (Berkeley: University of California Press), 144–74.

Giles, W. and Arat-Koc, S. (eds) (1994), *Maid in the Market.* (Halifax: Fernwood Publishing).

Gregson, N., and Lowe, M. (1994), *Servicing the Middle Classes: Class, Gender and Domestic Labour in Contemporary Britain.* (London: Routledge).

Gwynne, P. (1999), '"Brain Circulation" Replacing "Brain Drain" to US as Foreign-Born Scientists, Engineers Return Home,' *Research-Technology Management* 42:1, 2–3.

Hawthorne, L. (1997), 'The Question of Discrimination: Skilled Migrants' Access to Australian Employment', *Asian and Pacific Migration Journal* 35:3, 395–420.

Ho, C. (2006), 'Migration as feminization: Chinese women's experience of work and family in Australia,' *Journal of Ethnic and Migration Studies* 32**:** 497–514.

Hochschild, A. (2000), 'Global Care Chains and Emotional Surplus Value'. In *On The Edge: Living With Global Capitali*sm. W. Hutton and A. Giddens (eds). (London: Jonathan Cape), 130–46.

Hollway, W. (2006), *The Capacity to Care: Gender and Ethical Subjectivity.* (London: Routledge).

Hondagneu-Sotelo, P. (2005), 'Gendering Migration: Not for "feminists only" – and not only in the household', Centre for Migration and Development, Working Paper Series, January 2005.

Ip, D. (1993), 'Reluctant Entrepreneurs: Professionally Qualified Asian Migrants in Small Business', *Asian and Pacific Migration Journal* 2:1, 57–70.

Iredale, R. (2000), 'Migration Policies for the Highly Skilled in the Asia-Pacific Region', *International Migration Review* 34:3, 882–906.

Kingma, M. (2006), *Nurses on the move: migration and the global health care economy* (Ithaca: Cornell University Press).

Kofman, E., Phizacklea, A., Raghuram, P. and Sales, R. (2000), *Gender and International Migration in Europe: Employment, Welfare and Politics.* (London: Routledge).

Koser K., and Salt, J. (1997), 'The Geography of Highly Skilled International Migration', *International Journal of Population Geography* 3, 285–303.

Kupfer, L., Hofman, K., Jarwan, R., McDermott, J. and Bridbord, J. (2004), Strategies to discourage brain drain, *Bulletin of the World Health Organization*, 8:8, 613–23.

Kuska. M. and Gyarfasova O. (1997), 'Brain Drain: Causes and Context', *Sociologia* 29:2, 191–209.

Lan, P. (2003), 'Maid Or Madam? Filipina Migrant Workers and the Continuity of Domestic Labor', *Gender and Society* 17: 187–208.

Lethbridge, J. (2004), 'Brain drain: rethinking allocation', *Bulletin of the World Health Organization* 82: 8, 623.

Levy, L. (2003), 'The First World's role in the third world brain drain' *British Medical Journal* 327:170.

Man, G.C. (2004), 'Gender, work and migration: deskilling Chinese immigrant women in Canada', *Women's Studies International Forum* 27: 135– 48.

Man, G. (1995), 'The Experience of Women in Chinese Immigrant Families: An Inquiry Into Institutional and Organizational Processes', *Asian and Pacific Migration Journal*, 4:2–3, 303–26.

Marchal, B. and Kegels, G. (2003), 'Health workforce imbalances in times of globalization: brain drain or professional mobility', *International Journal of Health Planning and Management* Special Issue 18:1, 89–101.

McDonald, D. and Crush, J. (eds). (2002), *Destinations Unknown: Skilled Migration in Southern Africa* (Pretoria: Africa Institute and Kingston, Ontario: Southern African Migration Project).

McDowell L. (2001), 'Father and Ford revisited: Gender, class and employment change in the new millennium', *Transactions of the Institute of British Geographers* 26: 448–64.

McLaren, A. and Dyck, I. (2004), 'Mothering, human capital and the "ideal immigrant",' *Women's Studies International Forum* 27:1, 41–53.

Mejía, A. (1978), 'Migration of physicians and nurses', *International Journal of Epidemiology* 7:3, 207–15.

Meyer, J.B. and Brown, M. (1999), *Scientific diasporas: a new approach to the brain drain*, Management of Social Transformations, Discussion Paper No. 41 (Paris: UNESCO).

Morokvasic, M. (1984), 'Birds of Passage are Also Women', *International Migration Review* 18:4, 886–907.

Ono, H. and Piper, N. (2004), 'Japanese Women Studying Abroad: The Case of the United States', *Women's Studies International Forum* 27: 101–18.

Ouaked, S. (2002), 'Transatlantic roundtable on high-skilled migration and sending country issues,' *International Migration* 40: 4, 153–66.

Pang, T., Lansang, M.A.and Haines, A. (2003), 'Brain drain and health professionals', *British Medical Journal* 324: 499–500.

Parreñas R. (2001), *Servants of Globalization*. (Palo Alto: University of Stanford Press).

Pellizoni, L. (2003), 'Knowledge, Uncertainty and the Public Sphere', *European Journal of Social Theory* 6: 3, 327–55.

Phizacklea, A. (1983), *One Way Ticket: Migration and Female Labour.* (London: Routledge and Kegan Paul).

Radhakrishnan, S. (2008), 'Examining the global Indian middle class: gender and culture in the Silicon Valley/Bangalore circuit', *Journal of Intercultural Studies* 29:1, 7–20.

Raghuram, P. (forthcoming), Caring about the brain drain in a postcolonial world, *Geoforum*.

– (2008), 'Migrant women in male dominated sectors of the labour market: a research agenda', *Population, Space and Place* 14:1, 43–57.

– (2006), 'Asian women medical migrants in the UK', in Agrawal (ed.).

– (2004), 'The difference that skills make: gender, family migration strategies and regulated labour markets', *Journal of Ethnic and Migration Studies* 30:2, 303–23.

– (2000), 'Gendering skilled migratory streams: implications for conceptualizing migration', *Asian and Pacific Migration Journal* 9: 4, 429–57.

Rajesh, U. and Nagrani, R. (2004), 'Overseas registrars training in obstetrics and gynaecology', *Journal of Obstetrics and Gynaecology* 24:1, 78–80.

Ray, K.M., Lowell, B.L. and Spencer, S. (2006), 'International Health Worker Mobility: Causes, Consequences, and Best Practices', *International Migration* 44: 181–203.

Royal College of Physicians (2001), *Women in hospital medicine: career choices and opportunities*. (London: Royal College of Physicians).

Salaff, J. and Greve, A. (2003), 'Gendered structured barriers to job attainment for skilled Chinese emigrants in Canada', *International Journal of Population Geography* 9: 443–56.

Salt, J. (1992), 'Migration Processes Among the Highly Skilled in Europe', *International Migration Review* 26:2, 484–505.

Sassen S. (2003), 'Global cities and survival strategies' in Ehrenreich, B. and Hochschild, A. (eds).

Saxenian A. (2000), 'Silicon Valley's new immigrant entrepreneurs', CCIS working paper No. 15, (San Diego: University of California).

Shifrin, T. (2002), 'Changing the battle lines', *Health Service Journal* 13, at p. 14.

Stark, O. (2004), 'Rethinking the brain drain', *World Development* 32:1, 15–22.

Stillwell, B. and Adams, O. (2004), Health professionals and migration, *Bulletin of the World Health Organization* 82:8, 560.

UNIFEM (2002), *Progress of the World's Women.* (New York: United Nations Development Fund for Women).

Vizi, E.S. (1993), 'Reversing the Brain-drain from Eastern-European Countries: The Push and Pull Factors,' *Technology in Society*, 15:1, 101–9.

Vujicic, M., Zurn, P., Diallo, K., Adams, O. and Del Poz, M. (2004), The role of wages in the migration of health professionals from developing countries,

Human Resources for Health, 2: 3, <http://www.human-resources-health.com/content/2/1/3>, accessed 12 July 2004.

Wade, R. (2003), 'What strategies are viable for developing countries today? The World Trade Organization and the Shrinking of Development Space', *Review of International Political Economy* 10: 4, 621–44.

Wickramasekara, P. (2003), *Policy responses to skilled migration: retention, return and circulation.* (Geneva: ILO).

Willetts, A. and Martineau, T. (2004), *Ethical international recruitment of health professionals: will codes of practice protect developing country health systems?* (Liverpool: Liverpool School of Tropical Medicine).

Wibulpolprasert, S. and Pachanee, C. (2008), 'Addressing the Internal Brain Drain of Medical Doctors in Thailand: The Story and Lesson Learned', *Global Social Policy* 8: 12–15.

Winkelmann-Gleed, A. (2006), *Migrant Nurses, motivation, integration, contribution.* (Oxford: Radcliffe Medical Press).

Xiang, B. (2001), 'Structuration of Indian Information Technology Professionals Migration to Australia: An Ethnographic Story', *International Migration* 39: 73–90.

Yeates, N. (2004), 'Global Care Chains: critical reflections and lines of enquiry', *International Feminist Journal of Politics* 6:3, 369–91.

Yuval-Davis, N. (1997), *Gender and Nation.* (London: Sage).

Zweig,_D. (1997), 'To Return or Not to Return? Politics v Economics in China's Brain Drain', *Studies in Comparative International Development* 32:1, 92–125.

Chapter 6

Regular Migrants in the Irregular Workplace: Central and Eastern European Women in the UK after EU Enlargement

Samantha Currie

Since the fall of the Iron Curtain in 1989, the migration of women from the Central and Eastern European (CEE) region has been a very live and dynamic subject-area. As labour markets under the socialist regimes were frequently characterized by full employment, in many CEE countries the transition towards a market economy – and the inevitable restructuring of employment markets that runs simultaneously with it – fostered conditions that encouraged nationals to seek work elsewhere, often in European Union (EU) Member States (Morokvasic 2004: 7 Coyle 2007: 38-39). The dismantling of state-run industries contributed to an insecure labour market within which job losses and unemployment levels increased. Such conditions have obviously had adverse consequences for men and women alike but there is evidence that women were particularly affected by the economic restructuring (Gal and Kligman 2000; Coyle 2007: 40). For example, in Poland women's labour market participation decreased throughout the 1990s (in 1994 it stood at 52.2 per cent; by 2003 it was 47.9 per cent) and the rate of female unemployment has been higher than that of male unemployment (in 2003 the rate of unemployment was 20 per cent for women and 18 per cent for men) (all figures quoted in Coyle 2007: 40). This combined with high levels of gender discrimination in employment and falling government support for women in paid work – amidst suggestions that women should not 'take' scarce jobs away from men – has arguably acted as an additional 'push' factor motivating the migration of women (Ibid: 41).

It is notoriously difficult to quantify the extent of the migration that took place following the fall of the communist regimes in the CEE region. Jordan and Düvell (2002: 88) estimate that after 1989 approximately one million Polish nationals per year looked for undocumented work in EU countries. Notably, during some periods in the 1980s and 1990s Polish women migrants outnumbered men (Kofman et al. 2000: 282). Although the European Union concluded Europe Association Agreements with the CEE countries that then held EU applicant status, these did not extend any rights of residence or labour market access to CEE nationals.[1] Consequently, it is estimated that much of the movement that did take place was of an informal nature (a factor contributing to the unreliability of statistical estimates). Thus, prior to the 2004 EU enlargement many commentators had acknowledged the propensity for Polish (and other CEE) migrants to be situated in certain types of 'casualized labour in the informal sector' (Kofman 2000: 51 Morokvasic 2003; Phizacklea 1983). Such informal employment is often carried out by migrant workers with an undocumented, irregular, legal status and is characterized by its insecurity, poor working conditions and low pay. This 'informalization' in sectors such as construction, agriculture, and cleaning, has been described as 'the "dark" or dangerous side of globalization' (Munck 2005). With regards to the particular experiences of migrant women, Campani (1993: 192) has suggested that the global shift towards a service economy has led to an increased demand for 'female' labour in some of the more precarious sectors of the informal labour market. Domestic work, caring in private homes and prostitution – all examples of the 'expansion in the sector of "services to private persons"' (Campani 1993: 192) – represent work that CEE migrant women in 'western' states were found to be occupying in the 1990s (Friese 1995; Anderson 2000; Coyle 2007; Morokvasic 2003).

Situated against this historical backdrop of informality and irregularization, the aim of this chapter is to explore the more recent employment status and experiences of women from the CEE region working in the United Kingdom (UK). Specifically, the contribution focuses on migrants from those CEE states that have acceded to the EU in recent years. It explores whether, and to what extent, EU enlargement has altered the labour market position of migrant women from the accession states. By examining their post-accession status and experiences in the labour market, and highlighting ways in which the legal and policy framework has influenced their access to and experience of work, the contribution seeks to analyse the relationship that women from the CEE accession states have with formal/regular and, conversely, informal/irregular spheres of employment in the UK. Overall, it reflects on the extent to which there is a disparity between the security of the legal status available to the migrants following the accession of the CEE Member States to the EU and the insecurity associated with the work many of them undertake. Although the broader context is that of migration from the CEE accession states and the irregular labour market, to allow for a more focused analysis the discussion at times draws particularly on evidence pertaining to Polish migration and to domestic work as a sector of informal employment. Reference is made to qualitative interviews carried out by the author with Polish migrants in

1 For example, Europe Agreement establishing an association between the European Communities and their Member States, of the one part, and the Republic of Poland, of the other part, [1993] OJ L348/3. These agreements did enable CEE nationals to establish businesses in the then EU Member States. For those who did access lawful employment there were provisions outlawing discrimination on the grounds of nationality in employment.

2004–2005 to highlight particular features and consequences of the post-accession migration space.

EU Enlargement to the 'East' and the Regulation of Migration

In the first decade of the 21st century the EU's membership increased from 15 to 27 Member States bringing with it a significant number of new EU citizens. In 2004 the EU expanded for the fifth time in its history to take in the Czech Republic, Estonia, Hungary, Latvia, Lithuania, Poland, Slovenia and Slovakia (hereafter, the 'EU8'), along with Malta and Cyprus (hereafter, the 'EU8'). The sixth enlargement took place in 2007 as Romania and Bulgaria (the 'EU2') acceded to the EU. The scale of these enlargements is significant,[2] but they also hold broader symbolic and political significance owing to the particular historical circumstances of many of the countries involved, notably their communist associations.

The particular socio-economic circumstances of the EU8 and EU2 Member States also meant that the eastward enlargements took place against a backdrop of political tension, largely linked to concerns over the perceived likelihood of large-scale migration following the extension of EU free movement rights to citizens in the new Member States (Farkas and Rymkevitch 2004). The significant economic disparities between east and west/old and new, combined with high unemployment rates in the acceding states, were perceived as creating a powerful push-pull dynamic that could draw people towards the 15 pre–2004 Member States (the EU15) with potential adverse consequences for national labour markets, levels of social protection and welfare systems (Dougan 2004; Kvist 2004). Responding to these concerns, a free movement compromise was negotiated into the 2003 Accession Treaties[3] whereby the individual EU15 Member States were given the option of derogating from established EU law governing the free movement of persons with a view to preventing nationals of the CEE accession countries from accessing the national labour market.[4] Analogous transitional provisions were later

2 With the accession of the EU8 (along with Malta and Cyprus), the EU's population increased by 28 per cent to more than 500 million people (Vaughan-Whitehead 2003, 31). In January 2007 this figure rose by a further 29 million as the EU enlarged again to take in the EU2 (Lanzieri 2007: 1).

3 Treaty of Accession 2003 [2003] OJ L 236/17. Article 24 of the Act of Accession [2003] OJ L236/33 refers to a series of Annexes that contain details of the transitional arrangements in respect of each accession Member State (Annexes V-XIV). For example, in relation to Poland see Annex XII [2003] OJ L236/875.

4 Cyprus and Malta, also 2004 accession states, are not subject to such transitional restrictions. The primary Treaty provision on free movement of workers within the Member States is Article 39 EC. The Accession Treaties permit derogation from Article 1-6 of Regulation 1612/68, these provisions further detail the rights of EU nationals to access the labour markets of other Member States. Older Member States are able to govern migration from the CEE accession states by enacting 'national measures'.

also incorporated into the 2005 Accession Treaties governing the accession of the EU2.[5] The EU15 are granted significant discretion as regards the severity and scope of any national measures put in place in relation to free movement restrictions, (Adinolfi 2005, Currie 2006) resulting in a multiplicity of different migration regimes (including quota, work permit and registration schemes). Some Member States (such as Ireland, Sweden and the UK) have implemented relatively 'open' labour market rules, whereas others (such as Germany and Austria) have opted to restrict access to EU8 and EU2 nationals more severely.[6] Certain Member States have imposed different access rules for EU2 nationals than for EU8 nationals. For example, the UK has put in place a more closed regime to regulate the admission of Romanians and Bulgarians to the labour market.

The post-enlargement mobility restrictions, in many instances, curtail accession nationals' ability to access 'regular' employment in the older Member States. Interestingly, in a 2006 report the European Commission's Directorate-General for Economic and Financial Affairs suggested that many of the Member States that did impose transitional restrictions encountered increased numbers of EU8 migrants working in the irregular, 'black' labour market in the aftermath of enlargement (European Commission 2006, 6). Tamas and Münz (2006) echo this sentiment and argue that demand for labour, as opposed to migration control, has a greater influence over the number of migrants that enter a territory.[7] Thus, the suggestion on a pan-European level has been that closed labour markets can divert greater numbers into the shadow economy. This, essentially, would perpetuate the pre-accession trend of significant numbers of CEE migrants working in EU15 informal economies. One would assume, in contrast, that in those Member States with a more open labour market policy, CEE nationals regularize their status and are able to move into more 'formal' sectors of the economy. The following section tests this proposition by examining the experiences of CEE migrant women in the UK, particularly in the aftermath of the 2004 enlargement.

---

5 Treaty of Accession 2005 [2005] OJ L157/11, Act concerning the conditions of accession of Bulgaria and Romania [2005] OJ L157/203. The transitional arrangements on the free movement of workers have a maximum duration of seven years (2004-2011 in respect of the EU8; 2007-2014 in respect of the EU2).

6 For an overview of the current rules on free movement, see the Commission's summary at <http://ec.europa.eu/employment_social/free_movement/enlargement_en.htm> (last accessed 9 August 2008). Pollard et al. (2008, 14) also provide a useful table overview of the national transitional restrictions.

7 This notion of demand-driven migration resonates with the market-based migration theory devised by Favell and Hansen (2002). This theory contends that the market rather than the law is the primary driver behind migration processes in the EU and its Member States.

CEE Women and the Formal-Informal Work Continuum in the UK

The UK did not restrict the ability of EU8 migrants to access employment in its territory. To work lawfully in the UK EU8 migrants need only register their employment on the Workers' Registration Scheme (WRS) (and pay a £90 fee).[8] In contrast, EU2 nationals' rights to work are more circumscribed and reflect a stricter application of transitional mobility restrictions in response to concerns as to the existing influx of migrants stimulated by the 2004 accession.[9] In view of these developments, the following section compares the employment experiences of EU8 migrant women with those from the EU2.

Regular by Name but not by Nature: The Employment Status of Migrant Women from the EU8

The UK government's decision to enable EU8 nationals to access jobs in 2004 was, in part, motivated by a desire to eradicate the 'black' labour market and to promote greater engagement in legitimate employment by migrant workers.

This rationale is evidenced by the 'amnesty' offered to those EU8 nationals who were already in the UK prior to enlargement but working in the informal economy; such individuals were encouraged to regularize their status by registering on the WRS. One might presume that this opportunity for regularization would also enable those in the informal employment sector to enhance their overall position and experience in the UK. Coyle (2007: 39) makes a similar presumption in relation to migrant women post-accession: 'As they gain the right to live and work across the EU, many of the difficulties that Polish migrant women have experienced as a consequence of their undocumented and illegal status should ease. Skilled women should be better able to access higher level occupations.' (Coyle 2007: 39)

This can be challenged, however, by examining the post-accession experience of migrant women. First, the 'type' of work that CEE migrants, both male and female, have been carrying out does not, as yet, seem to have altered: informality still characterizes even their registered employment. Secondly, it is questionable whether the opportunities to regularize in the UK are as extensive for women

8 Accession (Immigration and Worker Registration) Regulations 2004. Note that the UK's open labour market policy was twinned with restrictions on social welfare entitlement of EU8 nationals (by amending the habitual residence test) under the Social Security (Habitual Residence) Amendment Regulations 2004. The effect of the system is to make legal residence dependent upon being in employment and, in turn, access to social benefits is restricted to those legally resident, in other words, those in work. For further details on the UK regime post-2004, see Currie 2006.

9 Pollard et al. (2008) have developed a methodology which combines different datasets (including the WRS and the International Passenger Survey) and estimate that, in 2008, the current population of EU8 and EU2 nationals in the UK is 650,000 (an increase of approximately 555,000 since early 2004). Polish nationals are the single largest foreign national group resident in the UK.

as they are for men from the EU8. It may be that female migrants in the post-enlargement climate face additional barriers which render it more likely that they enter irregular forms of work. Both of these contentions are considered below.

Caught in a Low-Status Work Trap Much of the literature on post-enlargement migration has commented on the tendency for EU8 migrants in general (Anderson et al. 2006), and EU8 migrant women in particular (Currie 2007), to experience downward occupational mobility in the UK. The archetypal migrant identified in the research has been young and university educated, yet has been working in jobs categorized as low-skilled, low-status and low-paid (Pollard et al. 2008; Anderson et al. 2006; Currie 2007; 2008; Traser 2006; Traser and Venables 2008; European Commission 2006a).[10] A report by the European Foundation for the Improvement of Living and Working Conditions pointed to the occurrence of both youth and brain drain in the enlarged EU, and defines a 'typical' EU8 migrant as 'young, well-educated or studying in third-level education and living as a single, non-cohabiting person' (Krieger 2004: 3).

The Accession Monitoring Report (Home Office UK Border Agency 2008: 14) also confirms that the list of top 20 occupations for which EU8 nationals have registered has remained stable from 2004 to 2008. 'Process operative (factory worker)' is the 'number one' occupation of EU8 nationals; 64,170 registrations in 2007. Warehouse operatives (19,875), packers (11,880), kitchen and catering assistants (11,115), cleaners/domestic staff (11,810), farm workers (8,595), waiters/waitresses (6,115), maids/room attendants (7,200), labourers (6,520) and sales assistants (6,130) make up the remaining top 10, with care assistants and home carers (4,335) at number 11 (Ibid: 15). Similarly, the percentage of those registered who were in the lowest earnings category remained broadly stable: 75 per cent of those who applied to the WRS between May 2004 and March 2008 stated that their hourly wage was between £4.50 and £5.99.

This statistical data seems to mirror the sentiment captured in the following statement by Favell (2008: 711): '[M]ost of these East European migrants – who are far from uneducated or unskilled – appear destined to languish in undervalued roles in temporary and low-paid labouring, domestic, agriculture or construction work.'

It is interesting that the supposedly regularized and 'privileged' status of the migrants who have entered the UK and registered their employment on the WRS has not yet translated into any change in their labour market position. This is in spite of the fact that UK law acknowledges that they qualify as migrant workers

10 Commission research confirms that post-accession migrants from the EU8, resident in the EU15, have high levels of educational attainment, see European Commission 2006c.

under EU law and are entitled to a variety of employment and social rights on the same basis as nationals.[11]

There are certain features of the UK system, and trends that have emerged from it, that render employment in low-skilled jobs more likely. For example, an EU8 national is only considered to be legally resident when in work and registered on the WRS. On arrival, there is only a 30 day period of grace within which a migrant can register and search for employment before UK law classifies him or her as being unlawfully resident.[12] Similarly, an EU8 worker who becomes unemployed during the first year can only retain the months of work already accumulated if she finds alternative work and re-registers within 30 days from the date the original employment relationship ceased.[13]

This 30 day deadline has consequences for the type of work EU8 migrants are initially able to access. Migrants may seek employment in the UK before leaving the home state, usually via an employment agency (Ward et al. 2005). However, those that fail to do so and arrive without a pre-arranged job are faced with the pressure of finding work quickly to avoid being categorized as an irregular migrant. It is sometimes difficult to access professional occupations in the formal economy within 30 days since the recruitment process for such posts often extends over a longer time-frame. Human resources departments have become increasingly formalized and many employers have detailed recruitment procedures which comprise a number of stages, utilize a number of different advertisement channels, and rely upon lengthy selection procedures (McKenna and Beech 2002: 140-51). By contrast, informal work in the lower-skilled sectors of the labour market is often more readily accessible (Düvell 2004). For EU8 migrants, taking up work in a low-skilled position may simply be the most pragmatic decision. This is illustrated by the following Polish respondent. She had hoped to secure work in marketing for which she held a degree. However her priorities changed after moving to the UK; after searching for work for over a month she eventually found employment as a cleaner with the help of a London-based agency: 'I started to look for a job in July and it was very difficult. For almost one month and a half I couldn't find anything [in marketing] so I tried looking for other work. I left my CV in shops, in cafés and in bars. I was so depressed.' (Interview 304.P).

---

11 EU migrant workers' residence, employment and social entitlement flows from Article 39 EC. It is given further expression in secondary legislation, notably Regulation 1612/68 [1968] OJ L257/2 and Directive 2004/38 OJ [2004] L158/77. The ECJ has also interpreted the rights of workers expansively, see *inter alia,* Case 316/85 *Lebon* [1987] ECR 2811; Case 207/78 *Even* [1979] ECR 2019; Case 139/85 *Kempf* [1986] ECR 1741; Case 53/81 *Levin* [1982] ECR 1035; Case C-357/89 *Raulin* [1992] ECR I-1027.

12 Regulation 7(2)(b)(i), Accession (Immigration and Worker Registration) Regulations 2004 ('WRR') SI 2004/121.

13 Regulation 2(4), WRR. This is important because after an EU8 migrant has complied with the registration process continuously for a year, the worker will be eligible for an EEA residence permit and will no longer be subject to any restrictions or registration conditions.

A significant amount of research conducted since 2004 confirms the rather negative labour market experiences of accession migrants. Concern has also been expressed, for example by trade unions, that some EU8 workers continue to be exploited by employers in terms of low-paid work, poor safety standards and insufficient enforcement of employment rights (TGWU 2006; TGWU 2005; TUC 2005). Research has found that some EU8 migrant workers in the UK, despite having the legal right to work and being registered on the WRS, are subject to such levels of exploitation and control that they fall within the international legal definition of 'forced labour' (Anderson and Rogaly 2005: 7 Jayaweera and Anderson 2008: 5). In other words, labour market patterns and conditions associated with informality are also playing a role in the lives of those with a legal immigration status.

The available statistical data, such as that referred to above, is not disaggregated by gender and so reveals little about the distinct experiences of women and men. Evidence from qualitative research, however, when analysed in conjunction with the interdisciplinary literature on gender and migration, can provide at least indicative evidence of wider trends pertaining to the experiences of CEE migrant women. The qualitative empirical work carried out by the author in 2004–2005 did evidence certain gender-specific features of the employment experiences of CEE migrants which link into broader arguments about female employment. For example, whereas the men interviewed were in occupations such as construction, driving and factory work, greater numbers of women were represented in caring and cleaning jobs. This observation obviously reflects a general trend within the labour market, and as such may appear trite, but this does carry specific connotations within the context of migration. First, it is arguable that EU8 migrant women face additional obstacles to regularization than EU8 migrant men in that their migration path will include greater incentives towards the taking up of informal work. Secondly, and following on from this point, informal 'female' employment – particularly that which is carried out in the private sphere – can be particularly undetectable and, as such, can lead to workers being placed in particularly vulnerable situations. It is to obstacles to regularization that attention now turns.

Restricted Opportunities to Regularize for EU8 Migrant Women Research suggests that a considerable number of EU8 migrants do not register their employment on the WRS and, as a result, their status is formally classified as irregular under UK law.[14] The majority of respondents interviewed by the author in 2004 and 2005 had not registered on the WRS, a tendency confirmed in subsequent research (Anderson et al, 2006: 97). In some cases, this is the choice of the individual migrant; many of those interviewed by the author were unhappy

14 Note that, under EU law, they may have rights of residence and equal treatment by virtue of their status as Union citizens and the interaction of Articles 18 and 12 EC. It is also possible that EU law would not recognize the UK's classification of illegality based on non-registration. On the interplay between EU and domestic law see Currie 2008.

with the registration fee which, especially in the initial phase after arrival, was viewed as being very costly. Some also stressed that there was 'no point' in registering as they did not intend to stay longer than a few months and had no interest in accumulating uninterrupted months of lawful employment. For others, non-registration had not been a conscious decision; they were simply not aware of the requirement to register or were misinformed about the applicability of the scheme to them.[15] Anderson et al. (2006) point to the lack of incentives for EU8 migrants to register, in particular the low probability that the UK authorities would actually carry out a deportation against such EU8 nationals (despite this being a theoretical possibility). On the other hand, it appears that in some instances it is at the employer's (or agency's) insistence that workers do not register. Despite the fact that employers commit an offence by employing unregistered EU8 workers,[16] there are very few checks conducted and legal enforcement is weak. Levels of prosecution against employers for violations of immigration law more generally are low, a trend reflected also in the operation of the WRS (Anderson et al. 2006: 97).

It is likely that some employers prefer to keep workers away from the 'legitimacy' associated with registration; after all, it is easier to offer poor work and pay conditions to those who exist outside of the official scheme away from even the most basic checks and balances.[17] The empirical data generated for the author's research would support this assertion; there were a number of examples of employers who preferred to 'keep the work illegal'. For example the following respondent, who worked in a café, was very aware of her employer's reasoning behind the decision to employ only irregular workers:

> I must confess that it was an illegal job because I didn't pay any insurance or tax or register myself. The money wasn't very good. I worked with a girl from Hungary and a girl from Brazil. It was illegal and I think that a lot of people work like that. Even though now it is legal you know the employers don't want to hire people legally because they can then pay less to workers and in such places there are only foreigners working there because no English people would accept that. It is not nice but they can always say: 'if you don't want a job there are plenty of people who would take your place' (Interview 304.P).

Given this context, it seems rather ironic that the government was seeking to eradicate the black labour market when it set up the WRS. Such findings indicate that availability of registration has not succeeded in regularizing illegal migrant workers, or in significantly reducing the black labour market.

---

15 The degree of confusion surrounding the scheme is elaborated on below.

16 Regulation 9(1), WRR.

17 EU8 workers should benefit from the protection of Directive 93/104/EC on the organization of working time [1993] *OJ L307/18;* as well as from equal remuneration provisions (Article 7(1), Regulation 1612/68).

Women from the accession countries are likely to face even greater difficulties than men in accessing regular employment and remain at greater risk of entering the informal and private economy. For example, one particular aspect of the climate that has emerged since 2004 and appears to operate in a gender-specific way is the popularity of organized migration schemes amongst employers. It has become common for employers with significant staff shortages to look towards the CEE accession countries for recruits. Such schemes generally involve an employer making contact with a partner of some kind, usually an employment agency, in Poland (or other EU8 Member State) and the subsequent recruitment of a group of migrants. The author's research, for example, incorporated a case study on a travel firm which recruited over 100 Polish drivers. Similar schemes operate in a number of other sectors (such as factory workers, doctors, drivers, engineers and IT professionals).[18] These are clearly of real benefit to migrants in assisting them in overcoming some of the hurdles associated with moving to a new country, language and housing in particular.[19] In addition, they often avoid 'occupational skidding' (Morawska and Spohn 1997: 36) by enabling the migrant to find the same employment in the UK as they occupied in Poland.

It seems, however, that these schemes may be operating in a gender-specific way that excludes many migrant women from such beneficial assistance.[20] This is undoubtedly related to the fact that many of the sectors in need of labour are associated with 'men's work', and so any associated training inevitably favours men also (Morokvasic 2004: 13 Kofman 2000: 50). The reduced opportunity to access such formal schemes is likely to increase the chances of a woman looking towards more casualized work in the informal sector, perhaps carrying out cleaning and domestic work. The lack of regulation by a formal agency or official employer and the absence of any official employment contract can leave migrant women in a particularly vulnerable situation. Women who take up casualized employment find themselves in a more isolated set-up with few formal support networks to turn to should problems arise in the host society. The reasons for the apparent lack of more formal recruitment schemes in areas such as domestic work and cleaning are not entirely clear. One suggestion is that such schemes do exist but that they target non-EU as opposed to EU migrants. Additionally, there are sectors which recruit through more informal migrant networks, creating less demand for formally organized schemes.

18 Based on Interview 401.S; Interview 402.B; Interview 403.I;, Interview 404.P and Interview 405.N.

19 This is not to deny that some agencies can be exploitative migration intermediaries, see Currie 2006. The employment agencies interviewed in Poland were all included on a national register and thus subject to, at least some, regulation. The same obviously would not apply to 'rogue' agencies in Poland and the UK.

20 This mirrors the way in which IT shortages in the 1990s favoured male migrants, see Kofman 2004: 654.

In any event, there is a point to be made here that stretches further than the existence of organized schemes per se. A number of more general factors contribute to the obstacles faced by women migrants in accessing formal employment. For example, the well-documented implications of family and domestic responsibilities (which continue to be borne in the main by women) for women's working life and employment prospects also holds relevance in the mobility context (Ackers and Stalford 2007). The cultural context within which the migration is situated is also clearly important; entrenched views on what are 'appropriate' jobs for women infiltrate the migration process perpetuating a demand for 'female' labour in the most vulnerable sectors.

Particularly precarious employment situated in the informal economy is that which operates largely in the private sphere and is, consequently, hidden from any rigorous public scrutiny. Such employment includes domestic and sex work, two areas dominated by women, and migrant women in particular (Anderson 2000). Domestic work certainly seems to have a continuing relevance to EU8 migrant women in the UK. This is interesting from the perspective of the discussion in this chapter as it is widely documented that a considerable number of these workers face poor living and exploitative working conditions and exist outside of any legal regulation (Schwenken 2005; Scullion this collection). There has been increased demand for female domestic workers in western industrialized countries, such as the UK, due to various demographic and social changes, the most notable of which are an ageing population and increased levels of female employment: 'The demand of "unprotected" female workers for employment in private households grows in the same measure as the trend of western middle-class women towards employment continues with increasing levels of education' (Friese 1995: 194).

The sample of migrants who took part in the author's study includes two female domestic workers employed by private households (one lived-in) and one female employed as a cleaner in a private household. In addition, three other women had previously worked as live-in domestic workers.[21] None of this work had been registered under the WRS.

As a result of its hidden nature it is difficult to estimate accurately the number of EU8 national women engaged in such employment. The WRS statistics tell us that 36,645 EU8 nationals had registered under the occupation category of 'cleaner/domestic staff in the first three years of the scheme's operation' (Home Office UK Border Agency 2007: 16).[22] Furthermore, it was estimated that there were 14,300 foreign (including third-country national) domestic workers in the UK in 2000 (Crawley 2001), although the actual number now is likely to be even greater. It may also be correct to say that there is an element of cultural heritage

21 Each subsequently took up the posts of nursery assistant, administrative assistant and waitress respectively.

22 There is no gender or occupation breakdown given of this figure.

at work here. For example, statistics on the au pair scheme in the UK[23] show that 3,490 of the 15,300 au pairs in the UK in 2003 were from Poland (Home Office 2003: 30). Given that a further 4,560 were from the Czech Republic and 2,690 were Slovakian it would appear that the trend for EU8 women to work in a domestic capacity has continued post-accession and, additionally, this cultural heritage of domestic work may have shaped the expectations of what constitute 'appropriate' jobs for EU8 women.

This is an area of employment that, in some instances, can be particularly negative, exploitative or even dangerous, precisely because the migrant worker is situated in the informal sphere. Of the six respondent domestic workers who took part in the study, one had found it to be a wholly negative experience. This woman worked as a domestic worker for one year in London and had since returned to Poland to work as a librarian. In the extract below she describes the manner in which the close proximity with her employer, which goes hand in hand with 'living in', led to her working excessive hours and essentially never being able to 'escape':

> They wanted someone to be a housekeeper and to take care of an old woman who was ill. She was from Poland and so that's why they wanted a Polish worker. She couldn't speak very well so it was very hard work … maybe not physical hard work but mental hard work. This woman had MS and she was also very depressed. I had only one free day, Sunday, and even then I was asked to do things for them. I had no time to myself (Interview 316.M).

The remaining domestic workers in the sample spoke in a more positive way about their time living in private households. Three expressed their relationship in the terms of being 'part of the family' although the literature suggests that this common perception may, in reality, work against domestic workers. For example, Hess and Puckhaber (2004: 65) have demonstrated that the more integrated a worker is into the family, the more difficult it becomes for them to take issue with poor working conditions. Workers are therefore entirely at the mercy of their employers who exercise exclusive authority to determine the terms of the employment.[24]

---

23 The current UK scheme, established by the Immigration Rules made under section 3(2) of the Immigration Act. 1971, C.77 enables single people between 17–27, with no dependents, come to the UK 'to study English' for up to two years while living with a family. The au pairs can help in the home for up to five hours per day and, although they do not receive a salary, they should be given an 'allowance' (£55 per week is recommended). They must not require any assistance from public funds and must not stay in the UK when the au pair period comes to an end. The EU8 (and EU2) countries were covered by the scheme prior to 2004 and, even though the scheme no longer formally applies to them, EU8 nationals can still enter the UK as au pairs (as can all EU nationals). For information on the working of the scheme see <http://www.bia.homeoffice.gov.uk/workingintheuk/aupairs/> (Accessed 20 February 2008).

24 There is also a question as to whether domestic workers in the private household would fall within the scope of the formal 'migrant worker' definition established by the

Relating to this are concerns as to the ability of workers to enforce employment-related rights. Under the UK regulations only registered EU8 workers are entitled to equality of treatment with national workers as regards employment[25] and social benefits.[26] Consequently, they may be denied access to work-related rights, such as parental leave and pension rights, or may be forced to work in conditions that do not meet adequate health and safety standards. Much of this entitlement is gender-specific. For example, maternity leave and access to health care associated with pregnancy are forms of valuable entitlement which may be restricted from those in more informal forms of employment with adverse personal, professional and financial consequences for those concerned.

Formal Access to Informal Work: EU2 Migrant Women in the UK

As noted above, the UK has imposed more restrictive conditions on Romanian and Bulgarian workers' right to work, with some notable consequences for women.

In order to work in the UK a Bulgarian or Romanian national must first apply for and be granted a worker authorization card.[27] Such cards can only be obtained by: those who carry out 'work permit employment' and have been granted a work permit under the national immigration rules;[28] individuals who take up work in an otherwise 'authorized category of employment' (notably such occupations include the female-dominated 'caring' occupations of domestic workers, nurses and au pairs);[29] or, those who gain a place on a low-skilled migration scheme (such as the Sectors Based Scheme and the Seasonal Agricultural Workers Scheme).[30] Furthermore, in most cases (across all categories) at the beginning of the application process an employer must first seek approval of the work arrangement under the work permit system. Only after this approval has been given can an individual apply for an accession worker card (Home Office UK Border Agency 2007b).

European Court of Justice to determine access to the panoply of rights that flow from Article 39 EC. See Currie 2007 and, *inter alia*, Case 66/85 *Lawrie Blum* [1986] ECR 2121, Case C-357/89 *Raulin* [1992] ECR I-1027, Case 53/81 *Levin* [1982] ECR.

25 Extended to those qualifying as EU migrant workers on the basis of Article 7(1), Regulation 1612/68 which provides that the principle of non-discrimination covers conditions of employment.

26 Pursuant to Article 7(2), Regulation 1612/68 which entitles migrant workers to the same 'social and tax advantages' as national workers (now supplemented by Article 24(1), Directive 2004/38).

27 Pursuant to the rules set out in the Accession (Immigration and Worker Authorization) Regulations 2006 SI 2006/3317.

28 Regulation 11, Accession (Immigration and Worker Authorization) Regulations 2006 SI 2006/3317.

29 Schedule 1, Accession (Immigration and Worker Authorization) Regulations 2006 SI 2006/3317.

30 Regulations 9 and 10, Accession (Immigration and Worker Authorization) Regulations 2006 SI 2006/3317.

This system is interesting on two counts. First, it is noteworthy that the decision of the UK government to impose transitional mobility restrictions on Romanians and Bulgarians, and hence to deny them free access to the employment market, was accompanied by the implementation of a policy which involved the reservation of all places on the low-skilled migration schemes for such EU2 nationals. This was announced by former Home Secretary John Reid when he confirmed the imposition of restrictions on Bulgarian and Romanian nationals:

> From 1 January 2007 we will be phasing out all low-skilled migration schemes from outside the EU. Places on the two low-skilled migration schemes (the seasonal agricultural workers scheme and the sectors based scheme which between them currently have 19,750 places) will now be restricted to nationals from Romania and Bulgaria.[31]

This decision, which reflects the preference clause in the Treaty of Accession's transitional provisions,[32] undoubtedly demonstrates the potential negative impact of EU enlargement on the position of third-country nationals in the Member States. Moreover, it highlights the expectation held by some of the Member States about the role the new EU citizens will fulfil; essentially they are expected to carry out the low-skilled, low-status and low-paid work.[33]

Secondly, the very specific provision made for domestic workers, au pairs in the UK's latest transitional rules, highlights the continuing 'demand' for such workers amongst middle-class working families. Perhaps this also demonstrates how the government is content to 'open up' an area of the labour market which it has, in practice, very little day-to-day regulation. This is reminiscent of Newcombe's (2004: 22) arguments in the context of au pairing: 'At the institutional level, the state sets up relationships between au pairs and host families and then walks away leaving an unregulated space, within which au pair agencies and families have the greatest room for manoeuvre.'

The potentially negative connotations of working in the private sphere have already been expounded above in the context of EU8 migration. As regards the rules on EU2 workers, a further point is worth noting: UK worker authorization cards are only issued in relation to specific jobs, effectively channelling Romanian and Bulgarian nationals into certain parts of the low-skilled employment market. Consequently, the worker is effectively 'tied' to the job (and the employer) in order to maintain their status of legality. Such dependency is a feature of many countries' formal migration channels for domestic workers (Anderson 2000: 176-8). Kofman et al. (2000: 123) cite the example of a 1980s scheme set up by the UK government which enabled migrating foreign employers and repatriated British

31 Hansard, HC, vol. 450, col. 84 (24 October 2006).

32 Para. 14, Annexes.

33 For further discussion of the experience of EU8 migrants working in the lower echelons of the UK labour market see Currie 2007, 83–116.

professionals to bring their domestic workers with them to the UK. These workers had no independent legal status and, in what was effectively a form of modern slavery, they too were tied to their employers. The authors (Ibid: 123) highlight some of the more unsavoury consequences arising from this earlier scheme: 'The system was widely abused with one agency alone handling over 4,000 reported cases of imprisonment, physical and sexual abuse, as well as widespread under and non-payment of workers by their employers.'

This illustrates the vulnerable and potentially dangerous situation in which some domestic workers can find themselves as a result of the domestic sphere's isolation from the mainstream, even those who have made use of formal, regular channels to enter a territory.

The available statistics suggest that between January 2007 and June 2008, there were 7,040 applications by Romanians and Bulgarians for Accession Worker Cards in the UK of which 4,730 were approved (Home Office UK Border Agency 2008a: 3).[34] 3,715 of these workers were in 'work permit employment'; whereas, 1,015 held cards for occupations classed as other 'authorized categories of employment' including au pairs, domestic workers and those in employment connected to the Sectors Based Scheme.[35]

Of course, Romanians and Bulgarians are also represented in other sectors. For example, the UK's monitoring statistics reveal that migrant women are entering the 'top five' sectors of: health and medical, manufacturing, administration business and management, financial, and educational and cultural. Unfortunately there are no indications as to what level of seniority or post they hold in these sectors (see also Raghuram, this collection), making it difficult to gain a complete picture of the actual work EU2 nationals are carrying out in the UK.[36] As with all migration statistics, there is also no way of knowing how many have bypassed this layer of regulation by entering unregulated employment without an accession worker card. Romanian and Bulgarian nationals have historically, like many other CEE nationals, accessed irregular employment in the labour markets of the older EU Member States (Horváth 2008: 772 Culic 2008: 150) and, for some, this experience will undoubtedly continue post-EU enlargement.

---

34 The UK Home Office publishes quarterly statistics on Bulgarian and Romanian nationals in the UK Home Office UK Border Agency 2008a).

<http://www.ukba.homeoffice.gov.uk/sitecontent/documents/aboutus/reports/bulgarianromanian/> (Accessed 19 February 2008).

35 The overall male:female ratio of those receiving accession worker cards between January 2007 and June 2008 was 55:45. The majority of applications are from Romanian nationals (*e.g.* 58 per cent of applicants in the first three months of 2008) (Home Office UK Border Agency 2008).

36 In addition, as the transitional restrictions do not apply to self-employed workers, many have opted to establish a business as opposed to obtaining a work permit. See *e.g.* Jayaweera and Anderson 2008; Pollard et al. 2008.

Aside from obtaining a worker authorization card, there is one other avenue open to EU2 nationals seeking to migrate to the UK during the transitional period: the 'highly skilled' (Accession (Immigration and Worker Authorization) Regulations 2006, Regulation 4).[37] 'Highly skilled' is defined quite narrowly on the basis of national immigration law rules applicable also to third-country nationals. Given that only 180 EU2 nationals obtained registration certificates on this basis between January 2007 and June 2008 (Home Office UK Border Agency 2008a: 6), it seems this route of entry is not benefitting many Bulgarians or Romanians, despite the fact that it is not conditional upon holding a specific job offer. At this point, it may be worth noting that the assumption of privilege often associated with highly-skilled migrants has been challenged. Ackers et al, in their work on mobile scientists from Poland and Bulgaria, have drawn attention to the (gender-)specific difficulties faced by many female migrants who have accessed higher sectors of the labour market (Ackers and Stalford 2007, Ackers and Oliver 2007, and Oliver this volume). This research has exposed the pressures imposed on women by an embedded long working hours culture in the scientific profession, and the difficulties this can cause in terms of reconciling work and family life. Related problems of arranging (and covering the costs of) child care in a country in which the migrant family may be rather isolated was also acknowledged. Such factors can stifle female progression in the various highly-skilled professions.

Thus far, the respective positions of EU8 and EU2 migrants have been considered in a relatively discrete fashion. The following section seeks to pull some of the strands of the discussion together and offer more of a holistic analysis of the (changing) nature of intra-EU east-west migration and what implications there might be for female migrants in particular.

A Fluid and Flexible Migration Space

The evidence that has emerged in the post-accession UK climate suggests that, in spite of the divergent legal rules which apply to the different groups, there is little distinctive variation between the type of work carried out by EU8 nationals on the one hand and EU2 nationals on the other hand. Further, it does not seem that membership of the EU is (yet) having any extensive qualitative impact on the day-to-day employment experience of CEE accession migrants in the UK, despite the enhanced security of legal status now available to such migrants. Traditionally, the positioning and experiences of migrants within the labour markets of EU

37 'Highly skilled' also includes those who, within the last 12 months, have obtained (i) a Higher National Diploma or degree awarded by a relevant institution in Scotland; or (ii) a degree with second class honours or above in a subject approved by the Department for Education and Skills for the purpose of participation in the Science and Engineering Graduates Scheme, or a master's degree or doctorate in any subject, awarded by a relevant institution in England, Wales or Northern Ireland.

Member States differed depending on their status as either privileged, internal EU-nationals or non-privileged, third-country nationals. There has been a general acceptance that third-country nationals have been undertaking the 3D – 'degrading, dangerous and dirty' – work in the Member states that EU-nationals 'are no longer prepared to do' (Kofman et al. 2000: 119). Similarly, Kofman et al. (Ibid: 122) have acknowledged the existence of a dual labour market, 'one for EU nationals and one for nationals of third countries who provide cheap and flexible labour power.' Clearly, third-country nationals within the EU are not a homogenous group; it would be inappropriate to equate the experience of US or Australian migrants with that of, for example, migrants from African countries. Nevertheless, the dual labour market notion is useful as a general indicator of migrants' status and entitlement within the EU. The recent EU enlargements have altered this established order on a scale unlike any accession that has gone before, however, and the current employment profile of CEE accession migrants is more akin to that of third-country nationals than that of nationals from the older EU Member States. Following the 'eastern' accessions then it would appear that divisions also exist within the traditionally 'privileged' group of EU nationals with regards to the work they undertake as migrant workers. Indeed, a discussion paper prepared on behalf of the 2005 UK Presidency by Patrick Weil used this trend rather unashamedly as an argument to support the lifting of labour market restrictions on EU8 migrants by the rest of the EU15:

> The countries who continue to close their labour markets find themselves in a counter-productive situation; with new European citizens immigrating anyway and working illegally. In the EU states that have opened their labour market, the new European citizens fill the jobs that are fulfilled in the rest of Europe by illegal migrants, either from the new Member States or non EU countries (Weil 2005).

Effectively, a new layer of disadvantaged migrants has been added to the hierarchy. The position of EU8 migrants in the UK's secondary labour market mirrors the secondary status granted to them at EU-level under the transitional arrangements on the free movement of persons. Seemingly, the position of third-country nationals has been further exacerbated as, in the UK at least, they are competing against EU8 and EU2 migrants for certain jobs.[38] Thus, under this

38 Particularly as the transitional arrangements oblige employers to give preference to EU8 and EU2 nationals over third-country nationals in access to jobs: para. 14, Annexes. The issue may not be quite so straightforward, however, due to the recent Directive on the position of third-country national long-term residents (Directive 2003/109/EC [2004] OJ L16/44). This Directive grants the right of equal treatment as regards access to employment to third-country nationals who have resided in an EU Member State for five years or more. Thus, in the older Member States fully applying the transitional restrictions on free movement, EU8 and EU2 nationals will occupy an inferior status to third-country

conceptualization, the CEE accession workers are forced into certain, specific sectors of employment, but TCN workers are potentially forced out completely.

This understanding assumes that EU8 and EU2 migrants currently have a largely assimilated work experience, a proposition endorsed by Favell (2008: 711):

> [T]here is little evidence that formal borders or barriers have made a lot of difference between, say, Poles and Romanians, although the latter are more likely to find themselves in precarious situations for want of official papers. But where their experiences are strikingly similar is in their strong sense of exclusion and exploitation ... The jobs they take are the ones that the West's citizens no longer want – those 3D jobs that have become a familiar range of employment 'opportunities' in the post-industrial service economy.

This conceptualization of the post-enlargement migration space certainly holds resonance but it would arguably be short-sighted to dismiss, or underestimate, the impact that the law – more specifically, a change in formal legal status – can have on the available employment options and opportunities for migrants. Domestic work again provides a pertinent example: Anderson (2007: 260-1) quotes examples of host families who made outright requests for Romanian, Bulgarian or Turkish au pairs, precisely because the legal status of EU8 nationals had been enhanced following the 2004 EU enlargement. Indeed, Anderson (Ibid: 260) also confirms that au pair agencies had reported substantial increases in the number of Romanian women they were placing in the UK. This is an interesting observation as, from one perspective, EU8 migrants' stronger legal rights are enabling them to 'escape' from certain jobs that have been characterizing their rather downtrodden employment experience. In other words it suggests that, although there has been no overnight transformation, EU membership does offer the promise of escape from the low-status work trap over a longer period (and would eventually also impact on EU2 nationals when transitional restrictions on their rights are eventually lifted). From another perspective, this might be taken as an indication of opportunities actually being closed-off to EU8 workers as a result of their fortified status, so that they effectively lose out to an even more flexible workforce.

One point this really does emphasize is that the intra-EU migration space is constantly evolving. The legal framework on free movement is extremely dynamic and will continue to shift as transitional arrangements applicable to both the EU8 and EU2 expire and the formal mobility status and rights of all present EU citizens equalize. Similarly, the political and economic context of both the newer and older Member States continues to alter shaping the supply and demand of the migrant workforce. The climate in the UK, for example, has already changed

---

nationals who fulfill the conditions in the Directive for securing long-term resident status (see Rettman 2006). The date for implementation was 23 January 2006. Note that the UK, Ireland and Denmark have opted-out and hence are not bound by the Directive. See more generally on the Directive Halleskov 2005.

somewhat since 2004 with the falling value of sterling weakening the economic impetus for EU8 nationals to work in the UK and, conversely, the economies of EU8 countries showing signs of growth and increases in wage-levels (Pollard et al. 2008). Structural changes such as these are contributing to a decrease in the numbers of EU8 nationals heading to the UK and an increase in those returning to their home states (Ibid).

Conclusion

CEE accession nationals with both regular and irregular statuses have continued to be situated in work traditionally associated with irregularity in the UK's 'flexible' labour market. This state of affairs can be traced back to the 'supply and demand' logic embodied in the transitional arrangements in the Accession Treaties. At EU level, CEE accession migrants have effectively been assigned the role of a flexible reserve army of labour for the EU15 when labour shortages so require. The corollary of this is that the work such a reserve army is frequently called upon to do is situated in the secondary labour market and, as such, is characterized by poor working conditions, and is often not significantly different to the employment experience of those with an unlawful migration or employment status.

The reserve army notion also raises the issue of the relationship between third-country nationals and CEE accession nationals in the post-accession climate. Previously, it has been third-country national migrants that have carried out much of the work in the UK (and other EU15 Member States') secondary labour markets. EU8 and EU2 nationals have made the formal transition from third-country national to EU national (or Union citizen), but the reality is that their employment experience continues to be characterized in a manner similar to that of third-country nationals. This reflects their transitional citizenship status in the immediate aftermath of enlargement; they are not yet full members of the free movement community and, hence, cannot expect their labour market experience to alter to any great extent initially. It would be naïve, however, to assume that this will automatically alter on expiry of the transitional arrangements. Although at this point the formal status of EU8 and EU2 nationals will mirror that of EU15 nationals, and the label of irregularity will no longer formally apply, it may be that longer-term social reconditioning will be necessary before stereotypes of what constitutes 'appropriate work' for CEE migrants, and the linked discrimination, on the part of employers in the EU15 for example, are eradicated. That being said, an enhanced legal status can undoubtedly contribute to a more secure and protected migration experience, particularly for those with a certain degree of rights awareness who are able to directly seek to enforce their rights in the event of default (by an employer for example). Furthermore, the potential of law to elicit more profound change, especially once it has time to filter through the layers of the EU polity, by impacting on perceptions of EU8 and EU2 nationals should not be underestimated.

There is no doubt that the labour market dynamics discussed in this chapter have affected women and men alike. It does, however, raise particular concerns in respect of the position of women from the EU8 and EU2 in the (live) climate of the post-accession migration space. The propensity of female migrants from the CEE region to migrate to the 'West' throughout the 1980s and particularly the 1990s – when opportunities to access a lawful, regular status were minimal – resulted in many such women moving into the private, unregulated sphere and living in a 'twilight zone' (Coyle 2007: 43). Although both men and women enter the informal labour market, the implications are often more precarious for women as a consequence of the hidden nature of the employment usually accessible to them.[39] Post-enlargement in the UK, these patterns have continued and have in some circumstances been encouraged by the legal and regulatory framework. The operation of employer-arranged schemes in respect of the EU8, and the UK's more relaxed rules as regards EU2 nationals' working as au pairs and domestic workers, evidence this. Much of this discussion of the particular consequences for migrant women relates to what is deemed as appropriate work for women (i.e. in the home). However, much of this also relates to what is considered to be suitable work for *migrant* women as, even in the 21st century, the experience of many continues to be characterized by precarious employment, often hidden from any public scrutiny, which in some way serves the needs of more privileged (and wealthy) members of the host society.

References

Ackers, L. and Stalford, H. (2007), 'Managing Multiple Life-Courses: The Influence of Children on Migration Processes in the European Union', *Social Policy Review* 19, 321–42.

– and Oliver, L. (2007), 'From Flexicurity to Flexsecquality? The Impact of the Fixed-term Contract Provisions on Employment in Science Research.' *International Studies of Management and Organization* 37:1, 53–79.

Adinolfi, A. (2005), 'Free Movement and Access to Work of Citizens of the New Member States: The Transitional Measures', *Common Market Law Review* 42:2, 469–98.

Anderson, B. (2007), 'A Very Private Business: Exploring the Demand for Migrant Domestic Workers', *European Journal of Women's Studies*, 14, 247–64.

– (2000), *Doing the Dirty Work? The Global Politics of Domestic Labour* (London: Zed Books).

– and Rogaly, B. (2005), *Forced Labour and Migration to the UK* (Oxford: Study prepared by COMPAS in collaboration with the Trades Union Congress).

39 Although domestic work has been used as a case study here, this is of course also true of sex work, an area of work with even greater chances of mistreatment and danger.

– et al. (2006), *Fair Enough? Central and East European Migrants in Low-Wage Employment in the UK* (Oxford: COMPAS).
– (2001), 'Why Madam has so Many Bathrobes: Demand for Migrant Domestic Workers in the EU', 22:1, 18–26.
Beck, U. (2000), *The Brave New World of Work* (Cambridge: Polity Press).
Bhagwati, J. (1976), The Brain Drain and Taxation – Theory and Empirical analysis, Amsterdam, North-Holland Publishing Co.
Boyer, D. (2006), "Gender and the Solvency of Professionalism: Eastern German Journalism before and after 1989." East European Politics and Societies. 20: 152-179.
Campani, G. (1993), 'Labour Markets and Family Networks: Filipino Women in Italy' in Rudolph, H. and Morokvasic, M. (eds).
Coyle, A., (2007), 'Resistance, Regulation and Rights: The Changing Status of Polish Women's Migration and Work in the "New" Europe', *European Journal of Women's Studies* 14, 37.
Crawley, H. (2001), *Refugees and Gender, Law and Process* (London: Jordans and Refugee Women's Legal Group).
Culic, I. (2008), 'Eluding Exit and Entry Controls: Romanian and Moldovan Immigrants in the European Union', 22:1, 145–70.
Currie, S. (2006), '"Free" movers? The Post-Accession Experience of Accession – 8 Migrant Workers in the UK', *European Law Review* 31:2 207–29.
– (2007), 'De-Skilled and Devalued: The Labour Market Experience of Polish Migrants in the UK Following EU Enlargement', *International Journal of Comparative Labour Law and Industrial Relations* 23:1, 83–116.
– (2008), Migration, Work and Citizenship in the Enlarged European Union (Aldershot, Ashgate).
Dougan, M. (2004), 'A Spectre is Haunting Europe … Free Movement of Persons and the Eastern Enlargement' in Hillion, C. (ed.).
Düvell, F. (2004), *Polish Undocumented Immigrants, Regular Highly-Skilled Workers and Entrepreneurs in the UK* (Warsaw: Institute for Social Studies Working Paper).
European Commission (Directorate-General for Economic and Financial Affairs) (2006), *Enlargement, Two Years After: An Economic Evaluation*, Occasional Paper 24 (Brussels: European Commission).
European Commission (2006a), *Report on the Functioning of the Transitional Arrangements set out in the 2003 Accession Treaty (period 1 May 2004–30 April 2006)*, COM (2006) 48 final.
Farkas, O. and Rymkevitch, O. (2004), 'Immigration and the Free Movement of Workers after Enlargement: Contrasting Choices', *International Journal of Comparative Labour Law and Industrial Relations* 20:3, 369–97.
Favell, A. and Hansen, R. (2002), 'Markets against Politics: Migration, EU Enlargement and the Idea of Europe', *Journal of Ethnic and Migration Studies* 28:4, 581–601.

Favell, A. (2008), 'The New Face of East-West Migration in Europe', *Journal of Ethnic and Migration Studies'* 34:5, 701–16.

Friese, M. (1995), 'East European Women as Domestics in Western Europe – New Social Inequality and Division of Labour Among Women', *Journal of Area Studies* 6, 194–201.

Gal, S. and Kligman, G. (2000), *The Politics of Gender after Socialism: A Comparative-Historical Essay* (Princeton, NJ: Princeton University Press).

Hagerstrand, T. (1982), Diorama path and project Tijdschrift voor economische en sociale geografie, 73, 6, 323-339.

Hess, S. and Puckhaber, A. (2004), '"Big sisters" are Better Domestic Servants? Comments on the Booming Au Pair Business', *Feminist Review* 77, 65–78.

Home Office (2003), *Control of Immigration: Statistics United Kingdom 2003* (London: Home Office).

Home Office et al. (2005), Department for Work and Pensions, the Inland Revenue and the Office of the Deputy Prime Minister, *Accession Monitoring Report, May 2004–March 2005*, 26 May 2005.

Home Office UK Border Agency (2007), *Accession Monitoring Report, May 2004–September 2007,* Joint Online Report between the Border and Immigration Agency, Department for Work and Pensions, HM Revenue and Customs and Communities and Local Government.

Home Office UK Border Agency (2007a), *Bulgarian and Romanian Accession Statistics* (July–September 2007), Joint Online Report between the Border and Immigration Agency, Department for Work and Pensions, HM Revenue and Customs and Communities and Local Government.

Home Office UK Border Agency (2007b), *Living and Working in the UK: Rights and Responsibilities of Nationals from Bulgaria and Romania from 1 January 2007,* (London: Border and Immigration Agency Communications).

Home Office UK Border Agency (2008), *Accession Monitoring Report, May 2004–June 2008,* Joint Online Report between the Border and Immigration Agency, Department for Work and Pensions, HM Revenue and Customs and Communities and Local Government.

Home Office UK Border Agency (2008a), *Bulgarian and Romanian Accession Statistics* (April–June 2008), Joint Online Report between the Border and Immigration Agency, Department for Work and Pensions, HM Revenue and Customs and Communities and Local Government.

Horvath, I. (2008), 'The Culture of Migration of Rural Romanian Youth', *Journal of Ethnic and Migration Studies,* 34:5, 771–86.

Jayaweera, H. and Anderson, B. (2008), *Migrant Workers and Vulnerable Employment: A Review of Existing Data*, Report for TUC Commission on Vulnerable Employment (Oxford: COMPAS).

Jordan, B. and Düvell, F. (2002), *Irregular Migration: The Dilemmas of Transnational Mobility* (Cheltenham and Northampton: Edward Elgar).

Kengerlinsky, M. (2004), 'Restrictions in EU Immigration Policies towards New Member States', *Journal of European Affairs* 2:4, 12–1.

Kofman, E. (1995), 'Citizenship for Some but not for Others: Spaces of Citizenship in Contemporary Europe', *Political Geography* 14:2, 121–37.

– (1999), 'Female "Birds of Passage" a Decade Later: Gender and Immigration in the European Union', *International Migration Review* 33:2, 269–99.

– (2000), 'The Invisibility of Skilled Female Migrants and Gender Relations in Studies of Skilled
Migration in Europe', *International Journal of Population Geography* 6:1, 45–59.

– et al. (2000), *Gender and International Migration in Europe: Employment, Welfare and Politics* (New York: Routledge).

– (2004a), 'Family-Related Migration: A Critical Review of European Studies', *Journal of Ethnic and Migration Studies* 30:2, 243–62.

– (2004b), 'Gendered Global Migrations', *International Feminist Journal of Politics* 6:4, 643–64.

– et al. (2005), *Gendered Migrations: Towards gender sensitive policies in the UK*, Institute for Public Policy Research, Asylum and Migration Working Paper 6.

Krieger, H. (2004), *Migration Trends in an Enlarged Europe* (Dublin: European Foundation for the Improvement of Living and Working Conditions).

Kvist, J. (2004), 'Does EU enlargement start a race to the bottom? Strategic interaction among EU member states in social policy', *Journal of European Social Policy* 14:3, 301–18.

Lanzieri, G. (2007), *First Demographic Estimates for 2006*, (Brussels: Eurostat, European Communities).

Maas, W. (2002), 'Free Movement and EU Enlargement', Paper prepared for the Fifth Biennial Conference of the European Community Studies Association, Toronto, Canada 31 May–1 June 2002.

McKenna, E. and Beech, N. (2002), *Human Resource Management: A Concise Analysis* (Harlow: Pearson Education).

Morawska, E. and Spohn, W. (1997), 'Moving Europeans in the Globalizing World: Contemporary Migrations in a Historical-Comparative Perspective (1955–1994 v 1870–1914)' in Gungwu, W. (ed.).

Morokvasic, M., (2004), 'Settled in Mobility': Engendering Post-wall Migration in Europe', 77 *Feminist Review* 77:1, 7–25.

– and de Tinguy, A. (1993), 'Between East and West: A New Migratory Space' in Rudolph, H. and Morokvasic, M. (eds).

– et al. (eds) (2003), *Crossing Borders and Shifting Boundaries. Vol I: Gender on the Move*, (Opalden: Leske and Budrich).

Munck, R. (2005), 'Irregular Migration and the Informal Labour Market: The "Underside" of Globalization or the New Norm?', Paper presented as the keynote address to the International Workshop on Irregular Migration, Informal Labour and Community in Europe, 1–2 December 2005, Istanbul.

Newcombe, E. (2004), *Temporary Migration to the UK as an 'Au Pair': Cultural Exchange or Reproductive Labour?*, Sussex Migration Working Paper no. 2 (Sussex: Centre for Migration Research).

Phizacklea, A. (1983), 'In the front line', in Phizacklea, A. (ed.) – *One way ticket. Migration and female labour* (London: Routledge).
Pollard, N. et al. (2008), *Floodgates or Turnstiles? Post–EU Enlargement Migration to (and from) the UK* (London: Institute for Public Policy Research).
Purcell, K. (2002), Qualifications and careers: equal opportunities and earnings amongst graduates, EOC.
Schwenken, H. (2005), *'Domestic Slavery' versus 'Workers Rights': Political Mobilizations of Migrant Domestic Workers in the European Union*, Centre for Comparative Immigration Studies, University of California, Working Paper 116.
Silverman, N. (2005), *Deserving of Decent Work: The Complications of Organizing Irregular Workers Without Legal Rights*, Working Paper 21 (Oxford: COMPAS).
Syrett, S. and Lyons, M. (2007), 'Migration, New Arrivals and Local Economies', *Local Economy,* 22:4, 325–34.
Tamas, K. and Münz, R. (2006b), *Labour Migrants Unbound? EU Enlargement, Transitional Measures and Labour Market Effects* (Stockholm: Institute for Futures Studies).
TGWU (2006) Press Release, *Shop steward suspended for speaking out against agency workers' abuse,* 27 June 2006. <http://www.tgwu.org.uk/Templates/News.asp?NodeID=92616> (last accessed 15 February 2008).
TGWU (2005) Press Release, *T&G Polish Members Join Nationwide Tesco Protest,* 3 September 2005. <http://www.tgwu.org.uk/Templates/News.asp?NodeID=91843> (last accessed 15 February 2008).
Traser J. (2006), *Who's Still Afraid of EU Enlargement* (Brussels: European Citizen Action Service).
Traser, J. and Venables, T. (2008), *Who's Afraid of the EU's Latest Enlargement? The Impact of Bulgaria and Romania Joining the Union on Free Movement of Persons* (Brussels: European Citizen Action Service).
TUC (2005), News Release, *Polish PM urged to join forces with UK to tackle bad employers,* 24 November 2005. <http://www.tuc.org.uk/h_and_s/tuc-11110-f0.cfm> (Accessed 15 February 2008).
Vaughan-Whitehead, D.C. (2003), *EU Enlargement versus Social Europe? The Uncertain Future of the European Social Model* (Cheltenham: Edward Elgar).
Velluti, S (2005), 'Implementing gender equality and mainstreaming in an enlarged European Union – some thoughts on prospects and challenges for Central Eastern Europe', *Journal of Social Welfare and Family Law* 27: 2, 221–33.[1]
Ward, K. et al. (2005), *The Role of Temporary Staffing Agencies in Facilitating Labour Mobility in Eastern and Central Europe* (Manchester: Vedior).
Weil, P. (2005), *A Flexible Framework for a Plural Europe*, Discussion paper prepared for the UK Presidency (Paris: Centre National de la Recherche Scientifique).

Chapter 7
Migrants in the Italian Labour Market: Gender Differences and Regional Disparities

Salvatore Strozza, Anna Paterno, Laura Bernardi, Giuseppe Gabrielli

For more than a century Italy has been one of the largest emigration countries in Europe contributing to a significant amount of labour force in the United States, Australia as well as in the richer European neighbouring countries (Favero and Tassello 1978; Birindelli 1984; Golini and Amato 2001; Casacchia and Strozza 2002). However, since the end of the 1970s, and particularly during the early 1990s after the fall of the Berlin Wall, Italy has become a recipient country. The migrants moving to Italy are mainly people from less developed countries (LDCs) outside of Europe and Central and Eastern Europe (CEE) (Di Comite 1991; Natale and Strozza 1997; Pugliese 2002; Bonifazi 2007).

Since the 1990s, migration flows have been increasing steadily. However, it has only been since the beginning of the 21st century that the phenomenon has grown quite significantly: Italy is second only to Germany and very similar to Spain in terms of absolute numbers of migrants living in the country supplanting countries with a long tradition of migration such as France and the United Kingdom (Cangiano and Strozza 2005).

The significant increase of migrants in Italy is an important element of social change not least because it triggers specific dynamics in the labour market (Bonifazi and Rinesi, 2008). One of the most visible dynamics is the existence of an ethnic stratification of the labour market increased by the specialization and segregation of different migrant communities in specific sectors of the economy (Strozza 2002). This form of ethnic segregation interacts and reinforces other existing forms of labour market segregation based on gender, education, residence, and professional qualifications. As a consequence, the already extant labour market segmentation is even more accentuated amongst migrants living in Italy. In particular, gender, legal status and nationality, as well as the selected region of residence represent important discriminatory elements in defining both migrants' degree of access to the labour market and types of employment.

In this chapter we focus on the discrimination of migrant workers based on gender as they emerge in the complex reality of the Italian regional labour markets. Recent studies (for instance, Carchedi 1999; Pugliese 1999; Ambrosini 2001; Reyneri 2001; Cangiano and Strozza 2005; Paterno et al. 2006) show that while in the Northern regions migrants are concentrated in the industry and services sector (classic 'Continental model'), in the Southern regions they work mainly in the agricultural sector or provide domestic work and family care services with less stable and thus more irregular forms of employment ('Mediterranean model').[1]

The micro data used has been taken from two separate sample surveys that have been analysed using specific statistical techniques.[2] On the basis of the Labour Force Survey of 2006 (for a description of the LFS methods, see ISTAT 2006; for a description of the LFS descriptive results, see ISTAT 2007), we examine the labour market performance of resident migrants in comparison with that of the Italian population. In particular, we consider differences in labour market access, activity rates, employment and unemployment rates, employment status and sectors of the economy in the four Italian macro-regions (North-West, North-East, Centre and South). As will be shown, gender plays an important role in distinguishing the labour market behaviour of migrants in comparison with that of the Italian population. In the second part of the chapter, we examine the employment status of migrants coming from LDCs and CEE countries distinguishing between regular and irregular migrants. In this context, we rely on the use of per capita data of the survey 'SUD' 2005, funded by Ministry of Labour and Social Policies and conducted by the ISMU (Fondazione per le Iniziative e lo Studio sulla Multietnicità) Foundation (Blangiardo and Farina 2006). This survey includes information on migrants living and working in Italy without taking into account the legal status of migrants, that is whether they are regular or irregular migrants. We analyse the determining factors of migrants' employment to show how gender and the peculiar characteristics of the region of residence strongly impact upon the possibility of becoming employed and the nature of employment, as well as other socio-demographic factors such as age, education, country of origin and duration of stay in Italy.

Data Sources Employed in this Analysis: Advantages and Disadvantages of the Two Surveys

The two main micro datasets on migrant workers in Italy have specific strengths and weaknesses which we outline below and thus only their combined use may

1 Before 1999 there was little academic acknowledgement of the 'Mediterranean model', even though a number of scholars identified, through schematic models, different work opportunities in certain Italian macro-regions (Pugliese 1990; Strozza 1995; Ambrosini 1996; Barsotti 1996; Frey and Livraghi 1996; Guarini and Natale 1996; Venturini and Villosio 1999).

2 Micro data or individual level data collect individual attributes like the person's age, gender, job-type etc. through survey interview. In the third section we aggregate the individual level data to produce macro level data which summarizes the situation of the Italian labour market. In the fourth section we analyse individual characteristics (micro level data) to study the main determinants of the occupational status.

provide an overall picture of the relationship between being a migrant, gender and employment status.

The Labour Force Survey 2006

The Italian Continuous Labour Force Survey (LFS) is a large national sample survey of the resident population which is continuously updated to take into account migrants who are resident in Italy since 2005 (Istat 2006). It is a cross-sectional survey that produces up-to-date estimates every three months (four times a year) with a quarterly sample of about 170,000 individuals of whom a mean number of 4,500 circa were migrants in 2006. In our analyses, we use the average values over the year of the four surveys of 2006. The great advantage of this data is that it draws on a large sample allowing for fine comparative analyses of occupational status by gender, age group, and macro-region of residence (Bonifazi 2007; Reyneri 2007; Sabbadini et al. 2007).[3] However the LSF also has two main limitations for our analyses: the first one is in relation to nature of the sample used and the second one is in relation to the type of information provided.

The sample only includes those migrants who possess a valid residence permit.[4] The LFS therefore does not provide information about migrants who are legally staying in the country but are not legally resident in Italy (350,000 in 2007) and irregular or illegal migrants (700,000 in 2007). A quarter of the migrant population living in Italy is thus not included in the data (Blangiardo 2008). As a consequence the estimates based on the LFS sample significantly underestimate the true presence of migrants in the labour market in absolute terms, despite the data covering three-quarters of the migrant population in the country. Most importantly, the LSF 'observes' a segment of the labour market which is selected for being more stable (as far as residence and employment are concerned). This narrow approach – particularly important in economic sectors characterized by high irregularity like agriculture, construction and household services – must be taken into consideration when interpreting the analyses of this data.

A second limitation of the LFS survey is that it does not contain information such as the date of entry into the country which is fundamental for an analytical and comparative study of individual migration trajectories. Both limitations are related to the fact that the survey was originally conceived with a view to examining mainly the labour market behaviour of the Italian population rather than that of the migrant population. Despite these limitations, the LSF survey remains one of the most reliable sources of information to carry out comparative studies of the labour force in Italy.

3 Because of the small size of foreigners in the sample and the relative large statistical sampling errors, we cannot run separate analyses for foreigners by country or macro geo-economic region of origin.

4 In the following we refer to the legally resident population as 'resident' *tout court.*

The SUD Survey 2005

In order to have a more comprehensive assessment of migrants in Italy, we also use a second type of survey, the 'SUD', carried out in 2005 by the ISMU Foundation and funded by the Minister of Labour and Social Policies as the LSF studies legally resident migrants and provides limited information on migration flows in Italy. The SUD survey, the largest survey on migrants in Italy, analyses the adult population originating from LDCs and CEE countries (Blangiardo and Farina 2006). The sample includes a total of 30,000 migrants of which 22,000 live in the Southern regions and islands of Italy. The remaining 8,000 are located in ten Northern and Central provinces which were selected for comparative purposes since they represent the most important areas of immigration in the country.

This sampling strategy responds to the central aim of the survey, which has been designed as a policy evaluation tool to estimate the effect of the 2002 regularization[5] in the Southern regions and islands and for which the Central and Northern regions should function as a comparative base. The great advantage of this survey is that it includes all categories of migrants living in the designated regions, independently of their legal status. This allows us to compare the labour market situation of all migrants as well as estimating the differential effects of gender, the duration of stay in the country and the ethnic community of belonging on migrants in the Italian labour market.

Resident Migrants in Italy's Varied Labour Market: Similarities and Differences with the Italian Labour Force

We now turn to the analysis of the employment status of the migrant labour force as described by their distribution in terms of economic participation, access to the labour market (indicated by unemployment rates), employment conditions (indicated by the professional position, part- or full-time employment and duration of the employment contract) and economic sectors of activity. We compare the occupational status of men and women both at national and regional levels (within the four macro-regions as described earlier) and discuss plausible interpretations for the main differences observed, taking into consideration any differences with the Italian labour force.

Data refers to migrants mainly issued from LDCs and MDCs; the migrants included from the latter data set constitute a small minority of the total group of

5 The 2002 regularization, associated with the *Bossi-Fini Law* (Law 189/2002), was the furthest-reaching measure to uncover illegal foreign work ever introduced in a European country (comparable only to the later 2005 regularization in Spain). More than 705,000 regularization applications were made, of which nearly 647,000 were accepted (approximately 92%).

migrants interviewed, and their patterns of labour market entry differ substantially from the first group (Bonifazi et al. 2008a).

Occupational Status

The active migrant labour force in Italy counts 2 million individuals in 2006, representing more than the 5 per cent of the total population aged 15–64 years old. There is about the same number of men and women (see Table 7.1); however their distribution across the country is quite uneven. Most of them (1.26 million, that is the 63 per cent of the migrants), are resident in the Northern regions (including the large urban agglomeration around Milan) where they represent 7 per cent of the Italian active labour force. In the Central regions of Italy (including the capital city of Rome) half a million migrants represent 7 per cent of the local labour force and 25 per cent of the total number of migrants in the country. On the contrary, in the South both absolute and relative measures are smaller: only a little more than one migrant out of ten lives here (250,000 individuals) representing only 2 per cent of the local labour force. If we look at the gender distribution, women are more represented in the Southern and Central regions than in the Northern regions.

This first general and descriptive overview already signals two important aspects of recent migration flows to Italy. First, and predictably so, the stable and legally resident migrant labour force represents an important share of the labour force in those regions with a better economic situation (more dynamic productive system, less extensive underground economy and low unemployment). Second, the marked gender distribution by regions may be considered as an indication of the gender stratification of employment opportunities in the different economic

Table 7.1 Migrant habitually resident population of 15–64 years old by gender and macro-regions. Italy, mean 2006. Absolute values (in thousands) and percentages.

Macro-regions	Absolute values (in thousands)			% by macro-regions			% migrants on the total population 15–64 years		
	Males	Females	Total	Males	Females	Total	Males	Females	Total
North West	367.9	360.1	728.1	37.1	35.8	36.4	7.1	7.1	7.1
North East	278.3	254.1	532.4	28.1	25.3	26.6	7.5	7.1	7.3
Centre	228.5	258.4	486.9	23.0	25.7	24.4	6.2	6.9	6.6
South	116.9	133.5	250.3	11.8	13.3	12.5	1.7	1.9	1.8
ITALY	**991.6**	**1.006.0**	**1.997.6**	**100.0**	**100.0**	**100.0**	**5.1**	**5.2**	**5.2**

Source: Our elaborations on Istat data, Continuous Labour Force Survey, 2006.

Table 7.2 Activity, employment and unemployment rates of migrant habitually resident population of 15–64 years old and differences with Italians by gender and macro-regions. Italy, mean 2006. Migrant rates and percentage differences with Italians.

Macro-regions	Rates (in %)			Differences with Italians		
	Males	Females	Total	Males	Females	Total
Rates of activity						
North West	89.6	56.3	73.1	13.0	–2.9	5.1
North East	90.6	60.6	76.3	12.7	0.5	7.2
Centre	89.0	61.9	74.6	13.6	6.3	9.2
South	82.8	54.8	67.9	13.8	17.8	15.0
ITALY	**89.0**	**58.6**	**73.7**	**15.1**	**8.2**	**11.6**
Rates of employment						
North West	86.0	49.6	68.0	11.7	–6.8	2.5
North East	85.2	51.3	69.0	9.1	–6.1	2.1
Centre	84.3	53.0	67.7	12.2	1.8	6.1
South	75.4	48.4	61.0	13.3	17.7	14.7
ITALY	**84.2**	**50.7**	**67.3**	**14.4**	**4.7**	**9.4**
Rates of unemployment						
North West	4.0	11.8	7.0	1.0	7.2	3.3
North East	5.9	15.5	9.5	3.7	11.0	6.4
Centre	5.3	14.3	9.3	0.9	6.6	3.4
South	9.0	11.6	10.1	–1.1	–5.1	–2.3
ITALY	**5.4**	**13.4**	**8.6**	**–0.1**	**4.9**	**1.9**

Source: see Table 7.1.

sectors of activity. Indeed, if we consider the distribution of activity, employment, and unemployment rates (see Table 7.2), we observe that the migrant labour force follows the typical gender and regional stratification of the Italian labour force. More specifically, the migrant labour force seems to highlight already existing problems and peculiarities of the Italian labour market, confirming the existence of a plurality of 'Italies' which, with some approximation, may be summarized in the differences between North and South. Also some indications, which considered separately, may seem not to fit this schema, appear as an integral part of it, when all pieces of information are pulled together.

The activity and employment rates of migrants, equal to 73.7 per cent and 67.3 per cent respectively, are clearly higher that those of the Italian active population, with a gap that varies between 11.6 per cent and 9.4 per cent (15.1 per cent and 14.1 per cent for men). Similar contrasts characterize other Mediterranean countries which have become recipient countries in recent years (namely Spain, Greece,

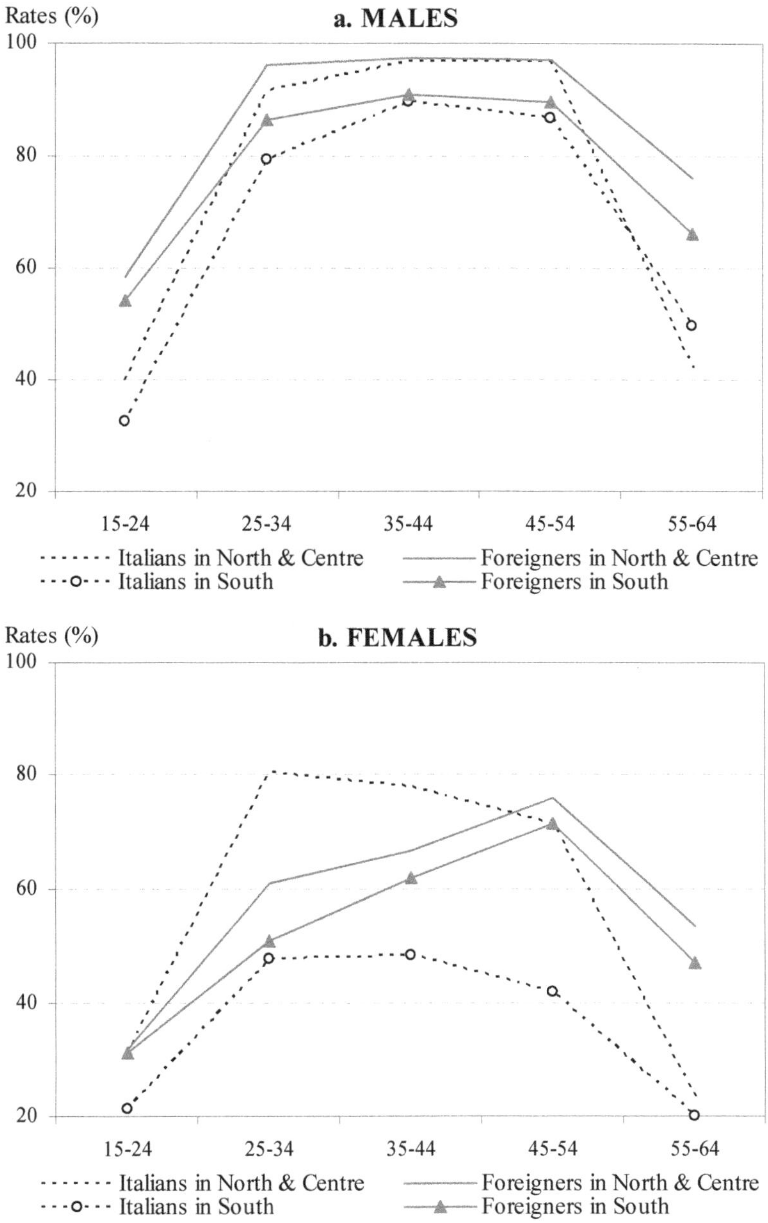

Figure 7.1 Activity rates per age groups of Italian and migrant habitually resident of 15-64 years old, by gender and macro-regions. Italy, mean 2006. Percentage values

Source: see Table 7.1

and Portugal). This is due to the fact that the migrant labour force is constituted mostly by migrants of the first generation, who moved mainly for employment reasons. In contrast, European countries with a longer immigration history register lower levels of migrants' activity and employment rates than those of the native population (Sabbadini et al. 2007).

Even when considering the activity rates by age group (see Figure 7.1) in order to take into account differences due to the for the older age structure of the Italian population, results do not change. Migrant men show higher levels of labour market participation than Italian men for any age group, with even larger differences in the youngest and oldest working age groups because of the higher share of young Italians in school and the early retirement of older adults between 50 and 60.

The large participation of young migrants (15–24 years old) in the labour market shows that immigration is mainly economically driven. The second generation of migrants constitutes still a minor part of the picture. In sum, migrants spend averagely 41 years being active in the labour market, of which 39 as employed, without significant differences across regions if we exclude the South (see Figure 7.2).[6] Remarkably, this period is six years shorter for Italian men.

Activity and employment rates of migrant women (58.6 per cent and 50.7 per cent, respectively) are considerably lower than those of men, partially because many women migrated for family reasons and have not (yet) entered the labour market. However, the number of migrant women is higher than that of Italian women in terms of average number of years spent in the labour market (28 years averagely, about 4 years more than Italian women) without relevant regional differences. The age profiles are different though: the activity peak is reached at ages 25–34 for Italian women and at 45–54 for migrant women (see Figure 7.1).

Regional differences also play a role: in the North, where unemployment is low, employment rates are higher for Italian women, while activity rates are similar in both populations; in the South instead both indicators are sensibly higher in the migrant population (the difference is of 18 per cent) mostly reflecting the scarce labour force participation of the Italian female population (only 3 per cent of them are active in the South, in contrast with the 60 per cent in the North). Remarkably, migrant women in the South are employed as much as other women in the rest of Italy: they are less active in the labour market but not unemployed as other Italian women.[7]

6 The average number of years spent in various professional statuses (employed, unemployed, inactive) during the 50 years of active life (15–64 years) is a period synthetic measure related to the year 2006 of employment, unemployment and activity rates of five year groups. Called also total rates, these measures control for the age structure of the population. For example, the employment rate is obtained multiplying by five the sum of ten employment rates (by five year groups). The sum of the total employment and the total unemployment rates is equivalent to the total activity rate.

7 Differences described here and in the following should be interpreted with extreme caution because of the low representative and the large confidence intervals (high level of

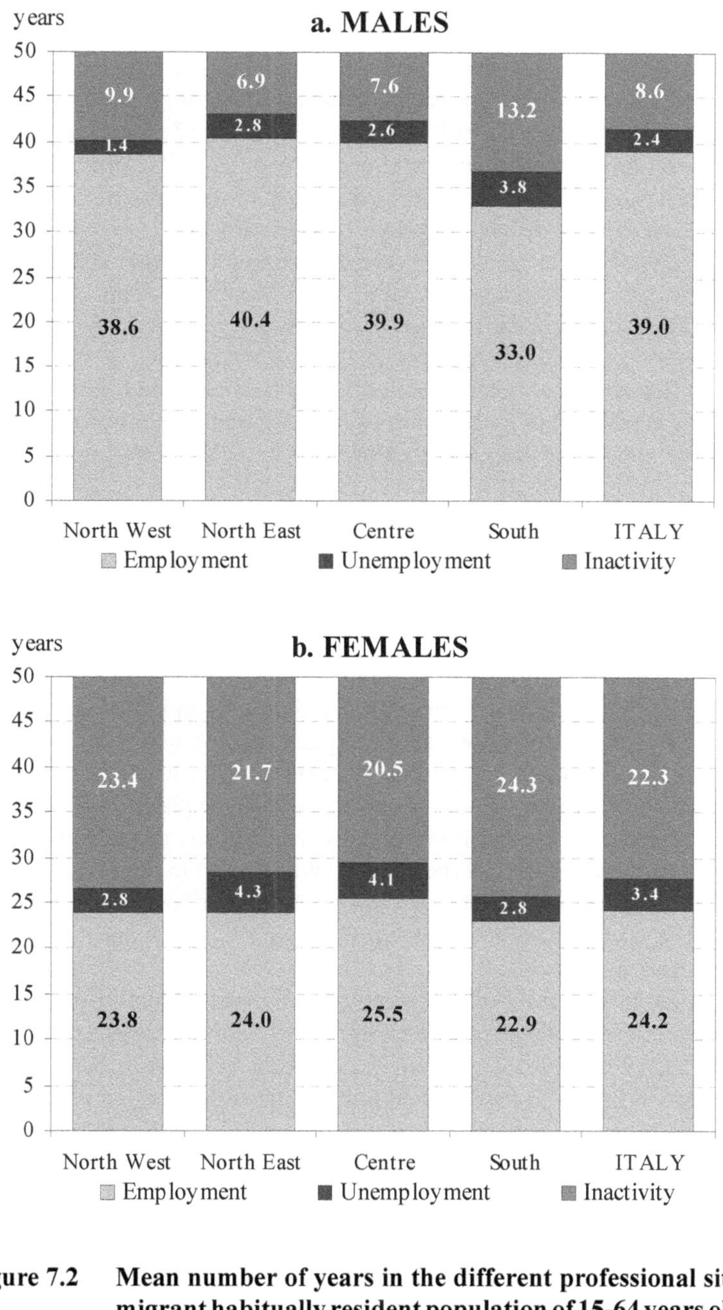

Figure 7.2 Mean number of years in the different professional situation of migrant habitually resident population of 15-64 years old distinct by gender and macro-regions. Italy, mean 2006. Percentage values

Source: see Table 7.1

The level of unemployment of the migrant population (8.6 per cent) is only slightly higher than the one of the Italian population (the gap is due exclusively to women) and it is lower than the unemployment rate of migrants in the main European receiving countries (about 19 per cent in Germany, 17 per cent in Belgium and similarly in France, more than 15 per cent in Sweden). This difference may only be temporary and due to the recent peculiarity of migration flows to Italy which covered an existing demand of labour (Reyneri 2007).

The analysis of variations across regions shows that the value of the unemployment rate of migrants increase from North to South apparently reproducing the same occupational geographical maps typical of the Italian population. However, some divergences in the differential rates of the migrant and the Italian labour force should be noted: in the Northern and Central regions unemployment is still higher for migrants (in a range from 3 to 6 per cent) while in the South the opposite is true, with the unemployment rate being higher for the Italians (12.4 per cent versus 10.4 per cent of migrants).

Unemployment rates by gender show that these figures depend mainly on foreign men's successful occupation: on a national level men's unemployment is only 5.4 per cent compared to the 13.4 per cent of women's, this gap being just smaller in the Southern regions where women's unemployment is the lower. The contrast among Italian and migrant women's rates reproduces the same situation we described for men but differences are more dramatic: the unemployment rates for migrants is higher in the Northern and Central regions and their employment levels is higher in the South. How can we explain that the unfavourable labour market and economic conditions of the Southern regions only affect migrant workers marginally? What seems to be a paradox is easily explained with mobility patterns in that migrants are much more likely than Italians to move where the employment opportunities are (Reyneri 2007). With regard to the South of Italy, chosen as first destination only by a minority, immigrants only remain if they are employed otherwise they move towards other regions which may offer better employment opportunities.

Data on internal migration of the migrant population resident in Italy shows how the typical migration flows from the Southern to Northern regions (Casacchia et al. 1999; Istat 2007) also characterizes migration flows from outside Italy. Those migrant workers who benefited from the 2002 regularization process and were still holding a residence permit to stay at the end of 2006 moved massively from Southern to North Eastern regions between 2004 and 2006 (Carfagna et al. 2008).

Once more, the data needs to be interpreted with caution because it does not include those regular migrants who do not live on a permanent basis in Italy or irregular/illegal migrants, two large categories which are likely to change the picture of those sectors of activity where the weight of the underground economy is larger (agriculture, construction, care and home services, food). With this in mind, we turn to the characteristics of employment and analyse the different economic sectors in which resident migrants are labour active.

Employment Conditions

An overview of the employment conditions of migrants shows their substantial 'employment frailty', that is a high precariousness in accessing job opportunities, which is particularly high for women. This depends on a series of inter-related causes among which the disadvantages of being a migrant, the legal status, employment opportunities, the characteristics of the immigrants and their communities, and last but not least the economic sectors in which migrants are employed.

First, migrating to another country generally entails a certain degree of family disruption and a series of difficulties. In particular, when employment is the main reason for migrating the major obstacles are represented by linguistic problems, problems with the recognition of educational and professional qualifications, or the lack of access to employment through social networking of relatives, friends and neighbours. Migrants can rely solely on ethnic networks (Ambrosini 1999; Reyneri 2007; Bonifazi and Rinesi 2008).

Second, local labour market opportunities and differences in the legal status of nationals and migrants may affect the employment stability of migrants. What we defined as 'employment frailty' is higher in the South where the low unemployment

Table 7.3 Percentages of self-employed between employed usual resident foreigners of 15–64 years old by gender and macro-regions. Italy, mean 2006. Percentage values and differences with Italians

Macro-regions	Total self-employed[(a)]			Of which: Single autonomous workers		
	Males	Females	Total	Males	Females	Total
Percentage values[(b)]						
North West	16.3	11.1	14.4	11.7	5.0	9.2
North East	14.8	13.3	14.3	11.4	5.6	9.3
Centre	16.2	11.0	14.0	12.8	5.4	9.7
South	26.4	12.1	20.3	24.3	8.6	17.7
ITALY	**16.9**	**11.8**	**15.0**	**13.2**	**5.7**	**10.3**
Differences with Italians						
North West	–12.4	–6.0	–9.3	–7.0	–4.0	–5.3
North East	–15.9	–5.0	–11.2	–9.6	–4.4	–7.0
Centre	–13.7	–7.5	–11.1	–5.5	–4.5	–5.1
South	–2.0	–7.5	–5.1	4.7	–3.4	0.6
ITALY	**–12.3**	**–6.5**	**–9.9**	**–6.2**	**–4.5**	**–5.4**

Note: (a) This category includes entrepreneur and freelance professional, single autonomous workers, family coadjutant and member of workers' cooperative. (b) Some estimates have a high sampling error.

Source: see Table 7.1.

rates of migrant workers are connected to their larger engagement in more diffused informal and less protected economic activities.

With regard to self-employment, which requires the necessary economic, professional, cultural and social resources to overcome the administrative and organizational steps to start a business or for being a professional, the share of migrants who are self-employed is equal to 15 per cent, nearly 10 per cent less than the share of Italians (see Table 7.3).

Such a difference seems to prove the 'employment frailty' of the migrant labour force in Italy. At the same time, self-employment in Italy is one of the highest in Europe in absolute terms (Greece being first) and even in countries where self employment does not discriminate migrants and nationals any longer (Germany, France, Belgium, and Netherlands), this result has been achieved slowly through decades and converged in the 1990s (Werner 2003). The difference between Italian and migrant self-employment shares may be explained by two factors: on the one hand, Italians perceive self-employment as a privileged channel of social mobility and are in competition with migrants in this field; on the other hand, the Italian regulation which prevented migrants from becoming self-employed in Italy was removed only towards the end of the 1990s (Reyneri 2007).

However, self-employment is not always a sign of ascendant social mobility or professional integration. Particularly among migrants there seems to be a plurality of situations ranging from *niche* activities such as begging and non-authorized street sales, small scale entrepreneurial-like activities, family-run businesses and real entrepreneurial activities. Migrant self-employment is often carried out without the necessary authorizations and it is generally a temporary survival measure while awaiting better employment opportunities in the official labour market to become a regular employee (Gesano 1993; Strozza 2006). The varied nature of migrant self-employment explains why it is necessary to distinguish entrepreneurial activity and freelance professionals from other forms of niche and pseudo self-employment, associates in family enterprise/business or cooperatives.

The rate of migrant men in self-employment is higher than that of women (16.9 per cent versus 11.8 per cent) which is made up mostly of autonomous workers. Self employment is particularly high in the South (26.4 per cent of men), mainly autonomous workers, while in the rest of the country the range goes from 14.8 per cent to 16.3 per cent among men. In the Central regions we count more than 3 per cent of entrepreneurs among men and in the North-East up to 6.5 per cent of the women are members of cooperatives and family enterprises. The particular type of self-employment, i.e. autonomous work, in the Southern part of the country suggests that migrant works have greater difficulty in accessing more stable jobs and it seems to represent a second best option. In the North, on the contrary, entrepreneurial work is on the rise even though this is still low in comparison with that of the native population (6 per cent difference) and mostly in the form of ethnic business.

For those who hold an employment contract it is important to analyse its duration and its type (whether it is a full- or a part-time job). Here gender does not play an important discriminatory role. Even if women in most cases have short-term employment contracts, at national level the share of migrants with non permanent contracts is comparable to that of Italians (Table 7.4 shows the difference in detail). In the South, such share is sensibly higher for migrant men. Once more, women in the South are outliers: migrant women have less often short-term contracts than their Italian counterpart and temporary contracts seem to be the norm. Women also tend to work part-time and this is even more so for migrant women than for Italian women. For the former, the gap with migrant men is over 30 per cent (see Table 7.4). The share of migrant women working part-time varies between the 43.8 per cent in the North-Western regions and 31.6 per cent in the Southern regions and is substantially higher than the share of Italian women working part-time. On the contrary, for men there is no significant difference in the type of employment contract.

Third, the 'emerging frailty' characterizing migrant workers not only depends on market opportunities and their local declination, but also on the characteristics of migrant workers and their communities. The large spectrum of nationalities to which migrants may belong means that there may be substantial variation in terms of demographic and social characteristics, migration projects and strategies, local

Table 7.4 Characteristics of the work contract of employed foreign usual resident population of 15–64 years old by gender and macro-regions. Italy, mean 2006. Percentages and differences with Italians

Macro-regions	Percentage values[(a)]			Differences with Italians		
	Males	Females	Total	Males	Females	Total
Non-permanent contract						
North West	11.5	14.1	12.5	3.7	2.8	3.1
North East	13.3	21.9	16.4	4.2	8.2	5.2
Centre	13.6	20.1	16.4	2.7	4.8	3.5
South	24.4	20.6	22.7	9.5	–2.5	4.9
ITALY	**13.7**	**18.5**	**15.6**	**2.7**	**2.9**	**2.6**
Part-time contract						
North West	5.2	43.8	19.1	1.8	18.7	6.4
North East	3.8	35.6	15.1	0.4	7.4	1.1
Centre	7.5	39.6	20.8	2.5	13.1	6.9
South	8.3	31.6	18.1	3.2	8.5	7.0
ITALY	**5.6**	**39.0**	**18.3**	**1.4**	**13.4**	**5.6**

Note: (a) Some estimates have a high sampling error.

Source: see Table 7.1.

integration models and sectors of activity. Indeed the differences noted across regions depend partially on the migrant population composition by nationality and the extent to which they are enrooted in the local community. In the Northern regions many women arrived following a successful family reconstitution application advanced by their partners whereas in the Southern regions most of the recent migration flows of women is due to the search for employment. The success of any migration project therefore depends directly on whether or not migrants find a job.

Concentration in Specific Sectors of Activity

The distribution of workers by sector of activity is a key aspect characterizing migrants' labour force participation. Gender differences are very marked here: men are mainly occupied in the industrial sector (57 per cent) meeting the demand of small and medium construction and manufacture enterprises; women are mainly employed in the service sector (about 83 per cent), particularly the household services sector (see Figure 7.3) meeting the demand for housekeepers and elderly caregivers coming from families. On the contrary, both migrant men and women have difficulty in entering more prestigious labour market sectors such as real estate, banks, insurance companies and public administration. Here, the share of migrants is negligible compared to that of Italians.

If this is the average situation at national level, regional differences are consistent with the characteristics of the local production systems and local labour markets. We identify two models of migrants' employment: the classic 'Continental model' of the Central and Northern regions where the contribution of the migrant labour force is concentrated in the small and medium size enterprises of the industrial sector and a 'Mediterranean model' in the Southern regions where the agriculture, household service, small commerce and restaurant sectors represent the largest share of employment opportunities for migrants.

In the 'Continental model' which is the typical model of migrant labour force participation to be found in the traditional receiving countries of continental Europe, we found that migrants' employment was more stable and that there were small differences between men and women. In Northern and Central Italy men are predominantly employed in the various branches of the industrial sector: construction accounts for the one fourth to one third of men's employment, while a substantial number of them are absorbed by the metallurgical industry (about 20 per cent in the North and 7 per cent in the Centre). In the North-East women are employed mainly in the household services (22.6 per cent), but they are well represented also in the other service activities and in the manufacturing industry where the 25 per cent of them are employed.

On the contrary, the 'Mediterranean model' seems to characterize the labour force participation in regions which have a Mediterranean economy (not only in Italy), characterized by seasonality and diffused irregularity of working relations. The migrant labour force in the Southern regions is less concentrated than in

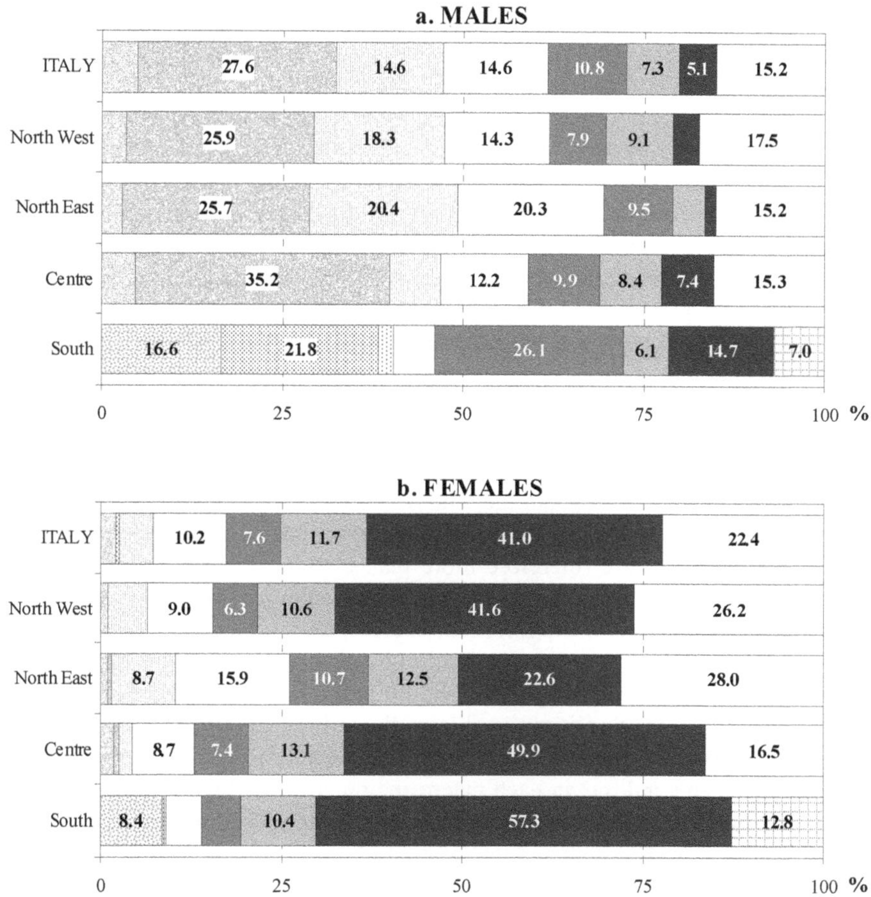

Figure 7.3 Sector of economic activity of employed migrant population of 15-64 years old, habitually resident, by gender and macro-regions. Italy, mean 2006. Percentage values

Source: see Table 7.1

other parts of the country. However, the main difference is not quantitative but qualitative as the distribution of men and women across the various sectors of activity is unique. For men, contrary to what happens in the Northern and Central regions, the manufacturing industry is a minor sector of employment (less than 8 per cent). The construction sector instead is also an important area of employment in the South (21.8 per cent), at least as a first step to employment (albeit irregular) and thus enables migrant workers to move eventually to better working conditions (Macioti and Pugliese 2003). However, migrants' employment in Southern regions is mainly concentrated in small commercial activities (26.1 per cent), in the agricultural sector (16.6 per cent), and household services (about 15 per cent) is definitively higher than anywhere else in the country.

One important factor explaining this difference lies in the economic structure of the regions: the relatively under-developed industrial and financial sectors in the South which reduces the employment opportunities available to the service sector where women are strongly preferred by the employers. Hence, men mainly work in the commercial and agricultural sectors (Strozza and Ferrara 2008), while the work of migrant women, which until the late 1980s was identifiable exclusively with household work in the urban areas, has rapidly expanded to include the provision of family care services and has expanded from the urban areas to smaller residential agglomerates.

Gender segregation in the labour market is a qualifying characteristic of the 'Mediterranean model' as is shown by the relatively high concentration of women workers in the household service sector in the South. Women in these regions have even less choice than men about the kind of job they can aspire to: more than 57 per cent of them are active in the household service sector and a little more than 8 per cent in agriculture (therefore more than elsewhere in the country). Such concentration is problematic if we think that these sectors are characterized mainly by precarious employment and informal, unprotected working arrangements.

An effective measure of the distribution by sector of activity between Italian and migrant labour force is the relative dissimilarity index (see Table 7.5).[8] Values for men already show that at national level the index is progressively increasing when we move from North to South going respectively from 27.8 per cent to 43 per cent. Women's indexes in each macro region are even higher because of the concentration of female work in the household sector. The highest dissimilarity index values are in the South and the Centre (58.7 per cent and 52.4 per cent).

In short, access and participation of the migrant labour force in the Italian labour market are strongly dependent on various *pull factors* which are differently distributed across regions. We saw for instance that women are often employed in the unstable and unprotected household service sector. Whereas in the Northern and Central regions this represents one among various employment opportunities, in the South it is almost the only type of employment for women. However, structural differences are just part of the story. The increasing demand for family care services by Italian families is explained by the demographic and social change experienced in the country in the last decade: since the 1960s there has been significant decline in the number of Italian women willing to carry out this type of work, a lack in the provision of care services for families, the increased feminization of the Italian labour market, the increasing ageing of the population

8 The Index is the result of the sum (divided by two) of the differences in absolute values of the percentage of employed of the two populations in each sector (Italian and foreigners by gender and macro-regions of residence). The distribution includes 28 activity sectors. Indexes vary from 0 (no dissimilarity) to 100 (maximal dissimilarity).

Table 7.5 Relative dissimilarity index (%) in the distribution by sector of economic activities between migrant and Italian employed population of 15–64 years old, distinctly by gender and macro-regions. Italy, mean 2006

Gender	North West	North East	Centre	South	ITALY
Males	26.5	27.0	38.5	45.3	**27.8**
Females	43.3	31.6	52.4	58.7	**43.0**

Note: It is considered a distribution in 28 sectors of economic activities.

Source: see Table 7.1.

and the diminished number of members of the family available to take care of elderly parents. These social changes are likely to increase in the coming years with a consequential increase in the demand of care services provided by migrant women.

In addition to the above there are also occupational *niches* filled by specific ethnic groups of migrant workers. Occupational niches are represented by specific entrepreneurial activities (ethnic restaurants, shops and artisan laboratories in the urban centres) and agricultural and zoo-technical activities in the rural areas are evidence of a strong tendency to specialization and *ethnicization* of the labour market. This phenomenon only concerns certain sectors of the economy and in some cases it reinforces the segmentation of the labour market. In the case of women, this *ethnicization* process, as shown in the employment of migrant women in the highly unstable and irregular care service sector could lead to occupational segregation which is not only difficult to eradicate but which may also hinder a real integration of migrant women (Ambrosini et al. 1995; Zanfrini 2002).

The differences by gender and region discussed so far only concern part of the migrant population which is habitually resident in the country and does not take into account those migrants who do not have their habitual residence in Italy or the irregular/illegal migrants. The exclusion of these two groups may lead to an underestimation of the active labour population. In the next section, therefore, we address these two groups and compare them with the resident one.

The Occupational Status of Migrants and their Determining Factors

In this section we use the individual level data of the 'SUD' survey of 2005, in order to provide a better understanding of the labour market characteristics of the migrant labour force described in the previous section. The usefulness of this survey is already evident from the sample characteristics: all non-Italian citizens from LDCs and CEE, aged eighteen or more, which were in the selected territorial

Table 7.6 Occupational status of migrant population of 15–64 years old – selected characteristics. Italy, mean 2006. Percentage values

Characteristics	Occupational status of foreign people aged 15–64			
	Unemployed	Irregular employed	Regular employed	TOTAL
Gender				
Males	9.5	18.6	72.0	100.0
Females	11.7	21.8	66.5	100.0
Age				
18–24	17.3	35.1	47.6	100.0
25–39	10.1	19.5	70.4	100.0
40–54	8.9	15.0	76.1	100.0
55+	11.0	26.8	62.2	100.0
Length of stay				
0–1	30.9	54.0	15.1	100.0
2–4	12.6	31.1	56.3	100.0
5–7	7.8	15.5	76.7	100.0
8+	6.6	7.6	85.9	100.0
Macro-regions				
North and Centre	10.4	18.3	71.2	100.0
South	10.3	32.8	56.9	100.0
Education				
No	13.0	24.5	62.5	100.0
Middle school	10.1	20.6	69.3	100.0
High school	10.6	19.2	70.2	100.0
Degree	8.7	16.9	74.4	100.0
Legal status				
Resident	8.0	8.5	83.6	100.0
Legal non-resident	21.4	30.4	48.2	100.0
Illegal	20.4	79.1	0.5	100.0

Source: Our elaborations on SUD data, 2005.

units at the moment of the data collection have interviewed independently of their legal status and country of residence. Women represent 37.6 per cent, resident migrants are 69.7 per cent, non-resident migrants are 5.7 per cent, and illegal migrants are 24.6per cent. In addition, 11.3 per cent of the active population are unemployed, 29.8 per cent irregularly employed and 58.9 per cent are regularly employed. The survey collects also important information on individual migration characteristics (like the duration of permanence in Italy or the country of origin) besides his or her socio-demographic characteristics such as gender and age.

Descriptive analyses (see Table 7.6) show in the first place a strong relation between the legal and the occupational status: residents are in the 84 per cent of the cases employed in regular activities, while 79 per cent of the illegal migrants are employed in irregular activities and a little more than 20 per cent of them are unemployed. Non resident migrants are in an intermediate situation: 48 per cent only works regularly. Italian legislation (for the present legislation see 'Bossi-Fini' Law n. 189/2002) strongly affects these distributions by defining the possession of a legal permit to stay (temporary or permanent) as a necessary requirement for obtaining regular employment.

As far as gender and regional stratification are concerned, women either tend to have an irregular employment or are unemployed and in the South migrant workers employed in the informal sector are almost double those in the Centre-North (33 per cent versus 18 per cent) while unemployment is uniformly spread across regions. Women working on an irregular basis, particularly in the South, are mostly employed as carers and cleaners. Men's irregular work is distributed across different sectors of the economy but comprises mostly unskilled workers (in the South) and blue collar workers as well sale, trade and service activities. It seems that at a descriptive level data on employment coming from the sample of official residents of the LFS and from the sample of actual residents of the 'SUD' survey are consistent with each other.[9] Similarly, the findings of the effects of age, education and duration of stay in Italy on the employment status of migrants are in line with the findings of the international migration literature. Unemployed and irregular migrant workers are usually prevalent among the very young or the over 55, the less educated, or newly arrived migrants. A longer duration of stay in the country and better qualifications generally ensure a better and more regular form of employment.

Migrants in Italy are a very heterogeneous group of different nationalities with diverse characteristics and migration patterns (Rossi and Strozza 2007). By disaggregating the data by nationality, we can analyse the occupational status (see Figures 7.4 and 7.5). We consider the fifteen most numerous nationalities.

The highest share of regular workers (87per cent) is registered among Philippinos, a group which is represented mainly by women active in the household sector (6 out of ten); a community which also has a very long migration history. A large share of regular male workers is represented by the Indian and the Chinese communities (respectively 83 per cent and 79 per cent) whose migration to Italy is relatively old. Half of the Indian community works in activities which require unskilled workers and half of the Chinese community works in sales, trade and service sectors (in particular, restaurants and shops). Finally, a high proportion of regular workers comes from the Balkan countries such as Serbia (84 per cent), Macedonia (77 per

9 In Section 2.3 the resident foreigners are defined on the basis of their legal status only; we do not know about their occupational status. They could include a quota of irregular workers as well.

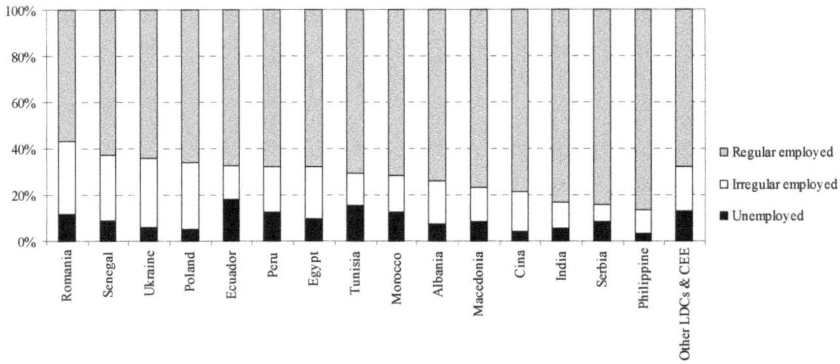

Figure 7.4 Occupational status of the migrant population, 15–64 years old, by country of origin. Italy, mean 2006. Percentage values

Source: see Table 7.6

cent) and Albania (74 per cent); they are mostly men who migrated to Italy during the early 1990s and employed as unskilled and blue collar workers.

The majority of irregular workers comes from Eastern European countries: Romania (32 per cent), Ukraine (30 per cent) and Poland (29 per cent). The migrants of these communities are largely women – particularly those from Ukraine and Poland – and they generally migrated to Italy in the last few years. However, while Ukrainians are mostly concentrated in the household sector, the other migrants coming from other countries are more evenly distributed across different sectors of the economy. In addition, there are also Senegalese migrants, mostly men who stay in Italy for a long period of time. They are generally irregular workers (28 per cent) and in most cases unskilled workers (mostly small-scale street commerce).

Ecuadorian (mainly women) and Tunisian (mainly men) migrants (18 per cent and 16 per cent) are generally unemployed. Those of them who work are mostly low-skilled workers. As expected, similar to the findings of the LFS, none of the biggest migrant communities is represented in significant ways among the 'white collar' or high professional jobs.

By using a multinomial logistic regression model we can now move on to assessing the effects of various factors on the occupational status of the migrant population (see Table 7.6, age, level of education, regional residence and so on).[10] We use employment

10 We apply a multinomial logistic regression in order to predict the value of the dependent variable at the variation of continuous and/or categorical independent variables. This model is the extension of the logistic regression model when the dependent variable is categorical; the factor response is not ordered (Hosmer, Lemeshow, 2000). Since we consider three occupational statuses, the multinomial logistic regression procedure produces two simultaneous logits: logit 1 refers here to the logistic regression which compares individuals with an irregular occupation to those who are unemployed; logit 2 refers to the logistic regression which compares individuals with a regular occupation to unemployed.

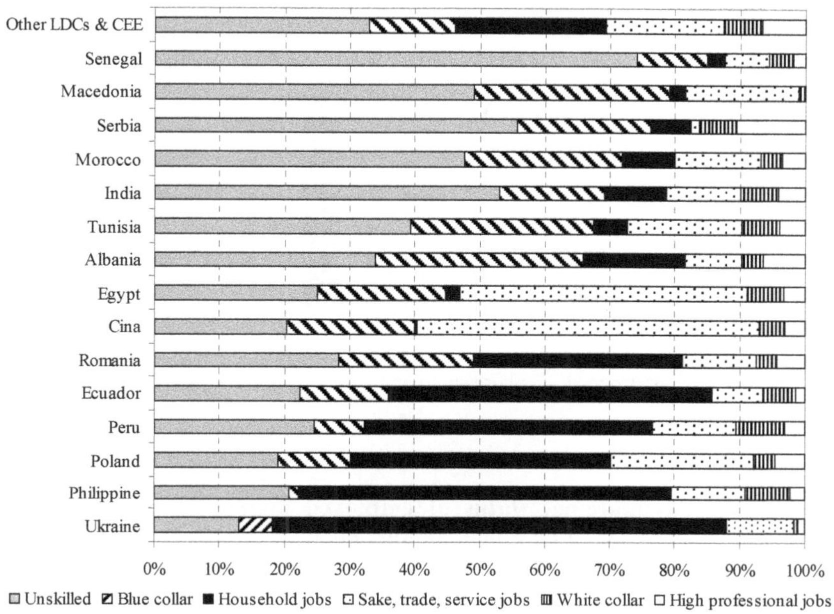

Figure 7.5 Professional level of employed migrant population of 15-64 years old by country of origin. Italy, mean 2006. Percentage values

Source: see Table 7.6

as our dependent variable which can be of three types: regular employment, irregular employment and unemployment.

The independent variables are gender, the Italian macro-regions where migrants live and their nationality,[11] and the control variables include age, the individual duration of stay in Italy[12] and education.[13] We could not include the legal and employment status in the labour market because of the Italian legislation on migrants (Law n. 189/2002): the possibility of being regularly employed is conditional on holding a legal permit to stay (temporary or permanent) and at the same time it is possible to renew the permit to stay only if holding a regular working contract. This circularity makes the direction of the causal relation between legal status and regular job difficult to define. In addition, as shown

11 This variable is a dummy that contrast one nationality against the group of others (collectively named Other Less Developed Countries and Central and Eastern Europe).

12 For continuous variables like age and duration of stay we insert a quadratic term as well, to control non linearity effects.

13 Education is a variable composed of three dummies: primary school, secondary school and university degree. The reference variable is the lowest educational category.

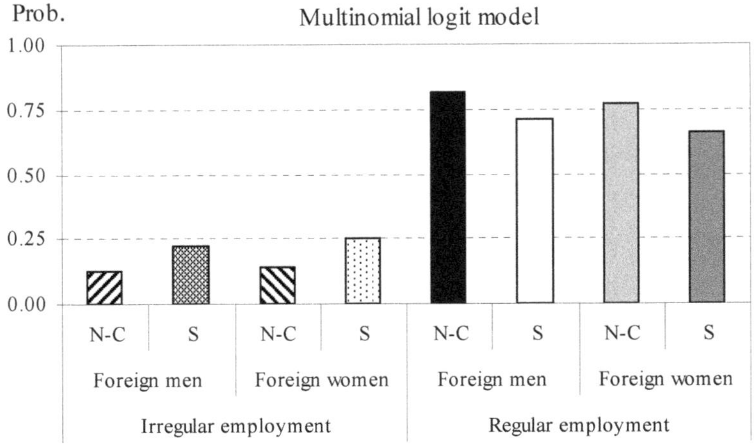

Figure 7.6 Occupational status of employed migrant population of 15-64 years old by gender and macro-regions. Italy, mean 2006. Probability

Note 1: (N-C) North and Centre (S) South

Note 2: educational level, age and length of stay are the control variables in the model

Source: see Table 7.6

in Table 7.6, in almost all cases the two conditions, legal residence and regular employment, overlap.

As far as the effect of control variables is concerned the results are almost in line with those of the aggregate analyses. Hence migrants tend to be employed on a regular basis in the North whereas in the South, migrants are more likely to work irregularly and this is particularly the case if they are women (see Figure 7.6). Moreover, women are generally forced to choose between irregular work and unemployment.

Age and education are relevant only for those migrants who are searching for a regular job. We notice that the duration of stay has a positive effect on the possibility of finding employment on a regular basis but is also an important determinant factor with regard to irregular work. However, these results do not change the evaluation made with the simple double entry table analyses (see Table 7.6). The theoretical possibility of each community group to be within one of the three types of employment (see Figure 7.7) is modified by the effect of other factors. It is the interaction of all these factors that determines the real distribution of employment shown in Figure 7.4.

The most illustrative case is that of the Ukrainians: due to the highly gendered structure of their migrant community and to the fact that they have only started migrating to Italy (and chiefly in the Southern regions) in recent years they have been unable to secure regular employment contracts and have therefore been

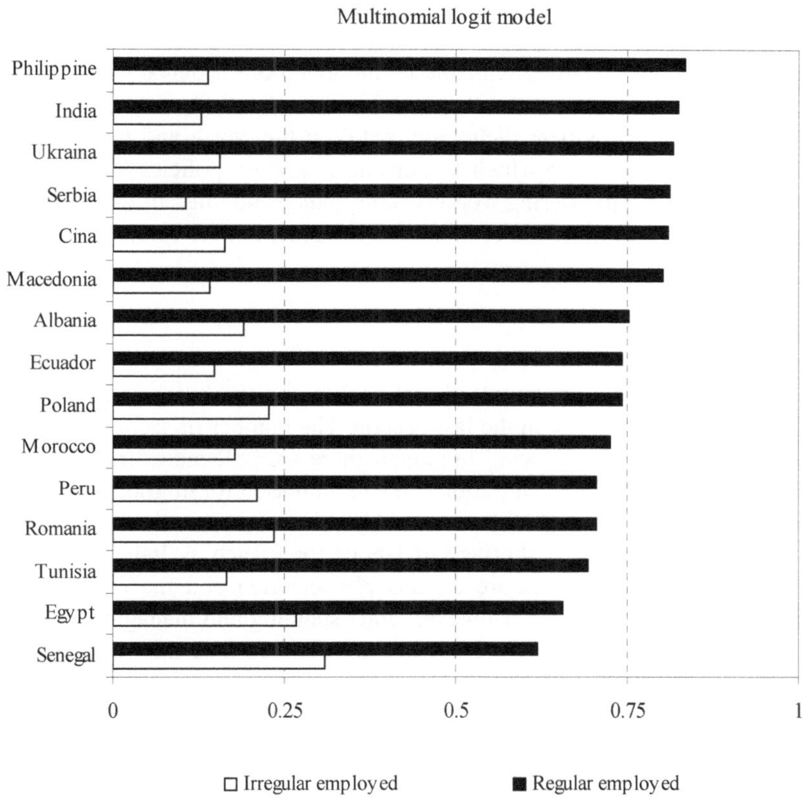

Figure 7.7 Occupational status of employed migrant population of 15-64 years old by country of origin. Italy, mean 2006. Probability

Note: gender, macro-regions, educational level, age and length of stay are the control variables

Source: see Table 7.6

working on an irregular basis. In addition, Ukrainian women mostly work as carers without regular contracts.

On the other hand, Tunisian and Egyptian migrants have been more successful in finding regular employment as they have been living in Italy for a longer period of time. Egyptians have been working mainly in sales, trade, and the service sector also as unskilled and irregular workers. However, Tunisians have a higher risk of unemployment.

The relationship between legal and employment status is significantly influenced by other factors, *in primis* gender and region of residence, particularly for certain communities of migrants. In many communities gender determines the field of specialization and the Italian labour market *ethnicization* of specific sectors of activity that we have discussed above.

The existing opportunities available in the region of residence will determine migrants' access to the labour market and the kind of activity they can perform. Our analyses confirm a clear dichotomy between the North and the South and they highlight the extent to which labour and migration policies have failed in reducing the gap and in offering workers (both Italian and migrant workers) equal opportunities with regard to the economic development of the country.

Summary and Discussion

Migration flows to Italy can be traced back to 30 years ago but they have become particularly significant only in the last decade. The number of second generation migrants is increasingly growing (although there are still more first generation migrants) and forced labour migration is the main reason for migrating to Italy.

The importance of labour migration world-wide which is particularly welcome in countries experiencing a shortage of labour force such as Italy explains the considerable volume of literature on this phenomenon and the attention it is receiving from policy makers. However, understanding and managing migration flows and migrant labour force requires more detailed data than that currently available.

Longitudinal micro data on migrants' labour and resident trajectories is crucial to examine the effects of selected factors determining the correlations between the legal and employment status (for example, irregular workers leaving the country after a period of time spent attempting to obtain a legal residence permit). More detailed retrospective data on changes affecting the legal and employment status of migrants would offer further insights into migration flows between states and for how long migrants remain in a certain legal and employment status.

More data on migrants' family background in the country of origin could also help in better understanding labour market performance (for example, single migrants may be more inclined to adopt labour market and migration strategies aimed at obtaining a permanent residence permit, while migrants with a family who are unlikely to follow them may prefer a renewal of the residence permit and be willing to accept seasonal work in comparison with migrants who are followed by their family in the destination country).

Another type of data which would greatly help in the understanding of how gender and regional differences affect migration in Italy would be more detailed studies on both migrants' and Italians' perception of regular and irregular employment and living conditions (for example, an illegal migrant living in a region where a significant amount of Italians are also irregular or undeclared workers may find themselves in a particularly inhospitable environment in comparison to other migrants living elsewhere).

Conclusion

Notwithstanding the above limitations, our analyses relied on the best currently available data on migrant labour force in Italy and provided a study by gender, territorial context and nationality. First, we showed how local and regional economies may determine migrants' access to the labour market and the type of work undertaken. We demonstrated how regional differences particularly in the economic structure have created two broad categories of migrant labour force due to different labour force demands across the Italian regions. In the Centre-North where most migrants live and work, we may talk of a 'continental model' according to which a large share of migrants is absorbed by the local industry, namely small and medium companies. On the contrary, there are less migrant workers in the South where the underground economy is widespread, unemployment rates are higher and levels of female employment the lowest than the rest of Italy. Here, we may refer to a 'Mediterranean' model of labour force participation whereby migrants work on a more irregular basis, particularly in the area of agriculture, care services, and small commerce.

Migrant workers reduce unemployment risks with a higher mobility across the country so that there are no observable differences in their rates by macro-regions. However, employment opportunities and conditions vary in important ways. In the Northern and Central regions migrants are in regular employment and in some cases are also self-employed. In the South, irregular work is more diffused and often self-employment activities only represent temporary subsistence strategies.

Second, we showed how migrant communities in Italy vary with different structural characteristics and migration patterns. By disaggregating the micro-data by migrants' citizenship we have identified two factors which have made the Italian labour market more multi-ethnic: on the one hand, the *ethnicization* is implicit in the existence of specific sub-sectors and activities in which there is a strong presence of the migrant labour force; on the other hand, the work specialization and labour segregation are present in many different communities each having their own specific migratory strategies, territorial distribution, and labour market participation.

Finally, from a gender perspective we have showed how there are also important differences between men and women in relation to employment opportunities. In general, migrant women are disadvantaged compared to men, as evidenced in the higher unemployment rates among migrant women and by their prevalence in more precarious and irregular service sectors where risks of exploitation, if not slavery, are higher (Carchedi et al. 2003). Those women who live with their employers are in a greater risk of being exploited and subjugated. The vicious circle created by a combination of long working hours, a lack of external support, isolation from other residents and their illegal status, works in favour of the employer perpetuating a state of exploitation (Carchedi et al. 2003). A 2001 sample survey on Rome showed that Philippine and Peruvian women are much more likely to experience exhausting working shifts when they share a house with their employer than when they have a house of their own. In the former case their salary is also substantially lower with unsatisfactory provision of food (Conti and Strozza 2006).

The large majority of migrant women in the South work in family care and thus experience, in addition to their status as women and often illegal migrants, the hardship of a strong occupational segregation. Often these women don't have a choice since many of them are the bread winner of the family and the only parent for their children. The increasing proportion of women, who are migrating alone without their partner and children, is a recognized contemporary international trend (Timur 2000; Oso and Garson 2005). Often migrant women working in family care have left their own children and relatives with someone else. As noted by many scholars, the increase in demand of household work in receiving countries has created a chain of care work which also includes sending countries (Ehrenreich and Hochschild 2002). This 'global care chain' made of personal links among people across different countries based on care work sustains an international division of reproductive labour (Hochschild 2000). Research on global care chains and migrants female headship focuses on two main explanations for care chain: on the one hand, these migrations are linked to the gender segregation in the labour market of the destination country (Hondagneu-Sotelo 1994; Menjivar 2000; Hagan 1998). On the other hand, the gender segregation typical of certain migrant communities may be associated with gender structures in the sending society (Massey et al. 2006).

With regard to gender labour migration this chapter showed how family migration plays an important role in explaining gender differences in labour force participation and employment conditions of women in recipient countries. Moreover, over time it has made the distinction between sending and destination countries more fuzzy. The trans-national nature and complexity of migration flows forces domestic policy makers to cooperate more actively on the international plane in designing labour migration and migrants' integration policies in the labour market.

Notes

A part of this chapter draws on research carried out within the project 'L'immigrazione euro-mediterranea nei nuovi paesi di accoglimento dell'Europa meridionale: evidenze empiriche per l'Italia', coordinated by Prof. Salvatore Strozza and carried out by Dipartimento di Scienze Statistiche (University of Naples Federico II) and co-financed by the Italian Ministero dell'Istruzione dell'Università e la Ricerca scientifica (MIUR) as part of the national project 'Dinamiche demografiche, migrazioni e loro impatto economico' (PRIN 2005).

References

Ambrosini, M. et al. (1995), *L'integrazione subalterna. Peruviani, Eritrei e Filippini nel mercato del lavoro milanese*, Quaderni-I.S.MU., 3.

Ambrosini, M. (1996), 'Segmentazione del mercato del lavoro e inserimento degli immigrati', *Rivista Italiana di Economia Demografia e Statistica*, a. L: 2, 63–90.

Ambrosini, M. (2001), 'Immigrati e lavoro indipendente', in Zincone G. (ed.), *Secondo rapporto sull'integrazione degli immigrati in Italia* (Bologna: Il Mulino), 366–92.

Ambrosini, M. (1999), *Utili invasori. L'inserimento degli immigrati nel mercato del lavoro italiano* (Milano: Franco Angeli).

Barsotti, O. (1996), 'L'inserimento lavorativo degli immigrati e il loro ruolo nei confronti della forza lavoro autoctona', *Rivista Italiana di Economia Demografia e Statistica*, a. L: 2, 37–51.

Birindelli, A.M. (1984), *Dalle grandi emigrazioni di massa all'arrivo dei lavoratori stranieri: un secolo di esperienza migratoria in Italia* (Roma: Dipartimento di Scienze Demografiche).

Blangiardo, G.C. (2008), 'Aspetti quantitativi e riflessioni su prospettive e convenienza dell'immigrazione straniera in Italia', in ISMU, Tredicesimo rapporto sulle migrazioni 2007 (Milano: Franco Angeli), 41–59.

Blangiardo G.C. and Farina, P. (eds) (2006), *Il Mezzogiorno dopo la grande regolarizzazione. Immagini e problematiche dell'immigrazione*, vol. III (Milano: Franco Angeli).

Bonifazi, C. (2007), *L'immigrazione straniera in Italia*, new edition (Bologna: Il Mulino).

Bonifazi, C. and Rinesi F. (2008), I nuovi contesti del lavoro: l'immigrazione straniera, Report on the labour issues (Roma: mimeo).

Bonifazi, C. et al. (2003), 'Measuring migrant integration in the nineties: the contribution of field surveys in Italy', *Studi Emigrazione/Migration Studies*, XL, n. 152, 855–84.

Bonifazi, C. et al. (2008a), *The Italian transition from emigration to immigration country*, IDEA Report (Roma: Mimeo).

Bonifazi, C. et al. (2008b), 'Popolazione straniera e mercato del lavoro: un'analisi per collettività', *Studi Emigrazione/Migration Studies*, n. 171, 549–72.

Cangiano, A. and Strozza, S. (2005), 'Gli immigrati extracomunitari nei mercati del lavoro italiani: alcune evidenze empiriche a livello territoriale', *Economia & Lavoro*, a. XXXIX: 1, 89–124.

Carchedi, F. (ed.) (1999), *La risorsa inaspettata. Lavoro e formazione degli immigrati nell'Europa mediterranea* (Roma: Ediesse).

Carfagna, S. et al. (2008), 'Changes of status of immigrants in Italy: results of a record-linkage on administrative sources', paper at the European Population Conference, EAPS, Barcelona, 9–12 July, (Updated 15 July 2008) http://epc2008.princeton.edu/abstractViewer.aspx? submissionId=80562.

Carchedi F., Mottura G., Pugliese E. (2003), Il lavoro servile e le nuoveschiavitù, Milano: Franco Angeli.

Casacchia, O. et al. (1999), 'Migrazioni interne e migrazioni internazionali: il nuovo ruolo del Mezzogiorno nel sistema migratorio nazionale', in Bonifazi, C. (ed.), *Mezzogiorno e migrazioni interne*, monografie n.10 (Roma: IRP-CNR), 237–72.

Casacchia, O. and Strozza, S. (2002), 'Migrations intérieures des italianes avec l'Europe au XIXème et au XXème siècle. L'Italie de pays d'émigration à pays d'immigration', in Roel, A.E., Gonzàlez Lopo, D.L. (eds), *Movilidad y migraciónes internas en Europa latina*, ACTAS del Coloquio Europeo (Universidade de Santiago de Compostela: Publicaciòns), 161–204.

Conti, C. and Strozza, S. (eds) (2006), *Gli immigrati stranieri e la capitale. Condizioni di vita e atteggiamenti dei filippini, marocchini, peruviani e romeni a Roma* (Milano: Franco Angeli).

Di Comite, L. (1991), 'Le migrazioni Sud-Nord nell'area del Bacino Mediterraneo e la transizione dell'Italia da paese di emigrazione a paese di immigrazione', in Ancona, G. (ed.), *Migrazioni mediterranee e mercato del lavoro*, (Bari: Cacucci), 43–58.

Ehrenreich, B. and Hochschild, A. (eds) (2002), *Global Woman: Nannies, Maids and Sex Workers in the New Economy* (New York: Henry Holt and Company/ Metropolitan Book).

Favero, L. and Tassello, G. (1978), 'Cent'anni di emigrazione italiana (1876–1976)', in Rosoli, G. (ed.), *Un secolo di emigrazione italiana 1876–1976* (Roma: Centro Studi Emigrazione).

Frey, L. and Livraghi, R. (1996), 'The Jobs and Effects of Migrant Workers in Italy', in Frey, L., et al. (eds), *The Jobs and the Effects of Migrant Workers in Italy. Three Essays* (Geneva ILO), 1–20.

Gesano, G. (1993), 'Immigrati e mercato del lavoro', in Birindelli, A.M. et al., (eds), *La presenza straniera in Italia. Il caso dell'area romana* (Milano: Franco Angeli), 53–97.

Golini, A. and Amato, F. (2001), 'Uno sguardo ad un secolo e mezzo di emigrazione italiana', in Bevilacqua, P. et al. (eds), *Storia dell'emigrazione italiana* (Roma: Donzelli Editore), 45–75.

Guarini, R. and Natale, M. (1996), 'Mercato del lavoro ed immigrazione straniera in Italia', *Rivista Italiana di Economia Demografia e Statistica*, a. L: 1, 13–65.

Hagan J.M., (1998), Social Networks, Gender and Immigrant Incorporation, American Sociological Review, 63(1):57-67.

Hochschild, A.R. (2000), 'Global Care Chains and Emotional Surplus Value', in Hutton, W. and Giddens, A. (eds), *On the Edge: Living with Global Capitalism* (London: Jonathan Cape).

Hondagneu-Sotelo, P. (1994), *Gendered Transitions: Mexican Experiences of Immigration* (Berkeley: University of California Press).

Hosmer, D.W. and Lemeshow, S. (2000), *Applied Logistic Regression*, 2nd ed. (New York: Wiley).

ISTAT (2006), *Gli stranieri nella rilevazione sulle forze di lavoro*, Metodi e Norme, n. 27 (Roma: Istat).
ISTAT (2007), *Forze di lavoro – Media 2006*, Annuario, n. 12 (Roma: Istat).
Macioti, M. I. and Pugliese, E. (2003), *L'esperienza migratoria. Immigrati e rifugiati in Italia* (Bari: Laterza).
Massey, D. (2006), 'Building a comprehensive model of international migration',in Howe, N. and Jackson, R. (eds), *Long-Term Immigration Projection Methods: Current Practice and How to Improve It* (Boston: Center for Retirement Research, Boston College), 4–28 (Updated 21 October 2008) <http://www.bc.edu/centers/ crr/papers/wp_2006–3A.pdf#page=6>.
Menjivar C., (2000), Fragmented Ties: Salvadoran Immigrant Networks in America, Berkeley: University of California.
Natale, M. and Strozza, S. (1997), *Gli immigrati stranieri in Italia: quanti sono, chi sono, come vivono?* (Bari: Cacucci Editore).
Oso, L. and Garson, J.P. (2005), 'The feminization of International Migration', OECD European Commission Seminar, *Migrant Women and the Labour Market: Diversity and Challenges* (Updated 21 October 2008) <http://www.ec.europa.eu/employment_social/employment_analysis/imm/imm_migrwom05_oso_gars_en.pdf>.
Paterno, A., Terzera, L. and Strozza, S. (eds) (2006), *Sospesi tra due rive. Migrazioni e insediamenti di albanesi e marocchini* (Milano: Franco Angeli).
Pugliese, E. (1990), 'Gli immigrati nel mercato del lavoro', *Polis*, a. IV: 1, 71–96.
Pugliese, E. (1999), 'Gli immigrati nel mercato del lavoro e i modelli regionali di inserimento', in Carchedi, F. (ed.), *La risorsa inaspettata. Lavoro e formazione degli immigrati nell'Europa mediterranea* (Roma: Ediesse), 37–58.
Pugliese, E. (2002), *L'Italia tra migrazioni internazionali e migrazioni interne* (Bologna: il Mulino).
Reyneri, E. (2000), 'Integrazione nel mercato del lavoro', in Zincone, G. (ed.), *Primo rapporto sull'integrazione degli immigrati in Italia* (Bologna: Il Mulino), 157–92.
Reyneri, E. (2001), 'L'integrazione nell'occupazione dipendente', in Zincone, G. (ed.), *Secondo rapporto sull'integrazione degli immigrati in Italia* (Bologna: Il Mulino), 331–65.
Reyneri, E. (2007a), 'La vulnerabilità degli immigrati', in Saraceno, C. and Brandolini, A. (eds), *Disuguaglianze economiche e vulnerabilità in Italia* (Bologna: Il Mulino).
Reyneri, E. (2007b), *Immigration in Italy: trends and perspectives*, Iom, Argo.
Rossi, F. and Strozza, S. (2007), 'Mobilità della popolazione, immigrazione e presenza straniera', in Gruppo di Coordinamento per la Demografia (ed.), *Rapporto sulla popolazione. L'Italia all'inizio del XXI secolo* (Bologna: Il Mulino), 111–37.
Sabbadini, L.L. et al. (2007), 'Il mercato del lavoro degli immigrati', in Ministero dell'Interno, *1° Rapporto sugli immigrati in Italia* (Roma: Ministero dell'Interno), 186–217.

Strozza, S. (1995), 'I lavoratori extracomunitari in Italia: esame della letteratura e tentativo di verifica di alcune ipotesi', *Studi Emigrazione/Migration Studies*, n. 119, 457–90.

Strozza, S. (2002), 'Gli immigrati stranieri in Italia: caratteristiche e inserimento lavorativo', in Natale M. (ed.), *Economia e Popolazione. Alcuni aspetti delle interrelazioni tra sviluppo demografico ed economico*, Nuova edizione aggiornata e integrata (Milano: Franco Angeli), 435–74.

Strozza, S. (2006), 'L'inserimento lavorativo degli immigrati stranieri nella capitale: il primo passo verso l'integrazione', in Conti C. and Strozza S. (eds.), *Gli immigrati stranieri e la capitale. Condizioni di vita e atteggiamenti dei filippini, marocchini, peruviani e romeni a Roma* (Milano: Franco Angeli), 106–27.

Strozza, S., Forcellati, L. and Ferrara R. (2008), *Il lavoro degli stranieri residenti nelle diverse Italie: differenze di genere e per nazionalità*, paper at the XLV Riunione Scientifica della S.I.E.D.S. 'Geopolitica del Mediterraneo' Bari 28–30 maggio 2008, forthcoming.

Strozza, S. and Ferrara, R. (2008), 'Gli immigrati esteuropei e nordafricani nel mercati del lavoro italiani: alcune evidenze empiriche', in Di Comite, L., Garavello, O. and Galizia, F., *Sviluppo demografico ed economico nel Mediterraneo* (Bari: Cacucci Editore), 431–59.

Timur, S. (2000), 'Changing Trends and Major Issues in International Migration: An Overview of UNESCO Programmes', *International Migration*, 165, 255–69.

Venturini, A. and Villosio, C. (1999), 'Foreign Workers in Italy: Are They Assimilating to Natives? Are They Competing Against Natives? An Analysis by the S.S.A. dataset', *Einwanderungsregion Europa?*, 33, Arbaitstagung der Deutschen Gesellschaft fur Bevolkerungswissenschaft in Zusammenarbeit mit dem Istitut fur Migrationsforschung und Interkulturelle Studien der Universitat Osnabruck.

Werner, H. (2003), 'The Integration of Immigrants into the Labour Market of the EU', *IAB Labour Market Research Topics*, n. 52, Institute for the Employment Research of the Federal Employment Services.

Zanfrini, L. (2002), 'Politiche delle 'quote' ed etnicizzazione del mercato del lavoro italiano', *Sociologia del Lavoro*, Fascicolo, Folder 88.

PART 3

Gender Perspectives on Immigration Control

Chapter 8
'Awkward Aliens': Female Migrants, Exploitation and the Trafficking Framework

Heli Askola

This chapter discusses the legal regimes devised by European migrant-receiving countries, in particular within the structures of the European Union (EU), to deal with migrant women who have experienced the kind of exploitation which is now commonly labelled 'trafficking in women'. As exploitation experienced by migrant women, especially in so-called 'commercial sex industries', has been viewed through the prism of 'trafficking', the response of many destination countries in Europe has been to construct a so-called 'trafficking framework' – a framework aimed at stemming what is viewed as a criminal trade by targeting traffickers and others involved in 'exploiting' migrant women (in prostitution and elsewhere). The typical European destination country response to the exploitation of female migrants is now commonly structured around three dimensions which are seen as necessary limbs of the trafficking framework: one focuses on the prosecution of traffickers, one on the protection of victims of trafficking, and one on the prevention of trafficking.

The 'awkward aliens' of the title refers to the apparent 'mismatch' between the notions that underlie existing legal strategies to address migrant exploitation in destination countries and the actual experiences of women who have faced the global realities of 'trafficking'. This chapter argues that the reality of such individuals corresponds awkwardly with the legal framework that has been developed to tackle 'trafficking' and provides insights into why the treatment 'trafficking victims' experience in destination countries is so inadequate. It is, of course, not a new argument to say that the law does not accommodate (certain) women's reality, at least for anyone familiar with feminist critiques of law; it is, after all, a staple of feminist writing on law that women do not 'fit in', that is, that the law uncomfortably incorporates specifically female experiences and interests, especially those that have no immediate male comparator (Lacey 1998; Réaume 1996). However, with trafficking one is, in some ways at least, dealing with a framework which has ostensibly been constructed for (these) women's benefit *and* with (some) women's participation. So how does one account for the inadequacies of the 'woman of trafficking' discourse (Smart 1992)?

The argument of this chapter proceeds as follows. First, the chapter briefly introduces the so-called 'trafficking framework'. It discusses why and how this kind of understanding came to frame the response to the phenomenon of (especially female) migrants' exploitation. It argues that the current trafficking framework came about owing to a combination of historical reasons and (sometimes conflicting) contemporary concerns, and that one of the factors that helps explain the relative success of the trafficking framework is its flexible nature. However, it is also this flexibility that is its main weakness. The second part of the chapter then considers the three limbs of the trafficking framework – prosecution, protection and prevention – with reference to how the experience of migrant women as 'trafficking victims' illuminates and contests the conceptual underpinnings of the framework. The fact that real-life 'trafficking victims' awkwardly fit within the legal categories of the trafficking framework or do not act in line with its underlying assumptions makes them difficult to 'manage' within the framework. This can be (and has been in the past) used to demonstrate the alleged inadequacies of the trafficking framework. However, this part of the chapter is particularly interested in interrogating the specific conditions for the construction of this framework and the limits that these conditions place on reforming the trafficking framework and pursuing alternatives to it.

The Development of the 'Trafficking Framework'

The so-called 'fight' against trafficking in human beings, which took off *de novo* in the 1990s, is an interesting example of the astonishing speed at which the often sluggish international community of states can react to a problem which is, for various reasons, perceived to be urgently in need of an international response and suitably receptive to legal regulation to achieve desired outcomes.

The problem, in short, was identified as one of criminal networks, which (allegedly) began to reap huge financial profits from the vulnerability of girls and young women from poor and destabilized countries. These networks, it was said, tempted women to migrate abroad, with the aim of driving them into prostitution (and other types of exploitative labour). The increase in this kind of criminal activity was linked to changed global circumstances in the 1990s, in particular the political and economic upheavals following the fall of the Iron Curtain and the various consequences of 'globalization', especially increased population mobility and inter-connectedness (Hughes 2000; van Impe 2000; von Struensee 2000). In Western Europe the perceived crisis was associated with specific concerns over the drastic economic and social transformations in Central and Eastern Europe and qualms about the consequences of increased freedom of movement in the Internal Market (Twomey 2000). The argument both at international, regional and national levels was that these circumstances created push and pull factors for migrants and provided (increasingly transnational) networks of criminals with ideal conditions to operate. In particular, these criminals were able to make vast profits (with minimal risk of being detected) by subverting migration controls and organizing vulnerable women and girls to journey to wealthy EU countries, ostensibly to work as nannies and entertainers but in reality for exploitation in prostitution.

In international, regional and national legislative terms, the last decade has involved what can only be described as a surge of activity to criminalize trafficking in human beings, to devise victim protection mechanisms and to take some kind of preventative action. Most notably, the so-called UN Trafficking Protocol[1] was adopted in 2000, entered into force a mere three years later, and currently has an astonishing 124 state parties, including the most important destination countries for migrants – most of the Member States of the EU as well as the United States (for further analysis of the Protocol, see Gallagher 2001). In Europe, EU Member States have become increasingly active in developing a regional and cross-national anti-trafficking framework. In some Member States the need for anti-trafficking strategies (and the desire for an increased EU role in these activities) stems from domestic concerns over increasing involvement of (irregular) migrants in unregulated sectors such as prostitution, while other Member States have been prompted to act by the EU itself following the introduction of binding anti-trafficking measures.[2] Whilst the EU has the most effective tools for harmonizing legal responses to trafficking, most recently the Council of Europe has sought to 'perfect' the regional European anti-trafficking framework by introducing its own Convention[3] which is more detailed than the UN Trafficking Protocol and, arguably, somewhat more sensitive to human rights than the EU's initiatives (Gallagher 2006).

The framework which has emerged reflects a particular view of the problem of migrant exploitation and the role of institutions, structures and processes necessary to counter it. This is underpinned by a set of understandings: 'trafficking in human beings' must be made a specific criminal offence subject to sufficiently heavy sanctions; associated offences and 'bad' practices contributing to trafficking, such as corruption, the use of fraudulent documents and money laundering, must also be tackled through tougher criminal justice measures and increased cooperation between states; more effective border control mechanisms are necessary to prevent unauthorized entry in general and, more specifically, to identify (potential) trafficking victims in transit; identified victims must be assisted and protected, especially if they are willing to cooperate with the authorities to help prosecute and convict those who have trafficked or 'exploited' them; after a temporary stay victims

1 The UN Trafficking Protocol, supplementing the UN Convention against Transnational Organized Crime (UN Doc A/53/383, Annex II, 2002), entered into force on 25 December 2003.

2 The two most important EU instruments, which are complemented by 'soft law', are the Council Framework Decision 2002/629/JHA of 19 July 2002 on combating trafficking in human beings (OJ L 203, 1 August 2002) and the Council Directive 2004/81/EC of 29 April 2004 on the residence permit issued to third-country nationals who are victims of trafficking in human beings or who have been the subject of an action to facilitate illegal immigration, who cooperate with the competent authorities (OJ L 261, 6 August 2004).

3 Council of Europe Convention on Action Against Trafficking in Human Beings, ETS no 197.

should in most cases be 'humanely repatriated' to their countries of origin (apart from exceptional cases where humanitarian reasons might necessitate permanent leave to remain or even granting asylum); and some preventative action is needed, for instance raising awareness of the risks of irregular migration amongst potential victims but also perhaps more broadly (and rather more vaguely) mitigating so-called 'root causes' of trafficking such as poverty, under-development and gender inequality.

It seems then that there is, superficially at least, an overwhelming external consensus on the need to 'fight trafficking', and on the steps necessary to do so, and this has expedited the process of adoption, ratification and, to some degree, implementation of legal instruments against trafficking. For the purposes of this analysis – which argues that some if not all of this activity in one way or another fails to understand the phenomenon it seeks to tackle – it is useful to ask why trafficking has been such a good modern folk enemy in terms of prompting this kind of response and what other possible frameworks have been ignored in the process of developing it.

As a starting point, it is worth noting (rather uncontroversially) that trafficking is, as a phenomenon, located at the intersection of a host of contemporary concerns. These range from, most prominently, concerns over transnational organized crime and increased freedom of movement globally and within the EU, to more diffuse anxieties over market liberalization, the global commodification of sexuality and socio-economic inequalities both within and between countries. It was, as noted, the specific concern over organized criminals organizing irregular migration which first pushed the issue back onto the international legal arena after an absence of half a century,[4] leading to the adoption of the UN Protocol which supplements the UN Convention against Transnational Organized Crime (Gallagher 2001). In Europe, underlying concerns about irregular migration into the borderless Internal Market, and the progressive enlargement towards the east served to make it a salient cooperation issue in the EU (Twomey 2000). Last but not least, whilst nobody nowadays contests that trafficking can occur for various purposes beyond the orthodox connection to exploitation in prostitution, it was again trafficking for commercial sex which first reignited the notoriously divided interest of feminists and other campaigners concerned about the women at the heart of this 'exploitation' (Outshoorn 2005). Indeed, it is the campaigns around trafficking for sexual exploitation in prostitution which have prompted the most substantial official response from European as well as other governments.

4 Until negotiations started in 1997 to include human trafficking (and eventually smuggling) in the so-called Vienna process, which culminated in the adoption of UN Convention against Transnational Organized Crime, concerns over trafficking had last been addressed in the international arena by the Convention for the Suppression of the Traffic in Persons and of the Exploitation of the Prostitution of Others, which was approved by the General Assembly of the United Nations in resolution in 1949.

Without questioning the good intentions of many campaigners genuinely concerned for the welfare of individuals affected by exploitation in the course of migration, it seems clear that trafficking has become a storage place for many contemporary anxieties which have little to do with the welfare of migrant women per se. Measures against 'trafficking' have such political purchase in part because the concept itself is in many ways an empty vessel, despite the long historical trajectory of the notion of 'traffic' in women.[5] Whilst, as a result of campaigning, the general public now have some idea of what commercial sexual exploitation of migrant women can involve (especially at its worst – newspaper stories of innocent girls lured into prostitution abroad have made sure of that), as a legal concept 'trafficking' is actually so imprecise that everyone can be said to be against it regardless of their views on the acceptability of prostitution, migrants' rights or the issue of global labour mobility. Moreover, nearly every kind of state measure – from stricter border controls to poverty reduction – can be characterized as an 'anti-trafficking measure'. This is not a new criticism: much has already been written on how many obligations regarding trafficking are flexible and discretionary and on how the celebrated international definition of trafficking[6] in the UN Trafficking Protocol (which was adopted, with slight modifications also in the EU Framework Decision and the Council of Europe Convention) involves an unhappy compromise (because of disputes over the nature and acceptability of prostitution), leading to crucial terms such as 'exploitation' and 'position of vulnerability' being left undefined (Gallagher 2001; Doezema 2002b; Raymond 2002; Munro 2005). However, the central point to highlight is that this definition and these obligations were adopted *precisely* because they are elusive enough to give (especially destination) states leeway to recast trafficking, and measures needed to tackle it, domestically as they please.

From a legal point of view the elusiveness of the concept of trafficking is extremely problematic, in particular because in the absence of a clear-cut definition of trafficking it is difficult to make distinctions between migrants and

5 For example see 1904 International Agreement for the Suppression of the Slave Trade (1 LNTS 83), 1910 International Convention for the Suppression of White Slave Traffic (III LNTS 278); 1921 Convention for the Suppression of Traffic in Women and Children (9 LNTS 415) and 1933 International Convention for the Suppression of the Traffic in Women of Full Age (150 LNTS 431).

6 Art. 3(a): 'Trafficking in persons' shall mean the recruitment, transportation, transfer, harbouring or receipt of persons, by means of the threat or use of force or other forms of coercion, of abduction, of fraud, of deception, of the abuse of power or of a position of vulnerability or of the giving or receiving of payments or benefits to achieve the consent of a person having control over another person, for the purpose of exploitation. Exploitation shall include, at a minimum, the exploitation of the prostitution of others or other forms of sexual exploitation, forced labour or services, slavery or practices similar to slavery, servitude or the removal of organs; (b) The consent of a victim of trafficking in persons to the intended exploitation set forth in subparagraph (a) of this article shall be irrelevant where any of the means set forth in subparagraph (a) have been used.'

to estimate the extent (and potential growth) of human trafficking. The adoption of a trafficking framework means that a determination has to be made about who is and who is not a 'victim of trafficking', as this resolves how individuals are treated in a destination country. Thanks to recent legislative developments, those identified as trafficking victims can expect (or at least hope) to be treated better than those who are merely identified as ordinary irregular or 'illegal'[7] migrants. Of course, even if an exact definition could be agreed on, gathering and comparing statistics on the scale of migrants' exploitation is always challenging (see e.g. Laczko and Gramegna 2003; Tyldum and Brunovskis 2005) which has lead to assertions that any officially recognized cases are the tip of the iceberg (Morris 2007). However, the real issue is surely that no one knows how big, or small, the iceberg is, particularly when there is no agreement as to how much one has to be 'exploited' to be considered as 'trafficked' rather than, for instance, as just having made the best available choices about migration when faced with grim alternatives. As such, the stereotypical images of 'modern-day slaves' now so prevalent in the media mask an infinitely more complex reality where many (in particular irregular) migrants make highly constrained choices about moving and working and face various degrees of 'exploitation' or forced labour, not only in prostitution but in sectors such as domestic labour, agriculture or construction (Anderson and Rogaly 2005).

Doubts about the usefulness of the concept of 'trafficking' have become increasingly significant as it has become evident that the imprecision of the term and the flexibility of the trafficking framework allow destination regions to adopt interpretations which can seem inimical to migrants' welfare in general and trafficking victims' situation in particular. From the point of view of migrant women's rights the trafficking framework can be criticized, for instance, for excessively focusing on the most egregious cases of violence and for de-emphasizing the need to empower migrant women. Some even advocate abandoning the trafficking framework altogether (Doezema 2002a: 7). More often it is suggested that more attention be given instead to human rights violations involved in coercive migration (or assisted movement for a fee) and gendered labour practices which together make up what are now characterized as trafficking-type practices. Implicit (and sometimes explicit) in these kinds of arguments is the idea that the trafficking framework came to be chosen by states (in particular destination states) over other and *better* alternatives to frame the issue – most notably, the International Convention on Migrant Workers, the (thus far) marginalized UN framework on migrants' human rights.[8] Other routes which could have been built on to develop

7 In EU jargon, the word 'illegal' is consistently used, despite widespread criticism of the term as stigmatizing and overbroad.

8 The International Convention on the Protection of the Rights of All Migrant Workers and Members of their Families (IMWC) was adopted in 1990 as one of the seven major UN human rights instruments – yet it only limped into force in 2003 and has a measly 41 parties (in April 2009).

a more rights-oriented approach are the labour migration rights framework of the ILO[9] or even the 'slavery-based' model where trafficking could be framed as 'modern slavery'.[10] These perspectives, it is assumed, would be a more fruitful way forward than the measures incorporated in the trafficking framework which are found to be profoundly inadequate to deal with the phenomenon: 'at worst they can cause repercussions which have repressive rather than emancipatory effects on the already precarious position of the women likely to be affected' (Wijers and van Doorninck 2002).

The 'Woman of Trafficking Discourse' and the Response to Her 'Exploitation'

Although it is easy to agree that the current European trafficking framework has major shortcomings and that alternatives such as the ones suggested above might provide a more appropriate basis for dealing with migrant exploitation, it seems essential to understand from where the problems with the current framework stem. Unless one establishes how and why the current 'solution' is flawed, it is a leap of faith to presume another solution could be introduced which would work better. Why is the trafficking framework so inadequate in practice? And is the problem simply one of bad practice or is the framework objectionable in principle as well? As stated above, the trafficking framework is vague and flexible, giving states leeway to *interpret* it in ways that overemphasize repressive measures and short-sighted stop-gap defensive action in preference for uniform respect for affected migrants' rights and consistent and sustained cooperation to reduce would-be migrants' vulnerability to exploitation. However, what this section explores is *why* this interpretation takes place, and what, if anything, can be learned about these reasons.

The following analysis discusses the 'three P's' that characterize the European trafficking framework – prosecution, protection and prevention. It examines the ways in which the actual experiences of migrant women never really seem to 'fit' with the victim-associated assumptions made in destination countries about 'the woman of trafficking discourse'. It is argued that as this incongruity stems from the fundamental underpinnings of the European trafficking framework, the framework might not be as susceptible to change as many reformists would like to believe.

---

9 Based on for example ILO Convention No. C 97 on migration for employment (1949) – ratified by 47 countries.

10 See for example the 1926 Slavery Convention (60 LNTS 253) and the 1956 Supplementary Convention on the Abolition of Slavery, the Slave Trade, and Institutions and Practices Similar to Slavery (266 UNTS 40).

Prosecution

The prosecution aspect of the 'trafficking framework' is, on the surface, fairly straightforward. The primary rationale for criminalization and criminal justice cooperation is linked to arguments about the need to punish traffickers/exploiters who subject people to 'violence, rape, battery and extreme cruelty as well as other types of pressure and coercion' and, in the transnational setting, to plug the gaps which exist in national law enforcement strategies through increased international/transnational cooperation (European Commission 2001). Thus the express aim of the prosecution dimension is to criminalize the practices of traffickers through a common definition which would iron out discrepancies and divergences in national penal legislation, thus paving the way for more effective investigation and prosecution not only within states but between them.[11] Indeed, because police and judicial cooperation between states is often seen as crucial for effective prosecution, it is commonly agreed that this must be improved through further developing law enforcement and judicial cooperation in areas which have a link to trafficking, for instance regarding corruption or money laundering. In the European framework, this task has, in particular, been taken up by the EU within its aim of creating an Area of Freedom, Security and Justice (for a summary of these activities, see European Commission 2005).

On the face of it, this dimension seems rather unobjectionable, at least if one takes seriously the accompanying rhetoric that this activity is about saving women from the 'misery behind the fantasy' (European Commission 2001). On that reading, 'victims of trafficking' have been deliberately lured with false promises by organized crime syndicates who have then dehumanized them into sellable commodities. This applies even to those women who knew, to a certain extent, what to expect: 'Even if a certain number of the trafficked women know they will work as prostitutes, they do not know that they will often be kept in slavery-like conditions being unable to escape from their exploiters' (European Commission 2001). Women who have experienced 'trafficking' are thus portrayed as 'innocent victims' who did not deserve the treatment they faced. Those who kept them under lock and key should face heavy penalties (why not?) and any measures that seek to facilitate better police and judicial cooperation are to be welcomed.

The woman of this trafficking discourse is a one-dimensional victim figure. This is essential as it is her innocence, acquired through her abuse and suffering, which serves to conceptually separate her from (and juxtapose her with) two other legal figures which are significantly more established than she is, and not innocent at all: the prostitute and the illegal immigrant (Goodey 2004: 32). The 'prostitute' is, of course, a well-established criminal figure, a 'legal leper' who 'contaminates' all who come in contact with her (Duncan 1994: 22-3). The old

11 See for instance the Legislative Recommendations on Police and Judicial Cooperation in the so-called Brussels Declaration (Council Conclusions of 8 May 2003, OJ C 137, 12 June 2003).

debates about the links between prostitution and trafficking were revived in many EU Member States by the early 1990s owing to the (perceived and in some cases real) influx of young foreign women into prostitution. Despite serious campaigning for prostitutes' rights, prostitution remains, in most EU Member States, a quasi-criminal activity. Even where it may be technically legal, most things connected with it (advertising, soliciting, streetwalking, etc) are not. Where the legal regulation around prostitution has been reformed to distance the issue partly from the criminal sphere (for instance in the Netherlands) the process has tended to be more about regulating prostitution-related activities and preventing migrants' involvement (Outshoorn 2004). In certain EU states, such as Sweden, the aim is explicitly that of suppression of prostitution altogether (Svanström 2004).

The criminal figure of the 'illegal immigrant' is a more contemporary construction. Whilst migrants may become irregular or 'illegal' because of irregular entry, residence or activities, these are often conflated into a single category of 'illegal immigration'. It is trite (but pertinent) to note that in European countries, which have become destination countries for migrants (in particular) from poorer countries, national electorates have become increasingly worried about the consequences of 'uncontrolled' migration. States have sought to police access into their areas and curb the 'influx' of undesirable economic migrants and have mobilized their migration (and asylum) laws to create increasingly complicated categories of legal and, by implication, illegal migration (Geddes 2003). In Europe this picture is made more complex by the added and shifting layers created by EU law (Bogusz et al. 2004).

In contrast, the woman of trafficking discourse is clearly distinguished from prostitutes and illegal immigrants by the emphasis on her innocence and suffering. The woman of trafficking discourse has been deceived or coerced into prostitution by (often foreign) criminals, pimps and brothel-owners – she has not chosen to be involved in prostitution or, at least, has not been aware of the conditions which await her. The woman of trafficking discourse is also distinguished from other irregular migrants: even though she may technically be 'illegal' because of irregular entry or irregular activities, unlike the 'migrant prostitute', the woman of trafficking discourse has (supposedly) not migrated with the specific aim of breaching immigration law or bringing social disorder. This conceptual move defines the woman of trafficking discourse through juxtaposing her 'victimhood' with the guilt of the other two figures. Thus a separate category is carved out for 'trafficking victims' who – unlike (migrant) prostitutes and illegal immigrants – are not criminals but victims of criminals (Goodey 2004). Thus the real criminals (traffickers) have to be caught as a matter of urgency while their victims deserve some protection (see later).

Of course, although the woman of trafficking discourse as a rhetorical figure is distinguished from the prostitute and the illegal immigrant, the similarities between them are clear; she works as a prostitute – even if this is perhaps against her will or under exploitative conditions – and she has, in one way or another, breached the legal rules on migration in the destination countries, and sometimes willingly collaborated to subvert migration controls in order to work in the EU. Furthermore, empirically speaking, making clear-cut distinctions between freely choosing prostitutes (or illegal immigrants) and non-consenting victims can be challenged as somewhat arbitrary. 'Non-trafficked' irregular migrants who are involved in prostitution rarely exercise unconstrained free choice and the causes behind prostitution are structural as well as individual in nature (O'Connell-Davidson 1998; Phoenix 1999). Similarly, many 'illegal immigrants' are, again for structural reasons, extremely vulnerable to exploitation or even forced labour even if they have not been 'trafficked' within the current definition provided by the law (Anderson and Rogaly 2005).

Thus the category of the woman of trafficking discourse is one that many real-life 'trafficked' women do not, and indeed cannot, fit. This explains why saving 'trafficking victims' appears to be relegated to a relatively low law enforcement priority and why in practice EU Member States' authorities often express relatively unsympathetic attitudes towards such individuals. In their eyes, very few female migrants found in prostitution fit the victim model of the deserving woman of trafficking discourse. As a result, to the extent that the prosecution dimension is interested in 'victims' of trafficking, it is alert to those women who are obviously 'innocent' or at least less criminal, those who are very young or clearly deceived, or literally forced into prostitution and abused through egregious violence. Migrant women who do not fit this conceptualization, even though they may have faced exploitation or violence, continue to be treated as (irregular) migrant prostitutes and expelled in order to send the message to (other) prospective illegal migrants.

What the prosecution limb of the trafficking framework is really interested in is not the abuse or exploitation migrant women may have experienced – laws on violence against women being notoriously under-enforced in most EU Member States – but the arguably worse crime which has been perpetrated by traffickers: assisting migrants to subvert national/regional territorial boundaries and making profits from criminal activities in the underbelly of the Common Market. Thus, if the irregular migrant (like the 'fake' asylum seeker who is in reality an 'economic migrant') is guilty of violating the integrity of sovereign borders, those who systematically organize such criminal migration for profit on a regional scale (and, at times, with use of violence) are guilty of a crime on a grander scale. The prosecution aspect is most concerned with identifying and pursuing these individuals – and protection for alleged 'victims' is highly conditional on their co-operation and assistance with this endeavour.[12]

12 See Art. 26 of the Council of Europe Convention which maintains that states shall (merely) 'provide for the possibility of not imposing penalties on victims for their involvement in unlawful activities, to the extent that they have been compelled to do so'.

Protection

Whatever the conceptual flaws of the prosecution limb, some of these could possibly be ameliorated by the construction of more robust protection and prevention dimensions. However, in the trafficking framework, both of these dimensions are not autonomous limbs. The protection aspect is defined through and linked to the priorities of the prosecution dimension. Similarly, the prevention dimension has been subordinated to the pursuit of prosecution (discussed later).

In some ways developing any kind of protection dimension is innovative as it treats, at least in theory, the woman of trafficking discourse as individuals as *deserving of* (if not entitled to) support and assistance, be it medical or psychological help to recover from abuse, or access to housing or other social assistance, or protection from those threatening harm. In Europe, early-affected destination countries began to develop national 'victim protection' systems in the early 1990s. Most notable efforts were made by Belgium, the Netherlands and Italy, often driven by and in collaboration with the volunteer sector. At the international level, obligations to protect and assist trafficking victims are mostly discretionary,[13] at the insistence of migrant-receiving countries. At the regional level, an EU Directive was adopted in 2004 and the Council of Europe Convention has provisions on victim protection, albeit with strict conditions attached.[14] The most significant aspects of the EU 'protection' dimension for victims who are migrants with an irregular migration status, are access to a temporary residence permit which delays expulsion (the normal fate of irregular migrants) and an associated entitlement to some services and temporary housing. The temporary permission to remain in the country of destination arguably aids victims' recovery and, more importantly for destination states, aims to encourage victims to cooperate with law enforcement authorities investigating and prosecuting traffickers.[15] Once identified trafficking victims have cooperated with law enforcement by providing evidence against their traffickers, they are then expected to return to countries of origin.[16] Only in exceptional cases is leave to remain on asylum and humanitarian grounds considered.

As discussed earlier, in the prosecution dimension 'trafficking victims' are seen on the surface as different from (migrant) prostitutes or irregular migrants, yet are in practice treated as marginalized objects of distrust. The same suspicions permeate the so-called protection dimension. Whilst in the UN Protocol the protection limb of the trafficking framework involves optional obligations towards *all* identified

---

13 See UN Trafficking Protocol, Articles 6–8.

14 See Council Directive 2004/81/EC, above n. 2. The Council of Europe aimed to introduce higher standards but the EU resisted this to maintain the (lower) standards embodied in its Directive (see above n. 2). See Recommendation 1695 (2005) by the Council of Europe Parliamentary Assembly.

15 See Article 8 of the Directive.

16 See Article 13 of the Directive.

trafficking victims, in the European framework access to protection and assistance and residence permits is specifically limited to those identified trafficking victims who are of use to the investigating and prosecution authorities. Moreover, the protection granted is very temporary and conditional in nature (Piotrowicz 2002). The EU Directive is (unusually) clear about this utilitarian exchange perhaps because of the potential implications of any ambiguity: so it specifically applies only to 'third-country nationals who are victims of trafficking in human beings or who have been the subject of an action to facilitate illegal immigration, *who cooperate with the competent authorities*'[17] (emphasis added).

The reciprocal exchange at the heart of the system has little to do with protection of exploited migrants. Instead, it is reminiscent of the treatment of the so-called *pentiti*[18] in the Italian legal system. *Pentiti*, that is, criminals who collaborate with the judicial system in investigations into a criminal organization, receive in exchange shorter sentences for their crimes, in some cases even freedom. In the Italian judicial system the *pentiti* can also obtain personal protection, a new identity, and some money to start a new life in another place, possibly abroad.[19] Applied to the trafficking context, *la pentita*, that is, the trafficking 'victim' who is, more often than not, an irregular migrant prostitute, has her 'punishment' for her activities (expulsion) deferred in exchange for providing information which is helpful to the investigation into and prosecution of those who organize criminal migration.[20] Whilst *la pentita* is not innocent, she is a minor player and less guilty than those who organized her migration. If she collaborates as a witness, her reward is that her expulsion is delayed by a few months and, in rare cases, can be removed altogether.

The conditional and discretionary nature of this 'protection' is thus directly linked to mistrust felt towards victims of trafficking as transgressing migrants. As with the prosecution dimension, this contradiction in the woman of trafficking discourse can have a devastating impact on the effectiveness of providing protection to migrants who are in need of assistance and support (Piotrowicz 2002). In practice, the EU Directive's 'protection' is more about bullying and bribing and is open to and likely to be taken up by the few migrant women who are not only identified and offered this opportunity but who can actually choose to co-operate. In offering little prospect of a

17 See the title of Council Directive 2004/81/EC, above n. 2.

18 Literally meaning 'repented' (masc. pl.) The category of the *pentiti* was first created in order to fight terrorism in the 1970s but is also relevant with regard to *mafiosi* (members of organized criminal groups).

19 This and special witness protection provisions from the organized crime context have also been floated as ideas to deal with trafficking.

20 The original Commission proposal for the Directive puts it this way: 'It should also be underlined that the Commission's proposal on trafficking in human beings for exploitative purposes is to be seen as to complement the initiatives presented by the French Presidency on facilitation of illegal entry, stay and residence' (COM(2002) 71 final, OJ C 126 E, 28 May 2002).

more permanent stay or access to the labour market, which would allow migrants to rebuild their lives or work for a living, the European protection dimension assumes rather too much. For many, the risks involved in collaborating, including providing evidence against potentially very dangerous people, far outweigh the potential short-term benefits to be gained.

There is, of course, an alternative route which could have been developed for protecting trafficking victims, that is, to channel trafficking victims through existing systems for international protection (Piotrowicz 2002). In other words, trafficking victims' claims for protection could be reframed as claims for asylum or other protection. Indeed, it could be argued that exploitation experienced by trafficked migrants can amount to persecution or (in Europe) inhuman or degrading treatment contrary to Article 3 of the European Convention on Human Rights. This possibility has been advocated by some commentators (Demir 2003), and there are some cases in which refugee status or Article 3-based protection from expulsion have even been granted to women as 'trafficking victims'.[21] This is not because the individuals in question were necessarily asylum-seekers before being trafficked – although some might have been – but because of what happened to them in the course of migration and, more importantly, what could still happen to them if they were repatriated back to their countries of origin. Return can be especially dangerous if traffickers have threatened retribution or if the returned migrant has few economic and social opportunities to survive without again resorting to assisted and potentially exploitative migration.

Asylum and humanitarian protection channels are a much less common way of providing 'protection' for exploited migrants, in part because the reality of trafficking victims again does not match the entrenched assumptions behind the law on such protection. Regarding asylum, there are many hurdles in the 1951 Convention on Refugees[22] that have to be overcome to apply it to a trafficking situation. Nonetheless, it could be argued that the threat of re-trafficking or retribution from traffickers is relevant for establishing a well-founded fear of persecution, that the category 'social group' included in Article 1A can be stretched to cover 'trafficked women' persecuted as a group and that treatment by non-state actors is relevant where there is no state protection against traffickers or complicity of state actors can be established (Demir 2003). Similarly, it could be argued that Article 3 of the European Convention, which involves a positive obligation to not expel people to situations where they might face torture or inhuman or degrading treatment, could be interpreted to assist some migrant women needing protection from ill-treatment by private individuals beyond the reach of the state. These avenues could be explored further and ideas of 'gender-specific persecution' (Anker 2002) built on

21 One of these cases was in the UK, where the Immigration Appeal Tribunal accepted that an Albanian woman faced a real risk of persecution (and violations of Articles 3 and 8 of the European Convention). *Secretary of State for the Home Department v K* [2003] UKIAT00023, 7 August 2003.

22 See 1951 Convention Relating to the Status of Refugees, 189 UNTS 150.

to challenge the entrenched assumptions behind international protection (types of persecution, actors behind it) with the gendered reality of 'trafficking victims'.

However, it is telling that the current interpretations of European destination states actually pull in the opposite direction and towards more narrow, rather than wide interpretations of these protection frameworks. The sheer exceptionality of successful international protection cases for trafficking victims (and the slowness of change in this regard) and the particular form that the EU 'protection' dimension takes, together tell their own story about the trafficking framework. It is evident that the European protection dimension is conceptually premised on assumptions that have little to do with actual protection needs (or indeed rights) of trafficking victims. Linking trafficking to asylum and humanitarian protection in an expansive way would conflict with the increasing efforts and desires of European destination states to generally restrict the refugee law framework, with a view to removing asylum-seekers, tightening up immigration controls and curbing channels for unwanted migration. This fragility of the protection dimension again points to deeper problems with the trafficking framework.

Prevention

Just as the protection limb of the trafficking framework derives its content from its link with the aims of the prosecution dimension, the third limb, prevention of trafficking, is aimed primarily at preventing 'criminal migration'. This point can be highlighted by examining prevention measures both in the short/medium term and in the long term.

Short(er)-term prevention in the European trafficking framework focuses on prevention in the sense of measures to increase the risks to traffickers and decrease the likelihood that migrants become victims: measures to develop the criminal justice response both domestically and through regional cooperation; improved migration controls and security of travel documents; training of officials; conventions and clauses on readmission of irregular migrants (to send a message that irregular migrants will be caught and sent back); and measures to raise awareness of the possibility of trafficking (that is, informing migrants about the potential dangers of migrating, like exploitation by unscrupulous criminals).[23] In the long term, prevention is linked with alleviating structural factors which make persons vulnerable to trafficking, such as lack of equal opportunity for women and discriminated groups, poverty and underdevelopment. Whilst short-term prevention includes specific measures, long-term prevention, when discussed, is formulated in a very general and legally imprecise way.[24] Though there are

23 See e.g. the Brussels Declaration's recommendations on prevention of trafficking (above n.11); see also UN Trafficking Protocol, Articles 9–13.

24 For instance, the UN Trafficking Protocol, Art. 9(4) provides that 'States Parties shall take or strengthen measures, including through bilateral or multilateral cooperation,

requirements on states to 'cooperate' for prevention purposes, any real obligations mostly target migrant-sending states, and there is little elaboration as to where destination countries' responsibility lies.

Short/medium-term prevention clearly builds on the notions already discussed above with regard to the prosecution and protection dimensions. The woman of this dimension of the trafficking framework is the potential victim who ought to be prevented from falling to the hands of traffickers who might exploit her. Yet beneath her innocent surface looms the shadow of the irregular migrant, the criminal. These concerns are evident for instance regarding measures raising potential migrants' awareness of the risks of trafficking. Most awareness-raising programmes designed and funded by European destination countries, and the EU in particular, target the woman of trafficking discourse by trying to frighten migrants with stories of trafficking in the hope that they decide not to migrate at all (Nieuwenhuys and Pécoud 2007). Whilst it is a good idea to inform people of the risks irregular forms of migration can entail, why does that translate into seeking to discourage migration *altogether* – why not advise women as to how to migrate more safely and provide legal opportunities to work in Europe, considering the demand for labour migrants in European economies? The only answer to that question is that short-term prevention of trafficking really is not so much about preventing exploitation of migrant women, but more about curbing any form of illicit migration.

Awareness-raising that is based on fears over migrants imposing an unwarranted burden on welfare states or destabilizing the labour market of receiving countries builds on notions about the right *and* capacity of states to frighten off potential migrants. Empirically, many of these measures seem to be based on false confidence about destination regions' capacity to control migration in a globalizing world. That awareness-raising campaigns appear to have had limited success in Europe is hardly surprising considering that migration is seen by many migrants as imperative for their success or survival, however risky and exploitative (Nieuwenhuys and Pécoud 2007). Many migrant women, wishing to send money back to families, work hard in the jobs EU nationals may detest and avoid (Wichterich 2000) – yet because legal labour migration is such a politically charged issue in most EU Member States, the only instrument to timidly mention safe and legal migration options is the Council of Europe Convention.[25]

To the extent that the trafficking framework has a long-term prevention angle, the woman of trafficking discourse becomes part of the 'starving third world masses' which underlie much of existing donor approach to development cooperation. The rhetoric perceives the woman of trafficking discourse to be in a position of vulnerability due to the feminization of poverty, gender discrimination,

---

to alleviate the factors that make persons, especially women and children, vulnerable to trafficking, such as poverty, underdevelopment and lack of equal opportunity'.

25 'Each Party shall take appropriate measures, as may be necessary, to enable migration to take place legally'. Council of Europe Convention, Art. 5(4).

and lack of educational and professional opportunities in countries of origin. While such observations are salient, they have yet to be accompanied by a commitment to do anything specific about these causes.[26] Long-term prevention also seems to involve assumptions that might not be accurate, considering that the links between migration and development are still poorly understood (Nyberg-Sørensen et al. 2002). Most notably, it is problematic to assume that economic development (or giving some pin money to women) quenches their desire to migrate; indeed, development and female empowerment can actually increase the allure of migration as a result of increased ties between countries, increased resources to migrate and the potential financial benefits to be gained (Martin and Taylor 2001).

Most importantly, when the problem is framed as that of 'bad' individuals exploiting inequalities in countries of origin, the burden to prevent trafficking lies on these countries which must simply strive to diminish the pool of potential trafficking victims. As a result, some issues become invisible, such as the role played by global economic structures, destination countries' migration policies which make legal migration difficult and the global economic advantage of regions such as the EU that lures migrants with promises of economic success. The long-term prevention agenda regarding *destination* areas studiously avoids any hard obligations – while it is admitted some individuals in destination countries may be contributing to the exploitation of migrants, the causes are seen to lie in the countries of destination. The 'man of trafficking discourse' is a shadowy figure which can sometimes be seen lurking in the prostitution-related corner of the trafficking framework[27] but apart from that, the trafficking discourse does not sustain other demand-side figures: directors of corporations, sweatshop owners, Western consumers and so on. Diffuse concerns about bad labour practices, global inequalities and unscrupulous employers remain peripheral add-ons in the European trafficking framework which is based on not disturbing the global balance of economic power.

Conclusion: Beyond the 'Woman of Trafficking Discourse'?

This chapter has examined the construction and the baggage of the 'trafficking framework'. To conclude, it is useful to discuss what implications this baggage might have for the framework's potential to reform and the viability of proposed alternatives to it.

---

26 For example 'Support programmes should aim at the strengthening of efforts to tackle poverty and further marginalization, particularly amongst the most vulnerable groups of the populations, including women and the girl child, in all countries of origin, transit and destination through measures designed to improve governance, material support, social protection and employment opportunities and sustainable economic developments' (Brussels Declaration, above n. 11).

27 See Art. 6 of the Council of Europe Convention.

Based on the above analysis, the European trafficking framework is problematic not only in practice but in principle. The prosecution dimension, which is at the heart of the trafficking framework, is not (primarily) premised on concern over abuse and violence faced by migrants (women or men), and its primacy over the other two dimensions means that 'protection' and 'prevention' rely on the prosecution dimension for their meaning. What is missing from the trafficking framework is, fundamentally, an understanding about the multitude of structural factors which contribute to global inequalities and through them to the migration experiences which could be classified as 'trafficking', 'exploitation' or 'forced labour'. In many respects, this trafficking framework is the near-inevitable product of a set of existing socio-political circumstances and concerns which are, in the setting of European destination countries' legal systems, linked to existing legal categories and assumptions behind them. As a result of the way in which the trafficking framework has been constructed on fears of 'criminal migration', its attempts to manage global migration patterns have very little room to recognize the bravery, the desperation and the multitude of reasons which impel migrants to take the risks they do. This in turn shows the inadequacy of the legal framework to capture injustices which are done to migrants in the course of migration.

This analysis of the problems of the three dimensions highlights the difficulty of improving the trafficking framework – if the problem is that of principle, tinkering with the trafficking framework is unlikely to solve anything as long as the socio-political and economic foundations on which the framework is built remain unchanged. At the same time, building alternatives to the trafficking framework is an equally daunting task – if the unsatisfactory foundation of the trafficking framework is dismantled or rejected, it may be that not much is left. Calls to protect vulnerable migrants and address global injustices are easily ignored. Is the only option then to exhort states to improve the flawed trafficking framework whilst recognizing it is not likely ever to be particularly good anyway? To some extent this is the case: realistically, European destination states and the EU simply lack the political will to devise a better framework so, at this point, to give up on the trafficking framework, inadequate as it is, might be a strategic mistake. This is not to say that campaigners should not for political purposes advocate alternative approaches, for instance focusing attention to the human rights obligations that bind states or even utilitarianist arguments, but whatever the alternative directions, recognition of *why* the framework has both done some good as well as bad work remains crucial for any proposal for moving *beyond* the trafficking framework.

References

Anderson, B. and Rogaly, B. (2005), *Forced Labour and Migration to the UK.* (Oxford: Centre for Migration, Policy and Society).

Anker, D. (2002), 'Refugee Law, Gender, and the Human Rights Paradigm', *Harvard Human Rights Journal* 15, 133–54.

Bogusz, B. et al. (eds) (2004), *Irregular Migration and Human Rights: Theoretical, European and International Perspectives*. (Leiden: Martinus Nijhoff Publishers).

Demir, J. (2003), 'Trafficking of women for sexual exploitation: a gender-based well-founded fear?', *New Issues in Refugee Research* (UNHCR) 80.

Doezema, J. (2002a), 'The ideology of trafficking', paper presented at: Work Conference 'Human Trafficking', 15 November 2002, Ghent University Center for Ethics and Value Inquiry, <http://www.nswp.org/pdf/DOEZEMA-IDEOLOGY.PDF>, accessed 3 December 2008.

Doezema, J. (2002b), 'Who gets to choose? Coercion, consent, and the UN Trafficking Protocol', *Gender and Development* 10:1, 20–7.

Duncan, S. (1994), '"Disrupting the Surface of Order and Innocence": Towards a Theory of Sexuality and the Law', *Feminist Legal Studies* II:1, 3–28.

European Commission (2001), 'Trafficking in Women. The misery behind the fantasy: from poverty to sex slavery. A Comprehensive European Strategy', <http://ec.europa.eu/justice_home/news/8mars_en.htm>, accessed 3 December 2008.

European Commission (2005), 'EU action against trafficking in human beings and the sexual exploitation of children', <http://ec.europa.eu/justice_home/fsj/crime/trafficking/fsj_crime_human_trafficking_en.htm>, accessed 3 December 2008.

Gallagher, A. (2001), 'Human Rights and the New UN Protocols on Trafficking and Migrant Smuggling: A Preliminary Analysis', *Human Rights Quarterly* 23:4, 975–1004.

Gallagher, A. (2006), 'Recent Legal Developments in the Field of Human Trafficking: A Critical Review of the 2005 European Convention and Related Instruments', *European Journal of Migration and Law* 8:2, 163–89.

Geddes, A. (2003), *The Politics of Migration and Immigration in Europe*. (London: Sage Publications).

Goodey, J. (2004), 'Sex trafficking in women from Central and East European countries: promoting a 'victim–centred' and 'woman–centred' approach to criminal justice intervention', *Feminist Review* 76, 26–45.

Hughes, D. (2000), 'The "Natasha" Trade: The Transnational Shadow Market of Trafficking in Women', *Journal of International Affairs* 53:2, 625–51.

Lacey, N. (1998), *Unspeakable Subjects: Feminist Essays in Legal and Social Theory*. (Oxford: Hart Publishing).

Laczko, F. and Gramegna, M. (2003), 'Developing Better Indicators of Human Trafficking', *Brown Journal of World Affairs* 10:1, 179–94.

Martin, P. and Taylor, J. (2001), 'Managing Migration: the Role of Economic Policies', in Zolberg and Benda (eds).

Morris, J. (2007), 'No boundaries in war on sex trafficking' BBC [website] <http://news.bbc.co.uk/2/hi/uk_news/england/devon/6354633.stm>, accessed 3 December 2008.

Munro, V. (2005), 'A Tale of Two Servitudes: Defining and Implementing a Domestic Response to Trafficking of Women for Prostitution in the UK and Australia', *Social & Legal Studies* 14:1, 91–114.

Nieuwenhuys, C. and Pécoud, A. (2007), 'Human Trafficking, Information Campaigns, and Strategies of Migration Control', *American Behavioral Scientist* 50:12, 1674–95.

Nyberg-Sørensen, N. et al. (2002), 'The Migration-Development Nexus. Evidence and Policy Options. State-of-the-Art Overview', *International Migration* 40:5, 3–45.

O'Connell Davidson, J. (1998), *Prostitution, Power and Freedom*. (Cambridge: Polity Press).

Outshoorn, J. (2004), 'Pragmatism in the Polder: Changing Prostitution Policy in The Netherlands', Journal of Contemporary European Studies 12:2, 165–76.

– (2004) (ed), *The Politics of Prostitution. Women's Movements, Democratic States and the Globalization of Sex Commerce.* (Cambridge: Cambridge University Press).

– (2005), 'The Political Debates on Prostitution and Trafficking of Women', Social Politics 12:1, 141–55.

Phoenix, J. (1999), *Making Sense of Prostitution*. (London: Macmillan).

Piotrowicz, R. (2002), 'European Initiatives in the Protection of Victims of Trafficking who Give Evidence Against Their Traffickers', *International Journal of Refugee Law* 14:2–3, 263–78.

Raymond, J. (2002), 'The New UN Trafficking Protocol', *Women's Studies International Forum* 25:5, 491–502.

Réaume, D. (1996), 'What's Distinctive About Feminist Analysis of Law?: A Conceptual Analysis of Women's Exclusion from Law', *Legal Theory* 2:4, 265–99.

Smart, C. (1992), 'The Woman of Legal Discourse', *Social & Legal Studies* 1: 29–44.

Svanström, Y. (2004), 'Criminalizing the john – a Swedish gender model?', in Outshoorn (ed.).

Twomey, P. (2000), 'Europe's Other Market: Trafficking in People', *European Journal of Migration and Law* 2:1, 1–36.

Tyldum, G. and Brunovskis, A. (2005), 'Describing the Unobserved: Methodological Challenges in Empirical Studies on Human Trafficking', *International Migration* 43:1–2, 17–34.

van Impe, K. (2000), 'People for Sale: The need for a Multidisciplinary Approach towards Human Trafficking', *International Migration* 38:3, 113–31.

von Struensee, V. (2000), 'Sex Trafficking: A Plea for Action', *European Law Journal* 6:4, 379–407.

Wichterich, C. (2000), *The Globalized Woman*. (London: Zed Books).

Wijers, M. and van Doorninck, M. (2002), 'Only Rights Can Stop Wrongs: A Critical Assessment of Anti–Trafficking Strategies', paper presented at: EU/IOM STOP European Conference on Preventing and Combating Trafficking in Human Beings – A Global Challenge for the 21st Century, 18–20 September 2002, European Parliament, Brussels, available at <http://www.walnet.org/csis/papers/wijers–rights.html>, accessed 3 December 2008.

Zolberg, A. and Benda, P. (eds) (2001), *Global Migrants, Global Refugees*. (New York: Berghahn Books).

Chapter 9
Foreign National Prisoners, Deportations, and Gender

Helen Toner

This chapter examines the situation of foreign national prisoners and their interaction with the immigration control system from a gender perspective. The subject matter is inspired by the scandal that erupted in 2006 when it was disclosed that the system of identifying and deporting foreign national prisoners at the end of their sentences was in disarray and that a significant number of prisoners had been released without being considered for removal. It begins by setting out the background to the issues and introducing the law and practice behind detention and removal of foreign national prisoners convicted of criminal offences. It considers how the concepts underlying the case law, particularly that of the European Court of Human Rights, may be seen to have hidden gender dimensions. It then considers the issues that gave rise to the high profile scandal in 2006 that ultimately ended in the departure of the then Home Secretary Charles Clarke. The chapter moves on to offer a gender perspective on criminal justice and female prisoners generally, and on the issue of female foreign national prisoners in particular, contrasting their profile and needs with the female prison population and the male foreign national prisoner population. It then examines the response to the 2006 'FNP scandal' and highlights some changes in law and practice in response to the difficulties that came to light. This enables some conclusions to be drawn as to whether and to what extent the needs of and problems faced by female foreign national prisoners are being addressed, and what if any, impact the changes in law and practice have had since 2006.

Migration Control and Criminal Justice

Deportation and Removal Law and Practice

First, it is necessary to review the law and practice relating to deportation of foreign nationals on the grounds that their criminal conduct makes their presence in the country undesirable.[1] This has long been, in principle, a ground to remove

1 Here, the procedure involved is deportation rather than administrative removal, which is a different procedure, having fewer longer-term negative implications for the individual's future immigration status and offering more rights to the individual being

an individual non-national, yet it has been controversial. Specifically, however much one insists that deportation is not a punishment or penalty (a term of imprisonment performing that function) many have pointed out the unfairness of the practical reality of the 'double penalty' of the threat of or actual deportation, often including the consequent separation from family, friends and loved ones, coming on top of imprisonment. Nationals, of course, are not subjected to this additional consequence in the event that they infringe the law in exactly the same way,[2] hence the term 'double penalty'.

For our purposes, there are two key grounds whereby an individual may be deported under the relevant legislative provisions – Sections 3(5) and (6) of the Immigration Act 1971 indicate when individuals become liable to the making of a deportation order under Section 5(1) (on deportation generally, before the most recent changes discussed later, see for example Clayton 2006). The first, under section 3(6), is following the recommendation of a court at the conclusion of a criminal trial, and the second under Section 3(5)(a) is on so-called 'conducive' grounds – that the presence of the individual is not conducive to the public good – often but not always on the basis of a criminal conviction. Another third ground (Section 3(5)(b)) relates to the family members (spouse or child) of a deportee. Deportation is a two-stage process, and these grounds make the individual liable to the first stage of that process, an initial decision to deport taken by the Secretary of State or on his behalf by certain immigration officers. The decision to deport carries a right of appeal to the Asylum and Immigration Tribunal, and authorizes the possible use of immigration detention (on immigration detention generally, Clayton 2008). This is later followed by a final deportation order which prevents return to the UK until it is lifted. It is significant to recall that immigration detention itself is different from imprisonment; detainees are held under different conditions and usually in immigration detention centres rather than prisons. The deportation decision has traditionally been discretionary and a sentence of 12 months should normally have been expected to trigger consideration for (but not any presumption of) removal – although as we shall see, this did not always happen in practice. A number of factors would be taken into account, including age, length of residence, connections with the UK, personal history, domestic circumstances, previous criminal record and nature of any offence for which the person has been convicted, compassionate circumstances, and any representations made on the person's behalf. These specific factors were, until recently, enumerated explicitly in Paragraph 364 of the Immigration Rules, but these have since been amended

threatened with deportation. Administrative removal is now used in the majority of cases of overstaying or being in breach of conditions attached to entry permission.

2 Save exceptionally in the case of naturalized citizens whose citizenship could in some situations be removed and then deportation could follow. Conversely, there are also some limited exceptions whereby certain non-nationals are exempt from deportation, (see Clayton 2006 Ch 16.6 p 549) but the normal long term settled residence status of Indefinite Leave to Remain does not in itself exempt the individual from being liable to be deported.

(see further later). Nonetheless, the importance of taking these factors into account properly can be seen in considering the two major sources of external constraint on the use of the power to deport non-nationals. These are the European Convention on Human Rights (ECHR) and European Community law. We shall now examine each in turn.

Article 8 ECHR

The European Convention on Human Rights guarantees respect for the individual's family and private life in Article 8, and protection against torture or inhuman and degrading treatment in Article 3.[3] The ECHR does not in and of itself contain provisions explicitly addressing the situation of migrants (or would-be migrants), and early case law indicated that there was no right to choose the location of residence of a married couple's family life. Indeed in some contracting states it would often be assumed that the couple would follow the (foreign national) husband to his country of nationality and the ECHR initially did little to counter this gendered assumption of family migration patterns. From a gender perspective, *Abdulaziz* (1983) was a key case establishing that although there was no general obligation under Article 8 for a contracting State to admit a non-national spouse for family reunification, discriminatory rules on family settlement could violate Articles 8 and 14 (with Article 14 guaranteeing a right to equal treatment in the enjoyment of other Convention rights, in this case Article 8). In that case, the different (and stricter) rules then in force in the UK pertaining to admission of husbands in comparison with wives were considered to be unjustified discrimination.

Article 8 on its own has, however, been of considerable significance to those resident in Contracting States wishing to resist deportation. Used successfully since the early 1990s, the case of *Moustaquim v Belgium* (1991) illustrates the general approach. Moustaquim, a Moroccan national, had lived in Belgium since infancy with his parents, brothers and sisters who all still lived there. He had a number of convictions (mainly offences of theft and robbery) during his teenage years and had been imprisoned on more than one occasion. The authorities made a deportation order and he left Belgium, although the order was later temporarily suspended and he returned. On application to the European Court of Human Rights in Strasbourg, it concluded that the order had been an unjustified infringement of his right to respect for his family life. In doing so it considered the balance between, on the one hand, the offences and the consequent degree of danger to public order (including the fact that those he was prosecuted for were during his adolescence and that there was a relatively substantial period between the last offence and his departure from Belgium) and on the other hand, his strong links with Belgium and his family members there. In fact he had only visited Morocco twice since his arrival in Belgium when he was two years old, and when he had to

3 The focus of this section will be on Article 8 as it raises more issues relevant to a gender perspective. This should not be taken to mean that Article 3 is not relevant.

leave Belgium he did not return there but lived in other European countries before he was able to return to Belgium later. A string of similar cases followed, some more favourable to applicants than others (see later). One of the major criticisms of the case law is that it was, and to some degree still remains, unpredictable and uncertain, with little consistency or particularly helpful guidance as to what factors should be taken into account and how they should be balanced in taking any decision on deportation or removal to ensure compliance with Article 8 (see generally Rogers 2003). *Boultif v Switzerland* (2000) attempted to set out some more coherent principles, the key paragraph reading as follows:

> The Court has only a limited number of decided cases where the main obstacle to expulsion was that it would entail difficulties for the spouses to stay together and, in particular, for one of them and/or the children to live in the other's country of origin. It is therefore called upon to establish guiding principles in order to examine whether the measure in question was necessary in a democratic society. In assessing the relevant criteria in such a case, the Court will consider the nature and seriousness of the offence committed by the applicant; the duration of the applicant's stay in the country from which he is going to be expelled; the time which has elapsed since the commission of the offence and the applicant's conduct during that period; the nationalities of the various persons concerned; the applicant's family situation, such as the length of the marriage; other factors revealing whether the couple lead a real and genuine family life; whether the spouse knew about the offence at the time when he or she entered into a family relationship; and whether there are children in the marriage and, if so, their age. Not least, the Court will also consider the seriousness of the difficulties which the spouse would be likely to encounter in the applicant's country of origin, although the mere fact that a person might face certain difficulties in accompanying her or his spouse cannot in itself preclude expulsion (Paragraph 48).

When examined from a gender perspective, many of these cases tell a similar story. Very often, it is a young male offender, sometimes barely beyond adolescence, who resists deportation on the basis of his family ties with his parents and/or siblings (for example *Moustaquim* (1991)), or a slightly older male offender resisting deportation on the basis of marriage or partnership with a woman resident or a national of the Host state (for example *Boultif v Switzerland* (2000) or *Amrollahi v Demark* (2002)). Sometimes the couple have had children and the relevance of the continued relationship between father and child comes under scrutiny. The female protagonists in the 'stories' behind these cases are mostly relegated to what could be described as a secondary (although not insignificant) role, not resisting deportation themselves but as the primary 'family' connection relied upon to resist the removal of another. Often the court considers whether there are insuperable obstacles to re-establishing family life elsewhere, such as linguistic or cultural barriers, presence or absence of other family members, employment prospects, whether there are children, and if so their ages, nationality status and stage of education. Although explicitly discriminatory assumptions about migration patterns (such as assuming a wife will follow the residence of the husband) are no longer seen, it is still worth paying some attention to the racial and gender dimension of these cases. Cases such as *Boultif* or *Amrollahi* are worth considering in this light. In these cases it was held in the circumstances that it would not be reasonable to expect the woman to follow the man to his country of origin, (Morocco or Iran respectively) if he were to be deported following conviction for armed robbery and importation of drugs. On one level, it is heartening to see the court taking into account the reality of the significant cultural adaptation that would have to take place in such cases if the woman were to relocate with her husband, a transition that would probably be more problematic and profound than would be the case if the proposed destination for the deported husband was a more developed and western country.

Nonetheless, in both cases, it is possible to read into the cases a sub-text of almost paternalistic protectiveness towards the position of (white, non-muslim, western) women who have married Middle-Eastern or North-African Muslim men, and something of a reluctance to expect such women to travel with their husbands to relocate in these areas.[4] Of some significance in the light of what is known about the profile of female foreign national prisoners (see further later), a number of these cases involve offences related to the importation of drugs, and the approach of the ECtHR to these cases suggests that such offences are regarded as being amongst those which merit a robust response from the State, including the possibility of long prison sentences and deportation.

Another example of gendered assumptions about family life is found in the case of *Carpenter*, in which the ECJ (European Court of Justice) applied the general principles behind Article 8 of the ECHR to a case under EU law (on this case see further Toner (2003), Acierno (2003), CMLRev Editorial comments (2001)). In particular, the approach of the court to what constitutes 'family life' in this case is interesting – it takes note that the family life between the couple is genuine and, in particular, mentions that Mrs Carpenter (not in fact convicted of any offence, merely in an irregular/overstaying immigration situation) cares for her step-children. Whilst not suggesting that this is necessary to the establishment of family life, conformity to a traditional gendered pattern of family responsibility

4 This trend should however not be overestimated or elevated to an unjustified degree of importance, and it is worth pointing out that there are of course, including in the UK, many women whose husbands are refused leave to remain on the grounds that it is not unreasonable for the couple to continue family life outside the UK. Many of these in the UK relate to failed asylum seekers or those in irregular immigration situation whose relationships have started when their immigration status was known to be uncertain, rather than partners with criminal convictions where the relationship precedes any liability to or threat of deportation, and many involve the requirement to return to the country of origin to secure entry clearance as a spouse through the normal procedures. See the website of the campaign group 'Brides Without Borders' www.brideswithoutborders.org.uk. *Chikwamba* (2008) however is a more generous approach to this issue.

is clearly a factor significant enough to be mentioned by the Court in gaining the protection of Article 8.

European Community Law

European Community law has always granted nationals of Member States and their family members superior protection against deportation compared to other non-nationals who have traditionally been able to rely only upon national law and the human rights standards in the ECHR. For some considerable time Community law (Directive 64/221) has provided that any proposed deportation had to be justified on the grounds of public policy, security and health, and subsequent case law elaborated on these principles by making clear that there had to be a genuine, present and sufficiently serious threat to one of the fundamental interests of society, based on the personal conduct of the individual concerned not simply on general deterrence, and that a robust test of proportionality should be applied. This has now been consolidated and updated in new legislation (Directive 2004/38), which incorporates many of the general principles set out in previous case law into the legislative scheme, as well as instituting a system of enhanced protection against expulsion for those who have been resident for five or ten years or who are minors (on this generally see Harvey 2007). After five years of residence, the new Directive insists that the individual (EU Citizen or family member) may only be removed for 'serious' reasons of public policy or security while removal of an EU Citizen is only possible for 'imperative grounds of pubic security' after ten years residence or if a minor, (unless, in the case of children, expulsion is deemed to be in the best interests of the child). From the little available case law on these new requirements,[5] it is clear that they are intended to enhance protection against removal and to ensure that two stricter tests than before are applied alongside the existing standard as and when appropriate, and that decisions concerning EEA nationals and their family members taken without due appreciation of these different standards will be quashed as being legally flawed.

Returning Home and the Transfer of Sentenced Prisoners

For many foreign nationals, particularly with strong family ties or long residence, the most serious concern is to prevent removal from the life they have built or wish to build in the UK. Consequently, from a typical migration law perspective, the focus of attention is often on the issues outlined above regarding the possibilities of resisting deportation and remaining in the UK. For others however, the concern is precisely the opposite – to return home. Some may wish to seek to return home either during their sentence (to serve part of their sentence in their country of origin) or may actively wish to depart at the earliest opportunity at the end of

5 In the UK, see *MG & VC (EEA Regulations 2006)* (2006), *LG (Italy) v Secretary of State for the Home Department* (2008).

their sentence. There are bilateral Prisoner Transfer Agreements with individual countries as well as the multilateral Council of Europe Convention on the Transfer of Sentenced Prisoners from 1983, given effect in the UK by the Repatriation of Prisoners Act 1984. Numbers transferred under these schemes, however, are relatively small (in 2006, 109 prisoners were transferred out of England and Wales: Home Office 2007b) and although the procedure is initiated by the request of the prisoner, there is no right to transfer, and the request must be accepted by both the sending and receiving States. Some individuals seeking to be transferred (both internally within and between countries) to be closer to family members have pursued cases in the Strasbourg Court under the ECHR on the basis of complaints that their right to respect for family and private life has been infringed (*Hacisuleymanoglu v Italy* (1994), *Ounias v France* (1988), *PK, MK & BK v UK* (1991), *McCotter v UK* (1991), *X v UK* (1972), *Wakefield v UK* (15817/89)).

The case law recognizes the importance of maintaining family ties during a prison sentence and that interferences with rights to family life under Article 8 must be necessary 'having regard to the ordinary and reasonable requirements of imprisonment' – yet this explicitly acknowledges the possibility of these rights to family life being limited by the very nature of the penalty of imprisonment. Londono points out that this test is vague and leaves open the fundamental question of what prison is for (Londono 2007) and what precisely are the 'ordinary and reasonable requirements of imprisonment'. In particular, does the separation of a single parent or primary carer from her children, and/or imprisonment in a foreign country making visits impossible and contact very difficult, constitute something that goes beyond the 'ordinary and reasonable requirements of imprisonment'?

As yet, none of these cases seeking to challenge a refusal to transfer have succeeded, the general response to any legal challenge being that the individual cannot expect to choose the location of his or her imprisonment and that it is only exceptionally that any refusal to transfer would amount to a breach of Article 8. The most recent case raising this point is *Shaheen* (2008), a case involving a transfer of a UK national prisoner back to the Netherlands, (his country of permanent residence for a number of years where he had a wife and two children) in the UK Administrative Court brought under the Human Rights Act[6] following a refusal of consent for transfer. This indicates that even when imprisonment outside the individual's country of normal residence makes visiting by family members difficult, (although not impossible), this will not necessarily in itself be considered to raise exceptional issues above and beyond the normal curtailment of family life inherent in deprivation of liberty.

The main obstacles to the operation of prisoner transfer agreements in particular cases where a prisoner does wish to return home are the lack of a bilateral or multilateral agreement with the relevant country of origin, security objections in the cases of prisoners convicted of terrorism-related offences seeking transfer

---

6 The UK legislation bringing into effect directly within UK law most of the provisions of the ECHR.

to Northern Ireland (see *PK, MK & BK v UK* (1991), *McCotter v UK* (1991)), and objections from the sending state that the remission from time served in the receiving state would result in an unacceptable leniency (see *Hacisuleymanoglu v Italy* (1994) and *Shaheen* (2008), where although a reduction of time to be served would not necessarily bar agreement to a transfer request, and a Dutch national co-accused had been transferred, the British national applicant would have been released earlier in the Netherlands than in the UK and, being a British National, could not have been prevented from returning to the UK to offend again).

The Situation of Foreign National Prisoners in the UK Prison System

The Background – How the Scandal Came About

The first major thread of inquiry to pursue is the situation of foreign national prisoners generally. The unfolding of the so-called 'FNP' saga has been explored elsewhere (Bhui 2007, Shah 2007, Home Office 2007, HMIP 2007). The main focus of the recent concern started with the 'revelation' in April 2006 that foreign national prisoners were not always being considered for deportation at the end of their sentences (Clarke 2006). Charles Clarke's statement indicated that 1,023 prisoners had been released without consideration of their removal from the UK over a period of seven years (Feb. 1999 to March 2006). Over the subsequent months 'the picture became even muddier, revealing a state of utter chaos in relation to the identification, handling and treatment of FNPs as far as their removal from the UK was concerned' (Shah 2007). The story became the focus for intense media attention. As the weeks and months progressed and attempts were made to get to grips with the problem, headlines veered between two extremes. Some were alarmist 'scare stories' portraying these prisoners as dangerous and menacing and calling for an uncompromising hard-line approach of automatic removal, whilst others highlighted the detention of hundreds of prisoners beyond their due release date pending removal or deportation decisions (Lyon 2006, Leppard 2006). Stories emerged of prisoners who were threatened with deportation in entirely inappropriate circumstances. In some cases, the individuals concerned were in fact British Citizens (Shah 2007, Vasagar 2007, Morris and Brown 2006) and in one such instance it was reported that a court order had to be obtained to prevent a threatened deportation (Dodd 2006). Much was made of the large numbers of prisoners involved, but as Clayton points out (Clayton 2008) media reports rarely went on to mention clearly the fact that these figures were over a period of seven years, nor that a sizeable proportion of these individuals could not be removed anyway. One of the striking, although perhaps not entirely surprising, things to note about these stories is their male focus. The majority of the prisoners were of course men, and this in itself is therefore perhaps not unsurprising, but as Shah notes (Shah 2007, see also Clayton 2008) the reporting often takes place in something of a sensationalized manner and this does seem to add an additional dimension. Concern over violent and sexual offences predominate, the 'foreign national prisoner' implicitly being portrayed as the threatening 'other' preying on 'our' (British) women. Indeed there was much speculation at the time about the possibility of serious violent and/or sexual offenders who had been released having committed further crimes since their release, how long it would take for a newsworthy story of this kind to appear, and the damage it would do to the reputation of the Home Office and those in charge (particularly Charles Clarke, the then Home Secretary) if and when such stories began to emerge. Eventually, it emerged that at least five had re-offended. Here, the woman implicitly becomes the victim, the target of the predatory threatening (and foreign) male, and the fear of the criminal and fear of the foreigner become bound together and legitimated in the public imagination. This is despite the fact that there seems to be little or no real difference between the prevalence of violent and sexual offences amongst the foreign national prisoner population than amongst the UK prisoner population (Shah 2007).

There were a number of reasons why this situation developed (Border and Immigration Agency 2007), despite the fact that in 2005 the IND (Immigration and Nationality Directorate, as it then was) 'was considering, deporting and removing more than three times as many criminals as three years earlier, and a significantly higher proportion of them, notwithstanding the growth in their numbers (Home Office 2007). In summary, the Home Office review identifies three significant factors contributing to the increasing backlog of cases and individuals 'slipping through the net' without their cases being considered. First, there was a large increase in the numbers of foreign national prisoners from 5,600 to 9,650 between 2000 and 2005, a 73 per cent increase compared to an 11 per cent increase in the general prison population. Second, there was a problem of insufficient resources, including but not limited to a financial crisis that prevented a planned increase in resources from being implemented in 2003, and third, conflicting priorities within the IND were identified that intermittently diverted attention from the prioritization of the cases of the most serious offenders.

Foreign Nationals – No Longer the 'Forgotten' Prisoners?

It has been noted above that the numbers of foreign nationals in prisons has risen disproportionately quickly in recent years. There have been a number of recent reports carrying out systematic and quite detailed study of the experiences, problems, and needs of this fast-growing group of prisoners. In 2004, the Prison Reform Trust published a report entitled 'Forgotten Prisoners' (Prison Reform Trust, 2004). It would no longer be correct to say that these prisoners are entirely 'forgotten' in the sense that their situation is better understood than before and good practice is slowly being developed. A detailed thematic report drawing on extensive primary research by the Prisons Inspectorate in 2006 is an excellent source of information (HMIP 2006). Yet, the report also discloses a series of problems and issues faced by foreign national prisoners, with inadequate immigration advice, limited contact with families and language difficulties identified as particularly problematic issues. This and other reports have gone some long way to bring this issue out from the shadows and to raise its profile – both within and beyond the prison system. But they also indicate that continued and sustained effort and resources (for example, the survey indicated that translation services were not used as often as they might be to deal with language issues, and this was attributed in part to cost) are needed to ensure that the foreign national population does not remain 'forgotten'. Again however, much of this research concerns male prisoners and it is important not to ignore the potential multiple and overlapping issues of gender and nationality.

Female Offenders and the Criminal Justice System

The second major thread of inquiry to pursue is to introduce, by way of background, some of the issues surrounding women in the criminal justice system generally. Although they constitute a small proportion of the prison population, there is increasing awareness of and understanding that female patterns of offending are different from male patterns of offending, and that the criminal justice system, and prison system in particular, have been designed largely by and for men. This can leave women trapped in a system that is not designed with their needs or offending patterns in mind. Baroness Corston has recently reviewed the position of women in prison (Corston/Home Office 2007) and her report provides a valuable insight into the operation of the prison system and the experiences of women within it. Overwhelmingly, the report (itself entitled 'A Review of Women with Particular Vulnerabilities in the Criminal Justice System') emphasizes strongly the vulnerability of many, indeed most, women within the criminal justice system. The report proceeds on the basis that women and men are equal but not necessarily identical in every respect, that women's criminal careers are different from those of men, and that they experience imprisonment differently from men, and that applying an identical regime to men and women will not necessarily always result in real equality – particularly if that regime has been designed by and for men who make up the majority of those within the prison system. This paper shares these underlying premises and also proceeds from this perspective. So, what are the key differences that can be detected between male and female offending, and male and female experiences in prison, and does foreign nationality present another significant variable?

The first and most obvious point to make is the much lower offending rate amongst women and the relatively small proportion of the prison population that is female. Figures from 2001 (Carlen and Worrall 2004) indicate on average approximately 5.6 per cent of the prison population but 8 per cent of the *receptions* into prison: as of July 2008 there were 4,449 females of a total population of 83,495, 5.3 per cent of all population in prison (Ministry of Justice 2008). From this point of view, (Walklate 2000) the most obvious question to address from a gender perspective might be not so much to consider female criminality but male criminality and what it is about masculinity that results in criminal behaviour in men at such a significantly higher rate than women. Yet for the relatively smaller number of women who offend, the relative rarity of their behaviour may result in them being doubly stigmatized, not only as criminal but as deviating from acceptable norms of female behaviour. The general profile of the female prisoner population is also different, with a large number reporting recent drug use and/or addiction problems and mental health needs. The offences for which these women are imprisoned are also of a different pattern from the male prison population, with a higher proportion being convicted of 'acquisitive' offences, theft and handling, and proportionately fewer being convicted of murder and other violent offences. There are of course exceptions and the number of offences of violence does seem to be increasing somewhat, but as a whole the picture is quite consistent over time and distance, as similar statistics are also obtained internationally (Carlen and Worrall 2004). It is also evident that a larger proportion of women than men are facing their first experience of imprisonment, that the peak age for female offending is in fact younger than for men, and that women's criminal 'careers' consequently tend to be shorter and less serious than those of men. The lengths of sentences being served by these women consequently is also shorter than the male prison population, with many serving sentences of less than six months – and this explains the disparity between the percentage of receptions (8 per cent) and prison population (5.6 per cent) figures quoted above (Carlen and Worrall 2004). This, together with the effect on the domestic and family lives of these women (see further later), has led to the objection that womens' lives are disproportionately and harshly disrupted by short periods of imprisonment which are unwarranted by any significant deterrent or rehabilitative effect, yet still long enough to cause significant damage and disruption to the lives of many women who are already in vulnerable situations.

The other issue that is of some real significance is the effect that imprisonment has on the families of those imprisoned. A significant proportion of female prisoners (about two thirds, 60–70 per cent) are mothers, many are single mothers, and it is perhaps in this area that the lived experiences of female prisoners differ most from male prisoners. For male prisoners, the 'norm' is that partners and other female relatives 'keep the home fires burning', taking care of dependents, particularly children, during any prison sentence. For many children (but admittedly not all), the imprisonment of their father will not result in any immediate change in their living arrangements other than the absence of one parent, if that. Some children would be cared for already separate from their father in single parent households headed by their mother, with or without the involvement of other relatives, and if the parents are together, the imprisonment of the father will not necessarily result in the child having to move home or lose their primary carer. In fact, 90 per cent of such children continue to be cared for by what is described as their 'mother or current mother' during their father's prison sentence. For the child whose mother is imprisoned, the experience is likely to be very different. These children are much more likely to lose their main or sole carer and in most cases, the other parent (here, the father) does not care for the child during the period of imprisonment in the same way that happens when a father is imprisoned. This is the experience of only about a quarter (some studies put it as low as 9 per cent – Munro 2002) of children whose mother is imprisoned compared to the 90 per cent of those whose father is imprisoned who continue to be cared for by their mother. For the others, care is undertaken by their grandparents, other relatives or social services. Thus a mother's imprisonment may legitimately be surmised to be a more disruptive life event for the child than a father's. And from the point of view of the parent rather than the child, it is not unreasonable to suggest that the experience of being separated from children may be more traumatic and worrying for the mother than the father. This is borne out by the research and studies that have examined women's lived experiences of imprisonment. For many women, motherhood is central to their identity, in a way that fatherhood is not necessarily for as many men. For these women, imprisonment which results in separation from children will have a particularly hard impact and is a source of great distress. As Corston points out, the consequent sense of failure as a mother is a very significant blow to these women, who often have low levels of educational achievement and disrupted family backgrounds (Corston/Home Office 2007). Parenthood may be an all too rare positive experience for these women and for many, especially single mothers, will have been as central to their identities and to their day-to-day activities and tasks as employment would have been to many male prisoners in work prior to their conviction. This gender distinction continues on release; obviously the more the individual can be re-integrated into society through successful engagement with constructive activities, the better the chance of avoiding re-offending, but the realistic and appropriate ways forward for men and women may not always be the same. Whilst not dismissing the importance of gainful employment as a medium to long-term goal for former female prisoners, Corston suggests that this may not always be a realistic short-term goal for many women on release (Corston/Home Office 2007), especially single mothers. The lives of these women, she argues, may be so chaotic and disrupted by previous abuse, drug-taking and mental health issues that immediate employment may not be a feasible goal, and this is made all the more complex by the demands of childcare and motherhood. There is evidence that one of the main priorities and worries of male prisoners on release is work or employment, whereas one of the critical concerns of female prisoners is accommodation and care of their children. Many express frustration at being caught in a catch-22 situation, that in order to regain custody of their children they need accommodation, but in order to get priority in securing accommodation they already need to have children in their custody.

Such is the reality of women's (and men's) experiences of imprisonment as it emerges from the research that has been carried out. There are certainly questions to be asked about the gendered nature of family life and why women continue to bear such a disproportionate burden of child and family responsibilities (and this applies not just to women who are imprisoned but those whose male partners or other family members are, and who are left to maintain the family: see Codd 2007) which are the root cause of the apparent gender differential in terms of the impact of imprisonment on women. Focusing on the caring responsibilities of imprisoned mothers undoubtedly risks entrenching and perpetuating gender-specific roles in a way that some may not welcome. Nonetheless, these questions should not prevent recognition in the meantime of the reality of the situations faced by female prisoners, former prisoners, and family members (Codd 2007).

Female Foreign National Prisoners – A Distinctive Group?

Having introduced both the situation of foreign national prisoners generally and the female prison population generally, this section brings these two threads of inquiry together to examine the distinctive profile, experiences and needs of the female foreign national prisoner population. The profile of female foreign national prisoners is indeed distinct and different both from the profile of the general female prison population, and from the male foreign national prison population. First and most obviously, the proportion of foreign national women is markedly higher than foreign national men. Currently around 18–20 per cent (one in five) women in prison at any one time is a foreign national, and it has been as high as 25 per cent (one in four), compared to 12–14 per cent (one in seven or eight) of the male prisoner population. The distinct profile of these prisoners emerges from various research reports (see Corston/Home Office 2007, HMIP 2005, 2006). A large majority are serving sentences that are longer than the average female prisoner (75 per cent serving more than four years, compared to only one third of UK national women), most for drug importation offences (80 per cent to 90 per cent), although increasingly also for offences related to unlawful entry, false documents or illegal working in breach of immigration rules (Corston/Home Office 2007, Hibiscus Interview). Many are in prison for the first time (83 per cent), again a markedly higher proportion than the rest of the female prisoner population (47 per cent) (HMIP 2005). As with the rest of the female prisoner population, many are mothers although the age profile is somewhat older than the general female prison population. Although many (in fact most) are imprisoned for drug-related offences, they are in fact significantly less likely to be problematic drug users or have mental health problems on entry to prison. Most significantly for our present purposes, a far larger proportion of them are non-resident (79 per cent reported in 2006 Review) compared to the male foreign national prisoner population (50 per cent) or young inmates (66 per cent). This is significant, amongst other things, for the experiences of women whilst they are imprisoned (according to the Thematic Review, the single most significant predictor of a prisoner experiencing problems during their time in prison is residence outside the UK) as well as post-sentence planning and any decision concerning return to the country of origin (either voluntary or under a deportation order). If one wished to construct a profile of the 'typical' female foreign national prisoner, it is relatively easy to do so: she is most likely to be Nigerian or Jamaican, (or from other Caribbean or West African countries), perhaps in her thirties, with children to support, in prison for a first drug smuggling offence committed when visiting the UK rather than while resident here. This has obvious implications for the situation of these women and their needs in terms of immigration advice, sentence planning, post-release supervision and support and so on. It is of course the case that for some, 'repatriation will not be a realistic option' (Corston/Home Office 2007) and some may not wish to return to what may be inferior prison conditions and the stigma of serving a prison sentence in their home country despite the closer proximity of family members (for a discussion of the difficulties faced by some of these women when they return home see Ash 2006). But it is certainly far from clear that what one might imagine as the 'stereotypical' classic situation of the foreign national prisoner faced with deportation – to resist being returned and seek to remain – is going to be the norm to the same degree as for male prisoners (and even then it must be acknowledged that some do not wish to contest removal and are keen to return home as soon as they are released). It is often said of female prisoners generally that they rarely abscond and if they do it is easy to locate them because for the most part they have gone home to deal with some domestic crisis. Similarly, the background and profile of the female foreign national prisoner population means that many – although by no means all – will want to return to their country of origin and doing so as quickly as possible may be one of their major concerns. However much progress is made towards much smaller units to ensure that female prisoners are able to serve sentences closer to home than is currently the case, (see recommendation in Corston/Home Office 2007), this is likely to have a limited impact on foreign national women in the prison system.

As seen above, the treatment and experiences of the foreign national prisoner population whilst in custody raises a clear set of needs and concerns. A significant amount of primary research has been carried out on this group of prisoners and the major issues are now quite well accepted (Prison Reform Trust 2004, HMIP 2006, 2007). These are language, contact with family, and immigration advice. However, some discernible differences between the responses of male and female prisoners do emerge. It is not surprising to find that family links are the major concern for female prisoners, more prominently than with men: the research carried out for the 2006 Thematic Review (HMIP 2006) identified this as a problem for 71 per cent of female FNPs compared to 59 per cent of men and only 32 per cent of younger prisoners. As the Thematic Review points out, this is likely to be the case because of the prevalence of primary childcare responsibilities, but comparison of the adult male and female figures also seem suggestive at least of what common sense may indicate, that those imprisoned outside their country of normal residence may be more likely to face problems in maintaining contact with family members (of whom few, if any, may also be resident) than those imprisoned in their country of normal residence. Women reported immigration issues as problematic more often than men (63 per cent compared to 49 per cent) or young people (28 per cent), which the Thematic Review suggests may be due to immigration detention causing delays in returning to family. Another interesting observation concerns the prevalence of language as an issue – it is not seen to be such a major problem amongst the female respondents. This may be related to different distribution of countries of origin of the male and female respondents.

One of the most important elements of a strategy to meet the specific needs of female FNPs is direct on the ground work in prisons – that of the prison service, liaison with immigration authorities, and others. Any exploration of the situation of foreign national prisoners from a gender perspective would not be complete without considering the work of Hibiscus.[7] Hibiscus is a charity set up in 1991 to provide welfare advice and advocacy for foreign national and BME (black and minority ethnic) female prisoners.[8] It now has a permanent full-time presence in two prisons (Holloway, Bronzefield), visits others regularly, and responds to inquiries from throughout the female prison estate. The scale of the work undertaken can be illustrated by the fact that they dealt with 6,000 inquiries in the most recent financial year. They deal with a range of practical issues faced by women in prison often far from home. As we have already seen above, by far the most important issue presented by the women they assist is concern for their families, children in particular (Hibiscus interview) – keeping in contact with them, ensuring that their children are cared for and looked after, ensuring their continued education, and providing for them financially. This is one of the major concerns of all women in custody, and the additional factor of being imprisoned in an unfamiliar country far from home renders it even more acute. Financial provision for their families – and particularly for children – is a particularly problematic issue for women who have often been tempted into carrying drugs as a way out of poverty. Their economic situation is precarious from the outset and imprisonment thousands of miles apart only exacerbates this situation. Family members, even if otherwise willing to assist, may be financially very hard pressed and taking on responsibility for an additional child or children may impose a severe financial strain. Prison work provides a small amount of money which is often a valuable way of doing something practical to support children from a distance – and Hibiscus provides a facility to remit money back to families without cost to the sender, so that every penny returns to the family (Hibiscus interview).

Response to the Events of 2006

Finally, we turn to examine the response to the FNP saga in 2006, with particular attention to the gender dimension in the light of what we know of the profile and experiences of female foreign national prisoners. The experience of foreign nationals in the prison system since 2006 has not been a universally positive one

7 I am grateful to Cherry Whittingham and one of her colleagues for taking time to discuss the work of Hibiscus.

8 On the origins and early work of Hibiscus see Heaven (1996).

(see generally Bhui 2007, HMIP 2007). There is obviously a significant distinction to be made between those who wish to resist deportation in order to remain in the UK (either on the grounds of family connections and/or long residence), and those who do not. For both, however, the situation has not necessarily improved. Those who wish to remain and seek to resist removal find themselves caught up in an increasingly strict legal regime (see further later), with increasing numbers being removed (4,200 in 2007, an increase of around 80% since 2006: Byrne 2007) and increasing difficulties in securing release on bail from immigration detention pending any decision on removal. Those who wish to return home have sometimes found themselves in an equally difficult situation. There have been many instances of prisoners being detained beyond their release dates while decisions are made due to the inability of the prison service and immigration authorities to liaise properly and complete decision-making processes in time.

Others have found themselves re-categorized within the prison system and recalled from open conditions to closed prison regimes, and uncertainty about whether and when individuals are to be removed or allowed to stay can have detrimental effects on sentence planning and preparing individuals for release. Access to legal advice continues to be problematic although groups working with female foreign nationals are able to go some way to ensuring that this group of prisoners have someone to act as a source of initial contact to assist in finding proper legal advice. Overcrowding generally continues to be a real issue, exacerbated in the 'female estate' specifically by the re-designation of Bulwood Hall and Brockhill as male prisons in 2006, and more generally by the detention of foreign nationals beyond expected release dates pending decisions. Early release has been extended to ease crowding and of particular relevance to foreign nationals, there is an early removal scheme for those subject to deportation (there has been some recent publicity with an announcement that nearly 1,400 have been released early into the UK as well as the 4,200 removed in the last year: Winnett 2008) the terms of which were extended in 2008.[9] A Facilitated Returns scheme is available to provide financial and other support on return to countries of origin, run in conjunction with the International Organization for Migration (IOM). Developments have also taken place in prisoner transfer agreements. A particular initiative has been the development of a multilateral prisoner exchange agreement under the framework of EU law as a Framework Decision (Council of the European Union 2007). Although not specifically prompted by the situation here in 2006, (it was in preparation before this and the government view on it does not seem to have changed fundamentally) the government is supportive of this initiative. In the UK there has always been a requirement of consent in transfer of prisoners to serve

9 Most recently amended by the provisions in the Criminal Justice and Immigration Act 2008 sections 33 and 34. See also the litigation in *R (Clift)* v *Secretary of State for the Home Department; Secretary of State for the Home Department* v *Hindawi and another* [2006] UKHL 54, [2007] 2 W.L.R. 24 discussed by Padfield (2007), concerning different treatment of different categories of prisoners (including foreign nationals).

sentences abroad, and this new framework, somewhat controversially, dispenses with that. Negotiations are at the final stage but the text has not been formally adopted yet by the Council. An Additional Protocol to the 1983 Council of Europe Convention dating from 1997 which the UK has not yet signed or ratified also removes the requirement of consent. The government has stated its intention to amend the law to enable this to be ratified (Home Office 2007b). Finally, more bilateral prisoner transfer agreements have been signed – with Jamaica, Pakistan, and negotiations continue with Nigeria.

There have also been significant changes to the law and practice relating to deportation, following various government announcements and statements in response to the crisis in 2006 (See Clayton 2008). These announcements have often focused on assurances, made in response to public concern, that deportation of convicted criminals will be 'automatic'– yet the reality is not quite as simple as that. Nor could it ever be, given the underlying context of human rights and other international obligations. Paragraph 364 of the Immigration Rules has also been amended in relation to the exercise of the Home Secretary's discretion to deport (HC 1337). This was amended in July 2006 to remove explicit mention of the factors that were enumerated before, and to institute what is better regarded as a 'presumption' in favour of deportation rather than 'automatic' deportation. Where an individual is liable to deportation the presumption will be that this is in the public interest and this will only be outweighed in exceptional cases, although all relevant factors will be considered in each case. An exception will be when international obligations are engaged (ECHR rights, obligations under the Refugee Convention, and Community law rights) and a deportation would be inconsistent with such obligations. However this only applies when the individual is liable to deportation, that is when a decision that the deportation is conducive to the public good has been made or a Court has recommended deportation. The ministerial statement made at the time (Byrne 2006) suggests that a sentence or combination of shorter sentences over a five year period of 12 months will normally result in removal. (EEA nationals are subject to this presumption only after a sentence of 24 months, although the compatibility of this whole approach with Community law is questionable and, as Harvey suggests, the UK is 'sailing close to the wind' here (Harvey 2007)). However, paragraph 364 applies to the decision to deport not the initial decision that the individual's removal would be conducive to the public good, and this does still seem to be a separate question (Clayton 2008, see *EO (Turkey)* (2007) and (2008), making this point implicitly even though it is a case under the old rules pre-July 2006). This theme of 'automatic deportation' has been continued and taken further with the enactment of the UK Borders Act 2007. Sections 32–39 deal with deportations and institute a statutory regime to similar but more extensive effect.[10] It does seem that this scheme will complete what the 2006 rule change did not at the earlier stage of the deportation process and attach more importance to the sentence at the stage of deciding what is conducive to the public good (Clayton 2008), even when no recommendation for deportation has been made by the sentencing court. Again there are significant exceptions including compliance with Community law, European Convention rights (including Articles 8 and 3, discussed above so these considerations will still have to be taken into account where relevant) or the UK's obligations under the Refugee Convention as well as provisions relating to orders under Mental Health legislation and those under 18. Note however that the exceptions merely remove the automatic *presumption* of deportation being conducive to the public good and subsequent *obligation* to make the deportation order. These particular sections of the Borders Act dealing with 'automatic deportations' came into force in August 2008.[11] The series of changes made since 2006 are complex and as Clayton (2008) suggests 'The approach under the 2006 rules and the 2007 Act will need decisions of the higher courts in order for the matter to be fully resolved'. In relation to the Borders Act provisions on automatic deportation the Equality Impact Assessment states in relation to Gender that 'The gender profile of those subject to automatic deportation will be directly proportionate to the gender profile of those committing a qualifying offence. The safeguards against gender discrimination inherent in our international obligations will continue to apply' (Home Office 2007).

There is evidence that the situation in female prisons in relation to foreign nationals remains mixed. Undoubtedly the permanent presence of Hibiscus in some prisons and their regular work in others is a significant positive factor, with the Prisons Inspectorate noting in its Thematic Review that 'in the women's prisons we visited there was a more organized approach to foreign national work and support organizations such as Hibiscus played an important role in this'. However, it has also warned in inspection reports that the prison service should not be over-reliant on such voluntary organizations to provide basic services that should be the responsibility of the prison itself. Turning to recent inspection reports, a brief examination illustrates the variable provision across the female prison estate. Each

---

10 The primary provision (which is of course subject to certain exceptions) is Section 32 which institutes a general rule that it is deemed conducive to the public good to deport a foreign national prisoner after a 12 month sentence (note, this does not apply to aggregate sentences of more than 12 months over a 5 year period) or a sentence of imprisonment for an offence specified in an order under the Nationality, Asylum and Immigration Act and then *obliges* the Secretary of State to make a deportation order in these circumstances.

11 UK Borders Act 2007 (Commencement No 3 and Transitional Provisions) Order 2008 (SI 2008 No 1818), see also HC 951. This however is only in relation to the provisions dealing with sentences of more than 12 months, not yet in relation to those dealing with any sentence of imprisonment for specified offences: IDIs Ch 13(6). At the time of writing further reforms to the immigration system are planned in the Immigration and Citizenship Bill, part 4 of which deal with expulsion and removal and retain the 'automatic' deportation provisions in the 2007 Act.

inspection report does specifically address provision for foreign national prisoners, and follow-up reports examine the extent to which previous recommendations have been implemented. The overall picture that emerges from examining the recent inspection and follow-up reports from the 'female estate' is mixed. In some there is recognition of good practice, improvement, and achievement of previous recommendations (New Hall 2006, Morton Hall 2006).

In others, however, (Styall 2005, Askham Grange 2006, Foston Hall 2007) the picture is less positive: provision is criticized and previous recommendations are not being implemented. In others the picture is mixed, with some progress but recommendations still outstanding (Bronzefield 2007, East Sutton Park 2006, Downview 2006) or policies in place but not enough awareness and involvement of prison staff (Holloway 2004). Some prisons are identified as centres for foreign national women and hold considerable numbers, but even in some of these, services are said to remain 'under-developed' (Drake Hall 2007).

Sentencing and Prisoner Transfer

The Corston report stresses that the work underway with Foreign National Prisoners 'must take account of the views expressed in my report. The strategy being developed should include measures designed to prevent prison becoming a serious option'. The government's response has been to accept this recommendation in principle (Ministry of Justice 2007). Sentencing and crime prevention strategies are both going to be key issues here. Given the predominance of drug couriers amongst female FNPs, an important issue will be the extent to which any move is made away from the long custodial sentences that are routinely imposed on women in the UK who, in many ways, are often just as much victims of the drug trafficking business as those who are more direct victims through drug addiction or being victims of the associated acquisitive crime (Hibiscus interview). At the time of writing, a review of sentencing guidelines is being undertaken in this area (drug related offences generally, including drug courier offences) by the Sentencing Guidelines Council. One major factor that may have some impact on this is the extent to which the limited value of deterrent sentences for offenders who come into the UK from abroad with little or no knowledge of the potential consequences of their action will be taken into account. A regularly repeated observation is that long deterrent sentences are of precious little proven value in relation to this particular group of offenders because they are often ignorant of the UK's legal system, and of the potential consequences of what they are doing (Heaven/Hibiscus 2007, Allen 2003).

Londono suggests another interesting argument of discriminatory impact on the basis of gender concerning sentencing of female prisoners generally and the impact of imprisoning mothers with primary childcare responsibilities (Londono 2007). For foreign nationals, there is of course the added dimension that this (already disruptive) impact is vastly complicated and exacerbated by the distances involved and the difficulties of maintaining contact with family members overseas, so the question becomes one of multiple discrimination, encompassing questions of nationality and race as well as gender. It is at present very much in the realms of speculation, and given the attitude of the European Court of Human Rights (and indeed the UK Courts), and the uncertain place of impact in sentencing and mitigation generally, (see Piper 2007, and a more sceptical approach in Easton 2008) it is not at all clear that there is any significant chance of a successful legal challenge to any sentencing policy or individual sentencing decisions on this basis. This is particularly the case when many of the offences of drug importation involved are ones which would normally be seen to be clearly past the threshold of seriousness for imprisonment rather than being on the borderline, as evidenced by the long sentences currently involved. To the limited extent that impact on family members may be relevant as mitigation (see Piper 2007, also discussion in Munro 2002, Londono 2007) unless there is a significant change in underlying sentencing policy, any impact is likely to be at the level of reducing a sentence of imprisonment rather than avoiding prison altogether. But the underlying issue is certainly one that can and should be considered in the sentencing review. Conclusion of prisoner transfer agreements is also a significant issue and the progress with Nigeria and Jamaica may be particularly significant and a welcome step forward for those women from these countries who actively wish to return to serve their sentences in their countries of origin even before release.

Prevention

The other important long-term issue that needs to be tackled as part of a strategy to address the situation of female foreign national prisoners generally, is prevention. Clearly, it is far better that women are not tempted by the offer of significant sums of money to embark on the risky and dangerous business of drug trafficking, the reason for the vast majority of the imprisonment of female foreign nationals, resulting in disproportionately long sentences in comparison with the rest of the female prison population. There is however some encouraging evidence that carefully targeted strategies can have some significant effect. Hibiscus works with the Foreign Office in selected countries of origin, and has conducted several information campaigns to raise awareness of the potential consequences of carrying drugs. Three campaigns have been run (Maame goes to London – Ghana, Bola gets rich quick – Nigeria, Eva goes to Foreign – Jamaica: see Hibiscus website) employing various media to communicate the dangers of drug smuggling to women who may not be aware of the potential consequences of the 'opportunities' being offered to them to make large sums of money. These campaigns have had significant effects on numbers being apprehended where they have been run. This will have to be an ongoing process, as the evidence suggests that the reduction of the numbers of women caught following successful programmes in specific countries is often followed and matched by increasing numbers from other locations as those recruiting couriers turn their attention elsewhere in response to falling numbers.

Conclusion

It is not difficult to detect a gendered dimension (or dimensions) to the issue of deportation and removal of foreign national prisoners. As with so many issues concerning criminal justice generally, what is immediately striking is the paradigm of the male foreign national offender and the way women are relegated to an apparently secondary caring and/or dependent role as the partners, wives, mothers or children of the offenders being threatened with deportation. Yet there is another gender dimension which is not so obvious at first sight but which quickly emerges. The female prison population consistently has 50 to 100 per cent higher proportion of foreign nationals than the male population, with the preponderance of these women being mothers, often single mothers imprisoned for the first time, and often thousands of miles from their vulnerable and dependent children. These women present a specific set of concerns and needs which are slowly being recognized and acted upon through the prison estate and through the work of Hibiscus in particular. The profile of the population of women concerned indicates that, in fact, resisting return to their country of origin may not be the immediate reaction of many of these women. Maintenance of family ties and a swift return to their country of origin with proper support before and after release may, for many, be the highest priority. Yet there remains little room for complacency in meeting the needs of these women in relation to maintaining contact with families, provision of adequate immigration advice and interpretation to overcome language difficulties, and the underlying issue of whether prison in the UK is really the appropriate place for these women remains as difficult as ever.

References

Authors

Acierno, S. (2003), 'The Carpenter judgment: fundamental rights and the limits of the Community legal order', European Law Review 28:3, 398–407.

Allen, R. (2003), 'A bitter pill to swallow – the sentencing of foreign drug couriers' (Rethinking Crime and punishment briefing: <http://rethinking.org.uk/informed/pdf/briefings5.pdf.pdf>).

Ash, L. (2006), 'Hard Return for Jamaica Drugs Mule', BBC News Online, 19 January 2006.

Bhui, H.S. (2007), 'Alien Experience: Foreign National Prisoners after the Deportation Crisis', Probation Journal 54:4, 368–82.

Border and Immigration Agency (2007), 'A Review of the Failure of the Immigration & Nationality Directorate to Consider Some Foreign National Prisoners for Deportation'.

Byrne, L. (2008), Written Answers in House of Commons Hansard 25 Feb 2008 Column 1263W.

Byrne, L. (2006), Ministerial Statement 19 July 2006 House of Commons Hansard 19 July 2006 Column 29WS.

Carlen, P. and Worral, A. (2004), Analysing Women's Imprisonment. (Devon: Willan Publishing).

Clarke, C. (2006), Home Secretary's Statement on Foreign Prisoners: http://www.homeoffice.gov.uk/ about-us/news/foreign-prisoners-statement.

Clayton, G. (2008), Textbook on Immigration and Asylum Law (Oxford: Oxford University Press, 3rd edition).

Clayton, G. (2006), Textbook on Immigration and Asylum Law (Oxford: Oxford University Press, 2nd edition).

CMLRev Editiorial (2003), 'Freedoms unlimited? Reflections on Mary Carpenter v Secretary of State', Common Market Law Review 40:3, 537–43.

Codd, H. (2007), In the Shadow of Prison: Families, Imprisonment and Criminal Justice (Devon: Willan Publishing).

Corston/Home Office (2007), The Corston Report – A Report by Baroness Jean Corston of a Review of Women with Particular Vulnerabilities in the Criminal Justice System.

Dodd, V. (2006), 'Home Office told to release Briton facing deportation because of criminal record' (Guardian 6 June 2006).

Easton, S. (2008), Dangerous WATERS: Taking Account of Impact in Sentencing, Criminal Law Reivew (2008), 105–20.

Farbey, J. (2007), 'Foreign National Prisoners: Current Law and Practice', 21:1, 6–13.

Harvey, A. (2007), 'Expulsion and Exclusion', Journal of Immigration, Asylum and Nationality Law 21:3, 208–22.

Heaven, O. (2007), 'Sentencing': paper on Hibiscus website <http://www.hibiscuslondon.org.uk/ SENTENCING. pdf?page=11447>.

– (1996), 'Hibiscus: Working with Nigerian Women Prisoners' in Penny Green (ed.) Drug Couriers, a New Perspective (Volume II) (Howard League Handbooks, 1996).

Her Majesty's Inspectorate of Prisons (2005), 'Women in Prison'.

Her Majesty's Inspectorate of Prisons (2007), 'Foreign National Prisoners: A Follow-up Report'.

Her Majesty's Inspectorate of Prisons (2006), 'Foreign National Prisoners: A Thematic Review'.

Home Office (2007), Equality Impact Assessment, UK Borders Act, available on the UK Border Agency website: http://www.ukba.homeoffice.gov.uk/sitecontent/documents/policyandlaw/legislation/ukbordersact/

Home Office (2007a), Press Release on Prison Transfer Agreements 23.15.2007, <http://www.homeoffice.gov.uk/about-us/freedom-of-information/released-information/foi-archive-offender-management/4692-Prison-transfer-agreements?version=1>.

Leppard, D. (2006), 'Foreigners kept in jail by delays to deportation' (Sunday Times, 24 Sept 2006).

Londono, P. (2007), 'Applying Convention Jurisprudence to the needs of women prisoners', Public Law 189–97.
Lyon, J. (2006), 'The foreigners still locked in our jails are the other scandal' (Guardian 27 April 2006).
Ministry of Justice (2008), Population in custody monthly tables July 2008 (Ministry of Justice, August 2008).
Ministry of Justice (2007), 'The Government's Response to the Report by Baroness Corston'.
Morris, C. and Brown, N. (2006), 'Prisons holding 200 foreigners after sentences served' (Independent, 5 May 2006).
Munro, V. (2002), 'The emerging rights of imprisoned mothers and their children', Child and Family Law Quarterly 14:3, 303–14.
Padfield, N. (2007), 'Distinguishing the unlawful from the unjustifiable in the rules on early release from prison', Cambridge Law Journal 66:2, 255–58.
Prison Reform Trust (2004), 'Forgotten Prisoners – the Plight of Foreign National Prisoners in England and Wales'.
Piper, C. (2007), 'Should Impact Constitute Mitigation?: Structured Discretion versus Mercy', Criminal Law Review, (2007), 141–55.
Rogers, N. (2003), 'Immigration and the European Convention on Human Rights: are new principles emerging?', European Human Rights Law Review 1, 53–64.
Shah, R. (2007), 'The FNP Saga', Journal of Immigration, Asylum and Nationality Law 21(1), 27–31.
Toner, H. (2003), 'Comments on Mary Carpenter v Secretary of State', European Journal of Migration and Law 5:1, 163–72.
Vasagar, J. (2007), 'British Asian faced deportation threat' (The Guardian March 1 2007).
Walklate, S (2004), Gender, Crime and Criminal Justice (Willan, 2004).
Winnett, R(2008), 'Foreign Prisoners: 1,400 given early release in the past year alone' Telegraph 4/06/2008.

Table of Legislation, Immigration Rules and other Materials

Council of Europe (1983), Convention on the Transfer of Sentenced Prisoners.
Council of the European Union (2007), Council Document 16754/07, Council Framework Decision on the application of the principle of mutual recognition to judgments in criminal matters imposing custodial sentences or measures involving deprivation of liberty for the purpose of their enforcement in the European Union.
Criminal Justice Act and Immigration Act 2008 (2003 c 4).
Directive 64/221: Council Directive 64/221/EEC of 25 February 1964 on the co-ordination of special measures concerning the movement and residence of foreign nationals which are justified on grounds of public policy, public

security or public health, [1964] Official Journal 056/850 04/04/1964, English special edition: Series I Chapter 1963–4 p 117.
Directive 2004/38 – Directive 2004/38/EC of the Parliament and Council of 29 April 2004 on the rights of citizens of the Union and their family members to move and reside freely within the territory of the Member States, [2004] Official Journal L158/77.
HC 951 (2008), Statement of Changes in Immigration Rules: HC 1337, 1 August 2008 (The Stationery Office).
HC 1337 (2006), Statement of Changes in Immigration Rules: HC 1337, 19 July 2006 (The Stationery Office).
IDIs – Immigration Directorate Instructions, UK Border Agency,
http://www.bia.homeoffice.gov.uk/policyandlaw/guidance/IDIs/
Repatriation of Prisoners Act 1984 (1984 c 47).
UK Borders Act 2007 (2007 c 30).

Table of Cases

United Kingdom
Chikwamba [2008] UKHL 40, [2008] HRLR 39, [2008] INLR 502, [2008] Imm AR 700, [2009] 1 All ER 363.
Beoku Betts [2008] UKHL 39, [2009] 1 AC 115.
EB (Kosovo) [2008] UKHL 41, [2008] 3 WLR 178, [2008] 4 All ER 28, [2008] HRLR 40, [2008] INLR 516, [2008] Imm AR 713.
EO (Turkey) (2008) [2007] UKAIT 00062.
EO (Turkey) (2008) [2008] EWCA Civ 671.
Huang (2007), [2007] 2 AC 167, [2007] 2 WLR 581, [2007] 4 All ER 15.
LG (Italy) v Secretary of State for the Home Department (2008) [2008] EWCA Civ 190.
MG & VC (EEA Regulations 2006) (2006), [2006] UKAIT 00053.
R (Clift) v Secretary of State for the Home Department; Secretary of State for the Home Department v Hindawi and another [2006] UKHL 54, [2007] 2 W.L.R. 24.
VW and MO (2008) [2008] UKAIT 00021, unreported.
European Court of Human Rights
Abdulaziz, Cabales & Balkandali (1983) Case 15/1983/71/108–109.
Moustaquim v Belgium (1991) Case 26/1989/196/246.
Amrollahi v Denmark (2002) Application 56811/00 [2002] ECHR 585.
Boultif v Switzerland (2000) Application 54273/00 [2001] EHRR 50.
Hacisuleymanoglu v Italy (1994) Application 23241/94.
Ounias v France (1988) Application 13756/88.
PK, MK,& BK v UK (1991) Application 19085/91.
McCotter v UK (1992) Application 20479/92.
X v UK (1972) Application 5712/71.

Venetucci v Italy (1996) Application 33830/96.
Wakefield v UK (1989) 15817/89.
European Court of Justice
Carpenter v Secretary of State for the Home Department, Case C-60/00, [2002] ECR I-6279.

Chapter 10
Categorical and Plastic Boundaries: Albanian Migration to Greece, Immigration Policies and their Gender Implications

Gabriella Lazaridis

Migration today is a global and globalizing phenomenon that renders national borders obsolete and calls into question the viability of nation states and national identities. As new flexible forms of migration are increasing and transnationalism is becoming a marked trend, female migration is recognized as an important phenomenon in scholarly research and policy making (Lenz, et al. 2002: 8). At the same time as undermining national structures, migration has contributed to the reconstruction of increasingly impenetrable borders. It is in local situations and contexts that the impact of migration is experienced, debated and contested most directly and urgently. Distinguishing between ethnic Greek Albanians and 'other' Albanians (that is two groups who, for reasons explained later, enjoy different statuses in Greece) this chapter focuses on the relationship between different relational processes and mechanisms for the production of boundaries. It examines ways in which boundaries are drawn across contexts and on how constructed institutionalized and heavily politicized boundaries are gendered and, although carefully policed, shift, are crossed or become fluid; the *plasticity of boundaries,* is important in ex(in)clusionary policies on the one hand and ex(in)clusionary practices on the other.

The concept of boundary is central to the study of ethnic and racial inequalities; it has been used as an alternative to cultural and biological theories of ethnic and racial differences (Lamont and Molnàr 2002: 174). Social boundaries are 'objectified forms of social differences manifested in unequal access to and unequal distribution of resources (material and nonmaterial) and social opportunities'. Symbolic boundaries are 'tools by which individuals and groups struggle over and come to agree upon definitions of reality ... they are an essential medium through which people acquire status and monopolize resources' (Lamont and Molnàr 2002: 168). In this chapter I focus on the articulation between social, symbolic and institutional boundaries and how these are created, maintained, contested and starting to change.

The chapter first concentrates on immigration policies and their different impact on these two groups, given the Greek government's favourable stance towards ethnic Greek Albanians; then it discusses the issue of racism(s) and how this has, in the past decade, impacted differently on Albanian men and women migrants and on the strategies employed by these migrants for carving out actual or imaginary spaces of control.

Methods

The empirical part of this chapter is based on the findings of the narratives collected in the greater Athens area during two projects researching migration issues in southern Europe. Athens was chosen because of the main concentration of Albanians, ethnic-Greek Albanians, a metropolis where low-cost migrant labour is much in demand in various sectors of the economy. A large number of in-depth, semi-structured interviews were conducted with migrants: 22 with Albanians, 19 with ethnic-Greek Albanians (with an equal proportion of men and women), 69 guided conversations with migrants' associations, anti-racist organizations, state agencies and other key informants. Given the acknowledged high level of suspicion towards anyone who asked questions amongst undocumented migrants in particular, the interview subjects were selected carefully and approached with sensitivity. The role of intermediaries was critical here, combined with carefully controlled snowball techniques. We tried to achieve intuitive representativeness by interviewing people across age groups and socio-occupational backgrounds. Reflexivity was maintained to allow for diversity of interpretations, attitudes, perceptions and behaviours. What is reported is based on the interviewees' subjective accounts and interpretations of events, and their view of reality as they experienced it and reported it at the time of the interview.

Policy Framework: Permeability of Categorical Boundaries and the Emergence of 'Plastic Boundaries'

In the early 1990s, Greece once a country of emigration experienced a mass influx of migrants, the majority of whom came from Albania. The Greek government, unprepared and influenced by the 'Fortress Europe' ideology that had emerged in the European Union (EU) policy agenda, reacted by introducing in 1991 the particularly restrictive 'Law 1975'. This, with its exaggerated emphasis on policing and border controls, left the majority of migrants under a clandestine status, thus presenting obstacles to the life-chances and rights of the newcomers. Characteristically, this 'closed doors' and 'non-tolerance' spirit led Le Pen, the French National Front leader to characterize this law as 'a paradigm for Europe to follow' (Deltion Thielis 1998). Another important point is that throughout the 1990s many undocumented Albanian migrants lived in fear of deportation. Deportations were frequent in the 1990s under the so called '*skoupa*' or 'broom' operations where migrants were literally 'swept-up' off the streets by the police and transported to the borders for deportation. Men were more vulnerable to police arrests and deportation than women. As Yannis, an Albanian migrant said: '*I have been deported three times; they put me in a bus full of other Albanians and took us to the borders. A couple of days later we came back. It's easy to cross back and forth as long as you have the money to pay* [he means to bribe] *someone*'. Soon the boundaries between 'legality' and 'illegality' became blurred, as more and more migrants either 'over-stayed' or 'crossed back'. As Trinikliniotis (2007: 357) writes, 'the "illegal immigrant" is faceless, timeless, country-less, thus characterized by his or her not being something, *not being* legal. The fascination with *the illegal* is that he/she assumes the same, unchanging characteristics, irrespective of context, time, space, setting, condition or continent. Whether we are referring to the "illegal worker", or the "over-stayer" ... the "bogus" asylum seeker ... they are all homogenized and excluded from legal devices erected to protect all individuals from false conviction or accusation'. In 1997 a bilateral agreement was signed between the Albanian and Greek governments regulating the 'invitation' of Albanian workers on a seasonal contract basis. After a lot of deliberation and lobbying from various pressure groups the government introduced a series of regularization programmes (Lazaridis and Poyago-Theotoky 1999); the first one was introduced in 1998 and three others have followed since. All these programmes have been beset by implementation problems at all levels, namely institutional bureaucratic ones, characterized by racist attitudes and corruption. But most importantly, although third country migrants who are regularized are entitled to equal rights at work (that is equal payment for same job as the Greek workers and welfare and social insurance coverage rights), the majority still get jobs in the informal sector, under exploitative conditions (Lazaridis and Koumandraki 2007). The majority of the respondents reported long working days, lack of insurance, poor wages, sexual harassment by male employers (Lazaridis 2003; 2007), weak bargaining position, with employers insisting on hiring them clandestinely in order to save on employers' contributions costs. Particularly vulnerable here are women many of which are concentrated in 'invisible' or highly stigmatized spaces of work such as domestic work or prostitution, exacerbating their social, legal and economic insecurity.

Regularization for many of the respondents did not manage to achieve the crossing of the boundary from informality to formality or avoid the adverse consequences associated with the undeclared labour market. What it did, is to perhaps eliminate extreme forms of slave-like exploitation, where undocumented migrants were threatened that they would be reported to the police and deported if they did not abide by the employer's requests. For example, migrant women working as domestic workers reported that their passports were held by employers who then refused to pay their wages (Lazaridis 2000). Similarly, undocumented migrant women working in the care sector as personal nurses and migrant quasi-nurses (Lazaridis 2007) mentioned that, although they were sexually harassed at work, they turned a blind eye from fear that if they reported this to the police, they would be arrested and deported. Moreover, regularization has granted them temporary, transient statuses, resulting in their entrapment in a 'regularization cycle'. For example, most work permits were issued for one year and had to be renewed but, due to bureaucratic delays, just as one received the permit, they had to start the procedure of applying for its renewal. To compensate for such delays, the government introduced during the 2001 and 2005 regularizations a 'semi-regularized' status by issuing 'certification of having submitted an application for a residence permit'. This document protects the applicant from deportation without however constituting a valid residence permit. One is entrapped in an *in-limbo status*, deprived from entitlement to social benefits and from the freedom of movement. '*Ke na thelo na pao stin Alvania, then moro' (Even if I wanted to go to Albania, I can't)*, an Albanian woman said.

Currently Greece's principal legal instrument governing immigration is Law 3386/2005.This deals with entry, residence and social integration of third country nationals. A positive aspect of this law has been the provision that third country migrants who have lawfully resided in Greece for a period of at least two years are permitted to request the entry and residence of their family members into the country. However, this law is discriminatory against 'family members' as it excludes the parents and grandparents of the primary immigrant, as well as spouses other than the first legal spouse (in the case of polygamy), and same-sex partners irrespective of whether they have performed a legal wedding or civil partnership in another EU Member State. Law 3386/2005 was revised by law 3536/2007, the most important provision of which relates to the procedures for the regularization of migrants. Now, a migrant can be legalized provided that s/he produces public documents certifying that one of the following occurred before the end of 2004: the birth of a child in the host country; marriage to a Greek or EU citizen; or a child's enrolment in primary or secondary school. It abolishes the obligation to supply an employment contract for the renewal of a residence permit for construction workers (mainly men), private nurses and domestic workers (mostly women) with more than one non-permanent employer. Moreover migrants can buy insurance stamps at 20 per cent of the number needed annually in order to renew their residence permit and not be forced, as in the past, to buy them at extremely high prices in the black market.

The policy towards ethnic-Greek-Albanians is different. These belong to the Greek Orthodox minority which has lived for centuries in the southern part of Albania, known as Northern Epirus. They are viewed as 'temporary guests' rather than 'intruding strangers'. Until 1998, they entered Greece with visas issued by the Greek consulates in their home country. Upon their arrival in Greece some were issued with residence permits by the police authorities (law 1975/1991). Special legislation was introduced in 1998 to regulate the employment and residence of those who entered the country illegally or overstayed when their visas or permits expired. Although the Greek state did not 'encourage' their permanent settlement in Greece (so as not to weaken the Greek presence in southern Albania which is regarded by many as 'traditionally Greek territory') it introduced a temporary privileged status to accommodate this group taking into account the long term 'national interests' and the short-term needs of the group. They were issued with a '*special identity card for foreigners of Hellenic Descent' (Ethiko Deltio Taftotita*

Omogenous) renewable every three years which functions as both a residence and work permit. Its temporary duration aims to discourage their permanent settlement in Greece. But at the same time it grants them equal rights to Greek nationals in terms of access to and conditions of employment (in both public and private sectors), welfare services and other entitlements with the exception of the right to vote and serve in the army.

It is worth noting here the different statuses granted to Albanian migrant women and ethnic-Greek-migrant women, that is *residence permit* to the former and *quasi-citizenship* to the latter. Thus boundaries are constructed between 'us' the 'other' (ethnic-Greek-Albanians) and the 'other-other' (other Albanians); both are granted a '*temporary belonging*' via regularization; but whereas the 'other' is temporarily treated as 'one of us' and being granted favourable legal status to facilitate their social and labour market inclusion, in the case of the 'other-other', they are subject to a '*functional inclusion*', treated in much the same way as the '*gastarbeiter of the new millennium*' for as long as the market needs them.

Social and Symbolic Boundaries

The media has contributed to the *production* of the Albanian criminal, their stereotyping as 'cunning, primitive and untrustworthy' (Lazaridis and Romaniszyn 1998; Lazaridis and Wickens 1999) and their stigmatization as the 'dangerous other'. This 'media amplification' has resulted in the development of particular stances towards migrants and widespread Albanophobia, finding expression in racist attitudes and practices in Greek society. As mentioned by Lazaridis and Koumandraki (2001: 287-288), anti-immigration agitation compounded by media discourse has meant that the word 'Albanian' has become synonymous with 'untrustworthy', 'rogue', 'someone who is likely to steal or to kill', a 'liar', a 'source of trouble', 'dangerous others'. Since, according to Foucault (1972) discourses are 'practices that systematically form objects of which we speak', such stereotypical images or metaphors hold the key to understanding people's emotions and have had consequences in shaping racist attitudes and practices. As a result, the Greeks seem to automatically and unconsciously categorize the Albanian as 'other' and when social roles are activated in the process of perceiving a specific person, they become nested within prior, automatic categorization of that person as an untrustworthy villain. Hence Albanians, and particularly men, are believed to be more likely to commit crime than those of other nationalities. In the cases of both men and women, the other Albanians' religion and culture, rather than their 'colour', constitute the main signifiers of their 'racialization'. Such signifiers have been used to construct racialized boundaries, although these boundaries remain gendered. In the growing work on masculinities within gender studies, it has been argued that masculinity is often associated with being 'tough' or violent (Johnson 2005; Kimmel 2004). Thus men are more likely than women to be mistrusted and, as a result, encounter forms of discrimination, suspicion and marginalization. However, although hegemonic masculinity may explain the 'other' Albanian's discriminatory treatment, this type of explanation is challenged when analysing ethnic-greek-albanian men's experiences of discrimination.

Wieviorka (1994) identifies four empirically observable manifestations of racism in hierarchical order: prejudice, segregation, discrimination and violence. Prejudice refers to a reality more or less expressed in everyday speech or in the media. Segregation involves keeping the racialized group apart, setting aside designated spaces for it. Discrimination encompasses differential treatment of the group in various fields of social life. Violence can take minor forms (such as anonymous letters and limited forms of aggression) or major forms (killings, attacks etc). As shown in detail by Lazaridis and Koumanrdaki (2001) and Lazaridis and Psimmenos (2000), Albanians in Greece experience prejudice and discrimination in the housing market, at school, in the labour market, in the legal system and so on. Levels of racism vary, with some cases revealing more acute forms than others. These empirical categories may function at four different levels, and are connected with one of the two logics of racism: the logic of *inferiority*, which aims to ensure that the racialized group received unequal treatment, and the logic of *differentiation*, which tends to set it apart and in extreme cases, expel or exterminate it. The criterion of analytical differentiation amongst the four levels of racism is whether or not racism is an organized, political and/or institutional phenomenon. In the case of the Albanians, at all levels each of the elementary forms of racism mentioned below, with the exception of 'ghettoization', is more or less apparent and observable. When Albanians first arrived in Greece in the early 1990s the prejudices against them were rather xenophobic than racist. Segregation did emerge but this was a social phenomenon arising from the socio-economic position of the migrants rather than it being the result of ghettoization. By the mid-1990s, prejudices became more widespread and could be observable for example in media discourse especially targeting Albanian men, and recorded. However, racism was now embodied in state practices (the so called mass expulsions of Albanians in the 1990s under the *skoupa* operations (whereby Albanians, mostly men, were literally swept off the streets, put into buses against their will, transported to the borders and often forcefully deported, which meant them living in constant hiding by the police) and new legal framework (immigration law of 1991), justified in terms of the state's responsibility as guarantor of social order internally and of Fortress Europe externally. Gradually Greece moved from a country proudly stressing its *philoxenia* (hospitality) towards 'strangers', to exhibiting xenophobia and what Essed (1990) calls 'everyday racism'.

The concept of 'everyday racism' refers to both structural forces of racism as well as routine situations in everyday life. The key features of everyday racism are: it presupposes everyday situations, that is racist practices are embodied in daily practices. In the case of Albanians, these are observed in routine situations like informal conversations, public transportation, etc. When we asked our interviewees to describe to us a situation where they felt unfairly treated, Eleni said: *'My relations with the police were bad. The police have arrested me a few times and deported me. One feels bad because one is put on a bus; everybody stares at you ... it is insulting.'* She added: *'I will now refer to an incident in Mytilene. Two Albanians went to a bar to dance and some people beat them up. Why are the Greeks allowed to have fun and not the Albanians?'* Another Albanian woman, Lina, added: *'I went to OAED* [Employment Agency Organization] *and a man there, as soon as he heard that I am from Albania he said: 'I can't stomach you'* [meaning in Greek, 'I despise you']. *I replied: 'Where is the guy who sells beverages here, I will ask him to bring you a soda to help you with your digestion'. The others started laughing. He said that even with a soda drink he wouldn't stomach me. I replied: 'Then you need to see a doctor to prescribe you something stronger,' and I laughed...* Another woman, Rita, said: *'For example, in the buses; If one Albanian and two Greeks are caught without a ticket, the inspector will embarrass and fine the Albanian ... whereas the Greeks will get away with it and won't be charged any fine. This has happened to me ... One encounters this sort of attitude wherever one goes. But I don't pay any attention'*. One often hears Greeks say, *'They take our jobs, our children are unemployed, and accept ridiculously low wages; they are responsible for falling wages; I am not using the bus anymore; it is full of Albanians'*.

Racist verbal acts are recurrent, they are familiar and considered normal by the dominant group. For example, it is nowadays considered normal in Greece to accuse an Albanian of a crime, not to trust an Albanian employee, or to tell an Albanian to go back to his/her country. In addition to the above mentioned experiences of discrimination and racism, Albanians reported discrimination and slave-like exploitation in the workplace. Sokratis and Alexis's experience illustrates this. They said: *'We were working for two weeks doing agricultural work in a farm and were waiting for our wages, when the boss said that he would pay us at the end of the month because he was short of cash. The end of the month came but we saw no money. When we asked for the money, the police arrived and took us to the police station and beat us up. They said that we were there because we stole something, which was not true. In the end they said they would let us free on the condition that we would go back to the same farm and work for free for another month in order to pay back whatever it was they said we stole. As soon as they took us back, we left the farm; the farmer had enemies in the village who went and testified that we did not steal anything and that the farmer was not telling the truth and hence we were left in peace and continued working in the village'*. However, this slave-like exploitation is starting to diminish as more and more migrants manage to get regularized. In the case of Albanian women who work as nurses or *quasi*-nurses (see Lazaridis 2007), often a dependency develops on the part of the patient giving the migrant woman an advantage over negotiations on how many hours she will work and the type of tasks she will perform. In some cases the power hierarchy implicit in the interdependent relationship between employer and employee is turned on its head, with the employer becoming dependent on the service provided by the migrant woman, both emotionally and in terms of provision of care. This enables Albanian carers to carve out some degree of personal autonomy.

But how did our interviewees react to experiences of prejudice, discrimination and violence? The analysis of the qualitative data pointed to *passive* and *active* coping strategies. *Passive* responses encompass reactions ranging from choosing not to argue and 'keeping their heads down', to concealing their ethnic identity or revealing it only when they got to know someone well, to paying no attention to comments. As Zahos said: *'I will go there and if he hires me he'll offer to pay me peanuts ... I know this now, I have accepted it because I know that there is no other way ....'*. Andonis said: *'What on earth shall I do? Pick an argument? ... I say nothing'*. Gianna added: *'I hear a lot of comments in the bus. That we are dirty, that we are liars, that we do not do our job well ... I say nothing ... I leave ... There are situations where I wish I said something ... but I think, better say nothing'*. Alexandra said: *'At work I do not say that I am an Albanian. People are suspicious'*. Ervin added: *'I was doing that, but only in the beginning. Later I thought that isn't right. I have to be myself'*. Eva said something similar: *'When I am sitting on the underground near an old lady, I cannot say I am an Albanian, because she will stand up and leave ... We avoid speaking in Albanian in places where Greeks can hear us. As soon as we open our mouths and say something in Albanian we feel that they turn and look at us and that their non-verbal behaviour changes. They either move away in the bus, or they start saying things like "they should get all these Albanians the hell out of here"'*. A friend of hers added: *'I choose not to speak Albanian when I am not at home, because I don't like being stared at in a strange way ... My daughter doesn't speak Albanian at all. She speaks Greek very well. I don't speak with my daughter in Albanian when we are out so as not to feel embarrassed'*. Albanians' attitude changed through time. Whereas in the beginning people felt annoyed, hurt and often angry, by negative comments of the type mentioned above, it seems that they gradually developed a thicker skin. As Leonardo put it: '*It is a reoccurring phenomenon nowadays to hear Greeks badmouth an Albanian. This is what they think, this is what they do. Let them do it. It used to upset me but now I don't pay any attention whatsoever. I don't care ...'*.

Active responses included: developing a tough skin, being assertive and arguing back, developing a rhetoric along the lines that not all Albanians are bad, overtly expressing disapproval of Albanian criminality, and carving out spaces of control by organizing in associations and approaching anti-racist organizations. Rita, trying to explain that not all Albanians are the same, said: *'Generally speaking, people here have a very bad opinion of Albanians. I remember that a lady I used to work for, she was a gynaecologist, asked me: "Why do Albanians steal?" I was shocked. I replied, "I never stole anything". She replied, "I am not talking about you". "But", I said, "you talked about all Albanians. Are there not any Greeks that are thieves"?, She replied: "Oh yes, there are Greeks who steal". And I said: "But I never ask you why do Greeks steal? Because there are good Greeks and bad Greeks". The ones one watches on the TV, the ones who kill and steal are Greeks. One guy killed his wife and dismantled her body. Another guy killed his children, another man killed his mother-in-law, a son killed his father-in-law, they are all Greeks. But I never generalize because everywhere there are bad people.*

One cannot speak of a whole nation based on 100, 1000 bad people'. Ervin said: *'There is racism ... migrants are facing discrimination to a higher degree because of ethnic divisions ... I have been fighting this issue ... Gradually you become tougher and face up to things. You realise that you are going to encounter this type of behaviour and attitude many times in the future. You have to face up to the problem. That is why we decided to organize ourselves and build the Forum* [an Albanian organization in Athens] – *we believe that different cultures can co-exist'*. Some Albanians got baptized in the Orthodox church in order to integrate themselves into Greek culture and society. As Rita said: *'We had to do it. It was necessary. We realised from the very beginning that people looked at someone differently if one wasn't baptized'*.

Although Albanian migrants seem to have developed processes of 'managing' their coexistence with racism, they are still unwilling to lodge formal complaints. Instead they rely on rhetorical devices to demonstrate to themselves and others the injustice of racism. In the case of Albanian migrants, as shown by the interview extracts above, three of the four of Wieviorka's (1994) 'elementary' forms of racism, namely prejudice, discrimination and minor violence, are apparent, visible and observable. Some forms of racism are more visible and others are more institutionalized. In practice these forms and levels of racism are overlapping and there is no clear distinction between them.

The situation with ethnic-Greek Albanians differs. Ethnic-Greeks (*omogenis*) are not treated as 'aliens' because they are part of the Greek nation; they have a more beneficial treatment which, as mentioned above, has recently been institutionalized, provided that they can 'prove their Greekness', that is as long as they can prove that they are part of the in-group. This is important in explaining the differential treatment of 'other Albanian women' and 'ethnic-Greek-Albanian women', those to be on the 'included' side of the *wall* which separates those who are 'included' from those who are 'excluded' and those to be on its 'excluded' side. It is clear that the boundaries between 'us' and the 'other' are fluid and flexible; the degree of their *plasticity* depending to a large extent to which category of migrant one belongs. The favourable legal conditions of ethnic-Greek-Albanians have led 'other' Albanians to adopt specific integration 'strategies': changing their names to Greek; converting to Orthodoxy and baptizing themselves; adopting in other words 'fictive identities' in an attempt to abandon attributes that are 'strange' or 'different' to 'us'. In other words, Albanian migrants like to identify with the Greek population which leads to adopting fictive identities and belongings. Such identities are the result of a process of self-definition and the construction of symbolic boundaries. It is a strategy of self-preservation. So they draw boundaries in relation to their own culture.

Once perceived as an homogeneous nation Greece has become a multicultural country. This change challenges national identity and forces it to confront 'difference' and to rethink people's sense of belonging. The first reactions towards the 'other' were manifested not only in a rise in racism and xenophobia but also in discussions about 'who we are' and 'where do we belong'. Immigration challenged the exclusionary construction of Greekness on the basis of Orthodox Christian religion, linguistic and genealogical criteria and a historical myth which lies on a historical continuity between ancient and modern Greece. The revival of nationalist ideology in the 1990s culminated in the 'Macedonian question' together with periodic crises in the Greco-Turkish relations and historical disputes between Greece and some of its neighbours (such as Albania) and a general perception that those in the Balkans are 'barbarians', 'inferior'. This and the attitude that 'we' after all can refer to our glorious ancient past, influenced the population's perception of the 'other' and have had a negative impact on the perception of the migrant as the 'dangerous other'.

National identity is changing as it is faced with the 'other' who represents a 'threat' to the 'authenticity' of the nation. Religious and nationalistic values re-emerged in the 1990s, in parallel with other political developments in the Balkans, such as the objections to the name Macedonia, and the support of the Orthodox Serbs during the civil war in Yugoslavia. Greek ethnocentrism, creates problems to the smooth integration of Albanians, as the right to difference in the Greek case is perceived as the right of the majority to retain 'our identity and culture', whereas the Balkan is the backward, the barbarian, the inferior 'other'. For instance, during national holidays all schools organize a parade where the top-ranking pupil carries the Greek flag. This happens on two occasions: on the 25 March, a day attributed to the symbolic initiation of the Greek struggle for independence from the Ottoman Empire in 1821, and on the 28 October, when Greece refused to allow the fascist Italian troops into the country in 1940. In 1999, in Thessaloniki, an Albanian pupil became the flag-bearer. This caused a strong xenophobic reaction that dominated media discourse. Such reactions reflect the exclusionary character of national identity and of an ethnically or culturally defined model of nationality and the populist discourse around the control of symbols and traditions that surrounds this. Hence, 'anti-immigrant nationalists are seen as patriots who "protect" the country from a co-ordinated plan by the West's main opponent, Islam, to Islamize Europe and from Greece's main opponent, Turkey, to take over Greece both territorially and symbolically' (Lazaridis and Koumandraki 2001: 297).

Immigration has become part of the political agendas of major parties; the two main parties, New Democracy and PASOK have developed a managerial approach to migration aiming at measures encouraging the smooth integration of migrants into the country balanced by an 'effective border control' approach aimed at balancing the national interests of peaceful coexistence within which the external pressures towards securitization of the borders. Although a small but strong extreme right-wing political party with an anti-immigrant manifesto exists (for example the LAOS party) other smaller parties such as SYNASPISMOS and the Communist Party of Greece (KKE) are advocates of migrants' rights. Also, non-governmental organizations (NGOs), trade unions, migrants' associations, the Network for Support of Immigrants and Refugees and various anti-racist organizations which have been lobbying and campaigning for migrants' rights, have had a growing influence. Moreover, although racist attitudes are still widespread in the country, the rhetoric of media discourse has shifted from aphorisms branding Albanian migrants as 'untrustworthy, dangerous and a threat to society' to embracing a debate and giving from time to time a voice to pro-migrant activists and migrant associations. After nearly 17 years of being in the country Albanians are now interacting with civil society organizations (for example, their children attend Greek schools). As interaction increases reciprocity between migrants and locals is growing at the informal level, and as the 'second generation' comes of age, hybrid identities and practices are beginning to emerge. At the same time, movements back and forth from country of destination to country of origin encourage and contribute to the emergence of translational identities. Nevertheless, a mistrust of the 'other' still exists.

Concluding Remarks: Boundaries are Permeable

Usually pressures to evaluate one's group positively lead social groups to attempt to differentiate themselves from each other in order to maintain and achieve superiority over an out-group (see Tajfel and Turner 1985; Hogg and Abrams 1988). In the case of the 'other Albanians', what we have is the opposite. Instead of differentiating themselves they attempt the opposite: they try to make the boundaries between the host society and themselves permeable in order to achieve mobility, not through social competition but through voluntary assimilation. So instead of differentiating themselves from others by drawing on criteria of community and a sense of shared belonging within their subgroup (see Jenkins 1996), they do the opposite in order to demolish definitions of 'us' and 'them'. Thus boundaries become permeable, resulting in the formation of new fictive identities. This is particularly interesting when it comes to women; the role of women as ethnic actors and definers of ethnic boundary has often been used in the gender and migration literature to explore how nationhood and belongingness are retained and expressed (see Anthians and Yuval-Davis 1989; Yuval-Davis 1997). More work is needed to integrate the psychological, cultural and social mechanisms involved in this process and on its impact or not on systematic patters of discrimination. Boundaries become fluid like a *muro di gomma*, a rubber wall, whose position is not static, but alters; it changes depending on the interplay between different social divisions enacted within the context of historically reproduced economic, political and cultural relations and shaped by racialized definitions of the 'Albanian migrant'; such definitions are constructed by the environment these people are exposed to, namely the media, law, populist discourse and other mechanisms, ideologies and institutions which construct their social position in the host country.

Symbolic boundaries/markers, valued by and generated by the host culture are central in the creation of racialized boundaries. Migrants come to see their culture and ways as inferior to those of the host country, through oppositions such as vulgar/distinguished, pure/impure, etc. The hosts thereby exercise 'symbolic violence', that is, impose specific meaning as legitimate while concealing the power relations that are the basis of its force (Bourdieu and Passeron 1972, trans 1977: 4). Migrants use the culture of the dominant society to mark cultural proximity, to acquire privileges and to avoid exclusion. Hence, through the reinvention of *habitus* or cultural dispositions, newly acquired cultural practices have inescapable effects that shape their social position by defining boundaries between 'us' and the 'others'. In this case, they define their identity in opposition to the privileged 'other'. Boundary crossing, blurring and shifting are central to negotiations between newcomers and hosts. The stranger, 'the man who comes today and stays tomorrow' (Simmel 1971: 143) becomes, according to Lamont and Molnàr (2002: 185), 'instrumental in redrawing the boundaries of national identities'.

Acknowledgments

This chapter is based on the findings of a research project funded by the Leverhulme Trust (Grant No: F/00230/D, 2001–3) in collaboration with Russell Kind. Maria Koumandraki and Nicola Mai worked as research assistants on the Greek and Italian parts of the project respectively.

References

Anthias, F. and Yuval-Davis, N. (1989), 'Introduction', in Yuval-Davis, N. and Anthias, F. (eds) *Woman, Nation, State*. (Basingstoke: Macmillan).

Bourdieu, P. and Passeron, J-C (1977), *Reproduction in Education, Society, and Culture.* Transl. R. Nice. (London, Beverly Hills, CA: Sage).

Deltion Thielis (1998), Magazine of the Network of Movements for Social and Political Rights.

Essed, P. (1990), *Everyday Racism: Reports from Women in Two Cultures*. (Claremont, CA: Hunter House).

Foucault, M. (1972), *The Archaeology of Knowledge*. (London: Tavistock).

Hogg, M.A. and Abrams, D. (1988), *Social Identification.* (London: Routledge).

Jenkins, R. (1996), *Social Identity*. (London: Routledge).

Johnson, A. (2005), *The Gender Knot: Unravelling our Patriarchal Legacy*. Philadelphia: (Temple University Press).

Kimmel, M.S. (2004), *The Gendered Society*. (New York: Oxford University Press).

Lamont, M. and Molnàr, V. (2002), 'The Study of Boundaries in the Social Sciences', *Annual Review of Sociology* l.28, 167–95.

Lazaridis, G. (2000), 'Filipino and Albanian Women Migrant Workers in Greece', in Anthias, F. and Lazaridis, G. (eds) *Gender and Migration in Southern Europe: Women on the Move.* (Oxford: Berg).

Lazaridis, G. (2003), 'From Maids to Entrepreneurs: Immigrant Women in Greece', in Freedman, J. (ed.) *Gender and Insecurity: Migrant Women in Europe*. (Aldershot: Ashgate).

Lazaridis, G. (2007), 'Les Infirmières Exclusives and Migrant Quasi-Nurses in Greece', in *European Journal of Women's Studies* 14:3, 227–45.

Lazaridis, G. and Koumandraki, M. (2001), 'Deconstructing Naturalism: the Racialization of Ethnic Minorities in Greece', in King, R. (ed.) *The Mediterranean Passage: Migration and New Cultural Encounters in Southern Europe*. (Liverpool: Liverpool University Press).

Lazaridis, G. and Koumandraki, M. (1997), 'Albanian Migration to Greece: Patterns and Processes of Inclusion and Exclusion in the Labour Market', *European Societies* 9:1, 91–111.

Lazaridis, G. and Psimmenos, I. (2000), 'Migrant Flows from Albania to Greece: Economic, Social and Spatial Exclusion' in King, R., Lazaridis, G. and Tsardanidis, Ch. (eds) *Eldorado or Fortress? Migration in Southern Europe*. (London: Macmillan).

Lazaridis, G. and Poyago-Theotoky, J. (1999), 'Undocumented Migrants in Greece: Issues of Regularization', *International Migration* 37:4, 715–38.

Lazaridis, G. and Romaniszyn, C. (1998), 'Albanian and Polish Undocumented Workers in Greece: a Comparative Analysis', *Journal of European Social Policy* 8:1, 5–22.

Lazaridis, G. and Wickens, E. (1999), 'Us and the Others: Ethnic Minorities in Greece', *Annals of Tourism Research* 26: 3, 623–55.

Lenz, I., Lutz, H., Morokvasic-Müller, M., Schöning-Kalender, C. and Schwenken, H. (2002), 'Crossing Borders and Shifting Boundaries', in Lutz, H., Morokvasic-Müller, M., Schöning-Kalender, C. and Schwenken, H. (eds) *Crossing Borders and Shifting Bounraries: Vol. II Gender, Identities and Networks*. (Leske, Burdich: Opladen).

Simmel, G. (1971), 'The Stranger', in Simmel, G. (ed.) *Individuality and Social Forms*. (Chicago: University of Chicago Press).

Tajfel, H. and Turner, J.C. (1985), 'The Social Identity Theory of Intergroup Behavior', in Worchel, S. and Austin, W.G. (eds) *Psychology of Intergroup Relations*. (Chicago: Nelson-Hall).

Trinikliniotis, N. (2007), 'Populism, Democracy and Social Citizenship: Discourses on "Illegal Migration" or Beyond the "Fortress" versus "Cosmopolitanism" Debate', in Berggren, E., Likic-Brboric, B., Toksoz, G. and Trinikliniotis, N., *Irregular Migration, Informal Labour and Community: a Challenge for Europe*. (Maastricht: Shaker Publisher).

Yuval-Davis, N. (1997), *Gender and Nation*. (London: Sage).

Wieviorka, M. (1994), 'Racism in Europe: Unity and Diversity', in Rattansi, A. and Westwood, S. (eds) *Racism, Modernity, Identity on the Western Front*. (Cambridge: Cambridge University Press).

Chapter 11
Gender, Family Unity and Migration: Discourses and Dilemmas

Catherine Sherlock

'Families are the lifeblood of our communities – the place where dreams are born, children are nurtured, adults find purpose, and life challenges are weathered.' (Rice 1994: 321) Families matter to the individual but they also matter to communities and to society. The phenomenon of migration is not a new one but what has been noticeable to those working to support families in recent decades is the impact of migration on family life. The choices made to migrate and the consequences of the ever decreasing rights and entitlements for many non EU migrants in host countries have made this phenomenon pervasively interesting and of critical concern at the same time. One such complex issue within the study of migration is that of family unity. Jastram (2003) points out that this issue goes beyond individual and family decision-making and involves State decisions in relation to admission, stay and expulsion. It is made up of the constraints placed on States in separating existing families through expulsion of a member, and the ever decreasing entitlement to family reunification for families already separated and who wish to reunite. This chapter evaluates the issue of family unity from a human rights perspective, considering the impact of current discourse around migration from a gendered perspective and attempts to name some of the dilemmas which exist today within this sphere of law and policy. By assessing the implications of many of these policies for family life the aim is to see whether, and to what extent, women are disproportionately affected or disadvantaged by them. The particular focus of this chapter is the situation of individuals and families who have been granted refugee status and other complementary forms of protection following their crossing of State boundaries.

In January 2006, third country nationals residing in the EU numbered approximately 18.5 million or about 3.8 per cent of the total population (European Commission 2007: 3). The numbers of those seeking asylum is decreasing due to restrictive travel laws and more rigorous determination processes in many States throughout Europe. While the issues around family unity are diverse and complex for all migrants there are further complexities faced by those who have migrated for protection, having utilized the asylum and consequently the human rights system, and the issues facing women migrants hold particular complexities. To illustrate some of the issues arising in contemporary Europe, the chapter will provide examples of some of the dilemmas faced by women with an undetermined status or with leave to remain status in Ireland in the context of their family choices at various junctures.

In this contribution the dilemma in defining 'family' is explored, as it is a culturally constructed concept, and the difficulties inherent in the search for a definition are discussed. This is particularly significant as immigration controls and systems can have a hugely destructive effect on family life when they are rigid and Eurocentric in their approaches. An assessment follows of how the family unit is seen in International Law and how the right to protection is enshrined in both binding and non-binding instruments. The chapter continues with an analysis of the relationship between family unity, family separation and family reunification. The question of protection in International human rights law and indeed under the European Convention on Human Rights for women in migration, with reference to family rights, is raised. The importance of family unity in relation to separated families and with particular reference to women is explored. The concern that family immigration policies and legislation are gender neutral in theory but are in fact developed and experienced by women in a manner which clearly excludes them and does not allow for their specific needs is also examined. Some particular issues that face women as family members, such as enjoyment of reproductive rights and the notion that women are more resource intensive as migrants, are also explored in the context of Ireland.

Notions of 'belonging' pose complexities which are beyond the scope of International human rights law and the European Convention on Human Rights to resolve easily. These issues are explored against the backdrop of contemporary discourses in migration law and policy and where conditions are placed on the right to family unity and families are granted greater or lesser rights, depending on their defined status. As Van Walsum and Spijkerboer (2007: 3) point out, the very fact that immigration is inherently a selective process means that the criteria used to select immigrants, and as a consequence retain or admit family members, are related to notions of social citizenship. If migrant women are considered more to be consumers of welfare and state resources than migrant men, then arguably the criteria of selection of family members for admission will have a gendered aspect. The chapter concludes by raising questions about the current and emerging discourse around migration and how the dilemmas outlined need to be considered from a more gendered perspective.

Discourses in Migration

The discourses involved in the concept of migration include competing interests and a myriad of paradoxical values and how the tensions between these conflicting values are resolved is a result of political agenda and public opinion. As Crosby (2006: 2) highlights, much of the mainstream discourse around immigration in general and asylum in particular is infused with water imagery as the 'flood' which threatens the privileged in their protected space. Immigration is thus seen as a potential natural disaster, which must be controlled by the State with the utmost urgency.

In recent years this climate of fear has been reinforced by the concept of the 'war on terror' and consequently migrants and specifically asylum seekers who move spontaneously and in an unregulated manner are seen as a threat to security. The 'war on terror' is widely publicized and these global security issues are extensively debated. However the illegalities and human rights abuses inherent in the undeclared 'war on refugees' manifested in the legal and procedural systems in which asylum seekers and refugees find themselves, are much less so (Fekete 2005). The plight of individuals and families seeking asylum and those seeking to reunite are issues of huge concern to those working with vulnerable families; however the gendered implications have tended to be overlooked in any discussions. As Van Walsum and Spijkerboer (2007) state, women who are subject to immigration control must contend with two models of exclusion; those of gender and nationality. That migrant rights activists and gender rights activists would understand more of the significance of each others' struggles is clearly one way forward.

Defining Family

'The smallest, closest and yet most important community to many persons is the family unit' (Cholewinski 2002: 274). To define what exactly is meant by the 'family' is a difficult task as it is fundamentally a culturally constructed entity. It is also a 'concept in transitional development' (Van Bueren 1995: 68). There exists an abundance of research and debate about definitions of families, family life and the significance of family across many disciplines. Family can be seen as 'any group of individuals who are bonded together through marriage, kinship, adoption, or mutual agreement. Just as every individual is unique; so is every family' (Goode 1997: 347). A family is therefore a group of people who have a bond which is defined by their society and it is an entity 'based on a variety of experiences, including cultural and legal' (Demleitner 2003: 273). This bond may differ across societies and indeed within any one society. The concept of family is constantly evolving so in attempting to define family 'a flexible rather than a rigid definition is clearly necessary to meet new and developing notions ...'. (Anderfuhren-Wayne 1996: 360). It is beyond the scope of this chapter to discuss in any great depth the issues involved in the definition of family and the manner in which family is constructed in various societies. For the purposes of this topic however, the definition of family as it is seen in international law and within immigration policy is of most relevance.

Henriech (1996) examines the dilemmas around the meaning of the term 'family' in an attempt to arrive at a legal definition. 'The family is above all a social group but a social group is not necessarily a family. A family in the legal sense exists where the law has provided for such family relations' (Ibid: 42). So the law, in terms of the concepts which are in existence in any one particular legal system, defines 'family'. This is problematic if an agreed upon definition is sought on an international level in that what may be an acceptable definition within one particular jurisdiction, may not be in another. So can international law offer further clarity here? Van Bueren (1995) sees the approach of international law as one which regards the family as a 'community of individuals possessing specific rights' (Ibid: 72).

The Geneva Conventions of 1949 and additional protocol of 1977 give some attempt to define family in the broadest sense deeming the family to be any group that lives together and wishes to live together (Demleitner 2003: 277). This encompasses a subjective as well as an objective element to the definition of family in law. The International Convention on the Rights of All Migrant Workers and Members of their Families offers a definition for interpretation. The family is seen as married or those in a relationship equivalent to marriage, as well as their dependent children and other dependent persons. [1] This classifies the definition of family in some legal terms but leaves a lot of room for a State to interpret their own workable definition, rather than providing international law with any one definition. This Convention relates only to migrant workers and does not afford any protection to refugees or persons with other forms of protection or residency rights. The Human Rights Committee through a General Comment provide some interpretation of the obligations of States in their definition of the family and state how the concept will differ from State to State and that there is no standard definition, but that when a group of persons is regarded as a family under the legislation and practice of a State, it must be given the protection referred to in international law. (HRC General Comment 19: para. 2). This specifically refers to Article 23 of International Convention on Civil and Political Rights which states that the family is the 'natural group unit of society' and this includes the right to marry and the right to found a family.

If a family exists only when a State says it exists, it is useful to look briefly at some comments in relation to immigration law. Demleitner (2003: 290) discusses how 'in recent decades Western democracies have conceived of family as a nuclear family consisting of mother, father, and one or more (biological or adopted) minor children.' This construct is generally seen as the dominant model despite the reality of many households who live and are connected as family, but do not necessarily fit into this model. For example, the existence of same sex relationships, polygamous marriages, unmarried partners etc. make up significant family members as much as extended family members such as grandparents and,

---

1 Article 4 states that 'for the purposes of the present Convention the term 'members of the family' refers to persons married to migrant workers or having with them a relationship that according to applicable law, produces effects equivalent to marriage, as well as their dependent children and other dependent persons who are recognized as members of the family by applicable legislation or applicable bi-lateral or multilateral agreements between States concerned.'(International Convention on the Protection of the Rights of all Migrant Workers and Their Families 1990).

indeed, the 'nuclear' family. For concrete policy and outcomes of decisions made, how the family is defined can have far reaching consequences. Indeed 'despite its diminished reality, immigration law is based on the assumptions of the dominant model' (Ibid: 291). For migrant women who are parenting alone the possibilities for exclusion are now arguably threefold and can be based on family form, gender and nationality.

Van Bueren (1995) pinpoints a further dilemma in international law; as to be effective it must be able to be 'flexible on one hand to accommodate a range of family and community structures and values, while simultaneously enshrining universally-agreed minimum standards' of international legal rights. The openness to interpret the definition of family can provide a State with the opportunity to further play out the dominant discourses in mainstream society about what is acceptable as a family unit. As Cohen (Cohen 2001: 37) points out, family relationships 'become the sacrificial lambs of immigration control with controls themselves becoming an ideological defence of the one true family – the nuclear family…'. Indeed as Van Walsum and Spijkerboer (2007: 9) point out those discourses which reflect the most stereotypical 'some Immigration Law in Europe is currently responsive to those gender issues that can serve to dramatize the perceived inadequacies of 'non-western cultures' and prove the need for increased immigration control.' These issues include the perception of the need to protect society from polygamy, forced and arranged marriages (which are often mistakenly considered to be the same thing) and issues of smuggling and trafficking. The value conflicts inherent in the discussions around family and, indeed, migration are often deep-rooted in anti-migrant sentiment, islamaphobia and gender discrimination. The portrayal of women as victims and the immigration system as the protector not only simplifies the complexities of the societies from which many migrant women travel but 'deflects attention from the gendered tensions in current EU societies – tensions that involve both citizen and immigrant women.' (Van Walsum and Spijkerboer 2007: 10) It can also serve to dismiss women's agency and the feminist struggles women embrace in their countries of origin (ibid. 2007; Askola, this collection). In some situations migrant women are scape-goated in relation to how society views an existing potential rights' violation and where it is further highlighted when needs and rights intensify when a non-dominant cultural aspect is added. For example, the assertion of reproductive rights in a country where the issues have not been resolved for citizen women, violations are rendered more stark when migrant women attempt to access those same rights and they can face blame for unearthing an issue which had remained relatively hidden.

The Family in International Law

Despite the difficulty of finding a universal definition of 'family', international law affords rights and protection to the family, which it views in general terms as 'the natural and fundamental group unit of society … entitled to protections by society and the State.' (Universal Declaration of Human Rights, Article 16.3) This is reiterated in Article 23 of the International Covenant on Civil and Political Rights, which uses the same wording. In Article 16 of the Universal Declaration of Human Rights, the right to marry and form a family is proclaimed.[2] The themes of respect and protection for the family unit are also clearly set out. Article 17 of the International Covenant on Civil and Political Rights (ICCPR) and Article 10 of the International Covenant on Economic Social and Cultural Rights also provide for protection against arbitrary or unlawful interference with privacy, family, home or correspondence.[3]

The International Convention on the Rights of the Child (CRC) also offers a more comprehensive detail of the obligations of signatory States in relation to protection of the family unit and the importance of the family unit to children.[4] It is interesting to note, however, that it is the term 'parents' which is discussed in relation to protection of family reunion and not extended family members, guardians etc. Another point to note in this Convention is the use of a newer concept in international law of 'family environment.'[5] This is not defined but leads to some recognition of broader notions of family life and that the *experience* of family is what may be important; which if it is a notion that is developed in immigration law and policy could more wholly embrace diversity of family forms and open the debates around the existence of cultural rights more progressively.

2 UDHR Art 16 'Men and women of full age, without any limitation due to race, nationality or religion have the right to marry and found a family.'

UDHR article 12 also states 'no one shall be subjected to arbitrary interference with his privacy, family and home or correspondence, nor to attacks upon his honour and reputation. Everyone has the right to the protection of the law against such interference or attacks.'

3 ICESCR Article 10 states that 'The widest possible protection and assistance should be accorded to the family which is the natural and fundamental group unit of society.'

4 The preamble states how 'the family as the fundamental group of society and the natural environment for growth and well-being of all its members and particularly children, should be afforded the necessary protection and assistance so that it can fully assume its responsibilities within the community' Article 5 sets out how State Parties afford respect to 'the rights responsibilities and duties of children's parents or guardians' Article 7 is the declaration that the child shall have 'as far as possible the right to know and be cared for by his or her parents.' Article 16 prohibits arbitrary or unlawful interference with the child's family but it is Articles 9 and 10, which deal specifically with the child's right to a continued relationship with their parents. In Article 9 (1) 'State Parties shall ensure that a child shall not be separated from his or her parents against their will, except when competent authorities subject to judicial review determine, in accordance with applicable law and procedures, that such separation is necessary for the best interests of the child.' Again in article 10 (1) 'applications by a child or his or her parents to enter or leave a State Party for the purpose of family reunification shall be dealt with by State Parties in a positive, humane and expeditious manner.'

5 CRC Article 20.

Regional instruments also uphold the idea of protection of family.[6] The European Convention for the protection of Human Rights and Fundamental Freedoms 1950 (ECHR) enshrines the protection of the family in Article 8 but it, again, is worded differently. Article 8(1) states that 'everyone has the right to respect for his private and family life his home and his correspondence'. Article 8 (2) states that 'there shall be no interference by a public authority with the exercise of this right except such as is in accordance with the law and is necessary in a democratic society in the interests of national security, public safety or the economic well-being of the country, for the provision of disorder or crime for the protection of health or morals, or for the protection of the rights and morals of others'. Comparably the African Charters imply positive obligations while the ECHR implies more negative obligations, that is those of non-interference. It allows for interference in certain circumstances but this interference must be lawful and deemed necessary under the outlined conditions, primarily national security and common good.

The principle of family unity then is very much enshrined in international documents and norms which are both binding and non-binding to States through the notions of the right to form a family and the protection from interference. While some interference can be lawful; such as in situations outlined above that is from the protection of the rights and morals of others to the issues involved in national security and public safety; the right to live together as a family within a Nation State in certain circumstances poses more complex questions. These questions involve notions of citizenship and belonging and perhaps the desire to send messages to potential migrant populations of the desirability of particular criteria of migrant and the power of the State to limit rights of those who have been uninvited.

Family Unity, Family Separation and Family Reunification

The value placed on family and the principle of family unity as outlined above embodies the legal relationship between family members and their right to any recognition of this relationship. There is a distinction between the right to family unity and a possible right to family reunification. A right to family unity encompasses the basic right to live together in whatever forms the family wish and for this right not to be under threat by any other party. This includes the right

---

6 Article 17 (1) of the American Convention on Human Rights uses similar wording to Article 23 of the ICCPR. The African Charter on Human and Peoples Rights words the protection somewhat differently in Article 18 (1) which states that 'The family shall be the natural unit and basis of society. It shall be protected by the State which shall take care of its physical health and moral *(well-being)*' The African Charter on the Rights and Welfare of the Child also provides for protection and support of the family Article 18 (1) 'The family shall be the natural unit and basis of society. It shall enjoy the protection and support of the State for its establishment and development.'

not to be separated if a family are already living together. The reality is that, in an era of increased security and moral panic around border control (Crosby 2006), if a family member is subject to immigration control the risk of separation by the State exists.

Family Reunification

It is estimated that family reunification makes up 60 per cent of migration to Western Europe. (Immigrant Council of Ireland 2006: 34) The issue of family reunification brings to the fore questions of the rights of entry for non-citizens and the further dilemmas around the right to travel. In order to reunify families there needs to be a movement of peoples between States. The right to leave one's own country is enshrined in many International human rights documents,[7] however there are no comparable rights to enter another country for any purpose including that of family reunification. Indeed 'outside the specific bilateral or multilateral treaties there is no right to immigrate and no specific duty placed on states to allow peoples into their territories for the purposes of family reunification.' (Anderfuhren-Wayne 1996: 351) Even the Convention on the Rights of the Child, the only convention where the notion of family reunification is expressly stated in Article 10, still 'stops short of requiring that States permit immigration for the purposes of family reunification' (Starr and Brilmayer 2003). There is 'no general right for non-nationals to enter a country other than the country of their nationality … and if 'rights' terminology is used, it is usually done so in the context of sovereign rights of States to determine the composition of the national community within defined territorial boundaries.' (Cholewinski 2002: 271) The issue of migration for family reunification purposes represents a special case in this conflict 'where there is the added consideration of the centrality of the family.' (Lahav 1997: 349) Where any family reunification policy exists States can put their own conditions on this.

The right to family reunification extends protection beyond the general right to family unity and refers more specifically to families who are separated and who wish to reunite. Interestingly the 1951 Convention Relating to the Status of Refugees, one convention which deals specifically with people in flight and in need of protection, does not refer explicitly to family reunification. However the final Conference of Plenipotentiaries does endorse family reunification in its Final Act (Final Act of the Conference of Plenipotentiaries Section IV). The Human Rights Committee's approach in General Comment 19 clearly states that 'the right to found a family implies, in principle, the possibility to procreate and live together' (HRC General Comment, para. 5), The Committee interpret a positive obligation on States and, in their view, 'the possibility to live together implies the adoption of appropriate measures, both at the internal level and as the case may be, in co-operation with other States, to ensure the unity or reunification of families particularly when their members are separated for political economic or similar

7 UDHR Article 13.2; ICCPR Article 12.2. as examples.

reasons' (Idem). 'Depending on the categories in which migrants find themselves, they have more or less generous family reunification rights' (Demleitner 2003: 277). The rights that someone with refugee status may have to family reunification may differ from the rights afforded to those more temporarily resident in a country. Families who are in the asylum system or who have not acquired refugee status but who cannot return to their country of origin are in a difficult position. As 'persons who cannot be returned to their country of origin by application of the principle of "non- refoulement"' (Lambert 1999: 431) this group who are granted some form of right to reside are usually granted lesser rights than refugees; notably a renewable but temporary residence permit, and often no right to family reunion. Immigration policies 'reflect who we are as citizens because they set the boundaries between 'us and them' who can belong and who cannot' (Crosby 2006: 2). People who move are granted more or less rights depending on how they are labelled, for example non-citizen, refugee, asylum seeker, economic migrant, illegal immigrant. People can move from one label to another at the permission of the State, and with the acquisition of these labels life experiences and life choices are mapped out. In the case of Ireland those with refugee status have an express right to reunification through the Refugee Act 1996. Those who have been granted humanitarian leave to remain for example have no *legal* right to reunification but can apply through policy provisions through the Department of Justice Equality and Law Reform and decisions are made on a case by case basis.

For children there is an express right not to be separated from parents unless it is in their best interests, as codified by Article 9 of the 1989 United Nations Convention on the Rights of the Child (CRC). For other family members there is no such express right and the issue is one which becomes hugely significant when the expulsion of one or more family members is a possibility either because their rights to reside are unstable or conditional and expire or because their rights to reside are revoked. These issues have huge implications for families, and the debates about the State's right to ensure security, public safety and enforce immigration laws versus the States obligations to respect family unity as outlined above, engender emotive public responses. When a family member has their right to reside revoked as the subject of criminal proceedings, for example, or because their initial right has expired, the 'elsewhere rule' is often utilized as the clear argument that the State is not interfering with a persons right to family life. This argues that expulsion is justified on the grounds that there is a possibility that the whole family can move together along with the member being expelled to another jurisdiction. In such circumstances it has been asserted that if the family remain separated it is because of choice (Jastram 2003). In reality there is often little choice in this matter for many families, as the family member may no longer have any ties with their country of origin, other members may never have been there, and the ability to set up a new life in a place which the family have not chosen, with few opportunities for education or employment, can create undue distress.

The Importance of Family Unity

The effects of family separation are worth a brief mention in that the denial of one human right can create violations of other human rights. Some commentators on the subject note how family separation 'threatens the cultural integrity of peoples' (Starr and Brilmayer 2003: 214). As previously discussed the fact that a State can define who constitutes a family causes the separation of self-defined families. There can be a disproportionate impact of 'family separation policies on women and ethnic or racial minoritie' (Starr and Brilmayer 2003: 214). When families are separated it is not necessarily by choice – dilemmas exist in the decision-making processes of many families; with the reality of a choice to be made between the chance for a better life and separation of family members, temporarily or otherwise.

Demleitner (2003) cites some of the reasons why a more restrictive trend in relation to family unity rights exists in Europe. She names the current thinking around overpopulation and environmental degradation, economic concern in periods of unemployment, changing culture through the admission of immigrants who do not assimilate, concern over the loss of a primary language, pressure on a welfare system and issues of concern regarding terrorism as issues of concern in Europe. Counter to this she notes what are considered to be the benefits of family unification. Firstly family unification should be supported in order to uphold international human rights standards as seen above. Secondly unification supports integration and speeds up the process of people establishing themselves in the host country. It is also imperative for refugees and asylum seekers in their process of healing, as worries about family left behind or further separations can impair their integration. Reduction of monies being sent home to family members so keeps funds within the country is an economic argument often cited. The state of a country's generosity in their family reunification policy will influence the choice of a country as a destination for immigration purposes. However it can be argued that family at risk of separation or who find themselves separated and unable to circumvent a reunification system will find a way to be together, often accessing the dangerous world of human smuggling in the process. 'In a more mobile world law will fail in keeping many individuals who have a strong emotional bond from joining each other in the country the family selects as more desirable' (Demleitner 2003: 276).

'That family reunion should be regarded as a fundamental right is not difficult to justify conceptually' (Cholewinski 2002: 274). However, since there are conditions placed on reunification, and certain criteria placed on right to reside for non-citizen members of a family it cannot be considered to be an absolute right. Family unity is a principle while family reunification is 'considered the means of implementation of such a principle.' (Lahav 1997: 360) In fact 'under general international law it is merely a policy, the force of which is vague and undefined … a right to unity without a clear means of executing it' (Anderfuhren-Wayne 1996: 351). What is significant is that 'law and policy reflect the priorities and concerns of those who enact and implement them,' (Cubie and Ryan 2004: ix) and nowhere is this more focused than in the area of immigration and asylum law and policy. The reality of placing conditions on family's rights to reunify is in clear contrast to the significance attached to the family in international human rights law.

Some cases raising these questions have come before the European Court of Human Rights in recent years. In the case of [*Amrollahi v Denmark (2002) 22 EHHR 585]* an Iranian man with refugee status was served with a deportation order following a criminal conviction and was to be separated from his family (all Danish nationals) were they not to follow him. This resulted in the court identifying the 'obvious and serious difficulties' which would be experienced by an Iranian man's wife and children were they to follow him subsequent to his proposed deportation to Iran. 'Accordingly, as a consequence of the applicant's permanent exclusion from Denmark the family will be separated, since it is *de facto* impossible for them to continue their family life outside Denmark' [*Amrollahi v Denmark (2002)* 22 EHHR 585 paragraph 43]. The action of the State was deemed to be in violation of Article 8 as a result.[8] However, as De Hart points out in her analysis of women's right to family unity, the cultural make-up of the family was evaluated in this instance. To continue with her line of argument in this case, what if Mr Amrollahi was to be returned to USA for example, or if Mrs Amrollahi was a second generation Iranian woman; would there have been a different outcome? (De Hart 2007)

The deportation process can, in itself, create the separation of families through the lack of planned systems, and certainly in Ireland many highly publicized cases have raised questions as to how migrant women are valued. Families separated through the process of deportation have included asylum-seeking families who have spent many years living in Ireland with an undetermined status due to the lengthy asylum determination process, an ad hoc and discretionary alternative right to reside system, and a recently established subsidiary protection system. It is useful to look at some outcomes of current policies. On 14 March 2005, 35 people were deported from Dublin to Nigeria, mainly individuals and families who had been through the asylum process and who had received a negative decision. This was not in itself an unusual occurrence, with six planned deportation operations completed in 2005, four of which went to Nigeria [9] (Garda Siochana Annual Report 2005). Among those deported were two mothers, Elizabeth Odunsi and Iyabo Nwanze (Reid 2005). Both women were parenting alone and had been in Ireland for over four years. They had been refused Refugee status but had applied for humanitarian leave to remain. Both women had one of their children with them at the time of deportation but four other children aged from eight to17 years

8 For a good discussion of the treatment of family life under the ECHR see Liddy J. 'The Concept of Family under the ECHR' 1998 1European Human Rights Law Review 15–25.

9 Garda Siochana Annual Report 2005 p9. The other two planned deportation operations involving charter flights in 2005 went to Romania.

who had been living with them in Ireland remained behind. Gardai had gone to the older children's schools to collect them but they were unable to trace them at the schools. It is unclear as to whether the children had left the schools earlier or the Gardai had arrived at the schools after the school day had ended. Mobile phones were taken from both women as was the usual procedure at a deportation operation at that time and there was no contact between the women and their older children. Despite the potential for separation of the families, the deportation operation went ahead and both women were deported leaving the older children behind in Ireland. The women said that the immigration officials had told them that their children would follow in two weeks. The children disappeared and, following some initial efforts by Gardai to trace the children, their whereabouts remains unknown to the authorities to date. Local support groups launched a campaign to bring Ms Odunsi and Ms Nwanze back to Ireland to reunite them with their families but as a deportation order can only be revoked at the discretion of the Minister, the then Minister did not agree to revoke their orders. An 18-year-old male Leaving Certificate student was also deported during that operation and following a similar public campaign was readmitted to the country. The Minister revoked his deportation order following public pressure in order that he could complete his studies. The same compromise was not made for Ms Odunsi and Ms Nwanze in order that they would be reunited with their children. They were both in the position that they were homeless on return to Nigeria and without access to legal support the opportunity to challenge the deportation has not been a practical option. Notwithstanding the importance of the revocation of the deportation order for this young man's life, the situation is interesting when observed through a gender lens in relation to the differing opportunities and expectations of migrant men and migrant women. The value placed by the State on the role these mothers held, in their contribution to their community and to their families, was arguably a lesser one than that of a single male student completing his education, who could become independent of state welfare more easily and more quickly once he was granted humanitarian leave to remain.

Serious concerns also relate to the lack of any transparency in the State's actions in the deportation process, the outcome for these families and the design of the various aspects of the alternative right to reside system which results in exclusion. Women finding themselves parenting alone and who are moving through the asylum system or awaiting determination of humanitarian leave to remain status (often for many years) are prohibited from working. This legal limbo has created serious situations of poverty and social isolation for women. In order to attain a secure status women need to be able to prove that they will not have to rely on the State for social assistance and as humanitarian leave to remain is granted temporarily the need to prove this at the point of reapplication demonstrates a level of gender insensitivity in the immigration process. For women parenting alone the lack of the availability of adequate childcare once the right to work was granted prohibits so many mothers from accessing employment. This gap in service provision routes many lone parents, both citizen and migrant mothers, into a circle of welfare dependency and consistent poverty (Coakley 2005). The added difficulties which migrant women experience may include the non-transferability of their educational qualifications, their asylum status often lasting many years, which prohibits them from building up work experience, and the existence of language barriers and racism. The lack of proof of this ability to independently support family has led to many mothers being turned down in their applications for family reunification to be joined by other children and this indefinite and temporary status creates a harsh reality for an already vulnerable and excluded minority. Worry about family left behind in a country of origin although not solely the concern of women migrants, can have a detrimental impact on mental health for many.

A further concern exists in relation to the clear reduction of rights relating to family unity in Ireland. A number of changes have taken place over the past few years in relation to citizenship rights and, as a consequence, in the family reunification rights affecting many immigrant families. A decision made in EU law in relation to EU citizenship rights in 2004 had an interesting outcome in the European Court of Justice. Catherine Chen, a child born in Northern Ireland to a Chinese national mother acquired Irish citizenship by virtue of being born on the island of Ireland as per citizenship law at this time. The family then moved to Wales where their application for long term residence was refused. The decision of the Court concluded that to deny Mrs Chen's right to residence in Wales would render her Irish citizen daughter's rights to reside in any EU State ineffective. [*Chen v Secretary of State for the Home Department* Case C-200/02] As Mullally (2007b) points out that this right was only deemed effective by virtue of the *economic viability* of the family where their residence in an EU member State would create no 'unreasonable burden' on the public finances of a State. This ruling only affects those who move across EU member state borders and doesn't apply to those applying for residency in the country of their child's birth. A recent change in Ireland in relation to citizenship rights following the 27th amendment to the Irish Constitution in 2004 has since reduced citizenship rights for children born on the island of Ireland and as a consequence residence rights of many migrant families, although residence rights had been reduced through policy decisions some months earlier. From 1 January 2005, children born in Ireland with non-citizen parents are no longer entitled to citizenship and their parents are no longer entitled to apply for residency on the basis of a child born in Ireland.[10] However for those families whose children were born before the 1 January 2005 and were still living in Ireland, a means was created for many who had been in a legal limbo, to regularize their situation by applying for residency under a time limited residence scheme IBC/05

10 The conditions attached to qualification for Irish citizenship now include if one parent is an Irish citizen or if non-national parents can prove a genuine link to Ireland, for example having lived in Ireland for three out of the four years immediately prior to the birth of the applicant. See Nationality and Citizenship Act 2004 No 38 of 2004 Government Publications Stationary Office Dublin.

scheme.[11] Applications are no longer accepted under this scheme which closed on March 31 2005. Along with the stringent paperwork required, a condition of this residency application was that applicants had to waiver any right to family reunification for any family members not in the country before the closing date of the application. This declaration had to be signed for the application to be accepted. This scheme has affected 17,000 people, approximately 10,000 of whom had been through the asylum system and many of whom were women parenting alone. The reduction of rights to citizenship and to family unity raises clear concerns about the dilemmas faced by families throughout a process such as this one.

For those with an express legal right to reunification in Ireland that is those with full refugee status, there can be delays of up to two years, from the date of their application, before families are reunited in reality. Thomas Hammerberg, the Council of Europe Commissioner for Human Rights, has noted that 'the administrative processing of applications is far from "expeditious" in a number of countries. In fact, the tendency is that they are extremely slow and unnecessarily bureaucratic.' (Hammerberg 2008)

Immigration Policy and Women's Family Rights

To return to the case of Ireland and the issue of women's autonomy and agency, a further interesting issue to assess is that of women's reproductive autonomy. In Ireland migrant women's assertion of their reproductive rights through giving birth within the state and before the citizenship laws changed, secured status for their children was judged as opportunistic and an abuse of the system. As Mullally points out migrant women became the 'demonized others' in the media-fuelled debates about the overstretched maternity services in Ireland and the notions attached to the resource-intensive characteristics of migrant women were made explicit. The migratory trajectory of women in these situations and their choice or lack of choice around a country of asylum was ignored. Indeed 'the voices of migrant women were rarely heard in the citizenship debates as legal interventions were designed and pursued solely from the perspective of the state's interest in immigration control' (Mullally 2007a: 235).

The reproductive rights of women have been the subject of complex and deeply contested debates in Ireland for many decades and have culminated in the movement of women who wish to terminate a pregnancy across national borders to do so (Mullally 2007a). This issue of travel has disproportionately affected migrant women, especially those who are in the asylum-seeking community and

11 Department of Justice Equality and Law Reform Application for permission to remain on the basis of parentage of an Irish-born Child born before 1 January 2005 Form IBC/05. It reads: 'I am aware that the granting of permission to remain in the state does not in any way give rise to any legitimate expectation on my part that any of my family members abroad will as a result be given permission to remain in the State.'

those awaiting decisions regarding the right to reside as they have no express right to leave the jurisdiction. This lack of a right to leave the jurisdiction, and the need to do so for the purposes of availing of a termination, has resulted in asylum-seeking women seeking permission from the Minister of Justice Equality and Law Reform for the right to travel, via a request for travel documents. This raises questions around confidentiality and creates further barriers to the right to choose this option and clearly demonstrates the deeply gendered elements surrounding family issues and rights of migrant women in Ireland.

Conclusions

'Devastating to the individuals involved and frequently destructive in its long term impact on cultural groups and entire societies, the involuntary separation of families is a widespread problem that deserves increased attention as an issue of international human rights' (Starr and Brilmar 2003: 213). The discourse around that of migration and in particular around those accessing the asylum system has been destructive and has often served to render invisible the real circumstances of those most marginalized. In a country like Ireland which is coming to terms with a new position on the world stage; that of a country of immigration rather than emigration there are huge opportunities to develop policies immersed in best practice which honour all families and respect the human rights of those most disadvantaged. The opportunity to consider the rights and voices of women in particular has been lost to date.

The nature of family life is steeped in diversity. For migrant families the dilemmas are real and the discourses are significant. Jones describes immigration policy as referring to 'the objectives, procedures and systems designed for the regulation of immigration. It applies to both published and unpublished intention and in some cases may only be ascertained by examining its effects' (Jones 2001: 255). When policy is unpublished or has a largely discretionary element to it the dilemmas intensify and value base of this intention becomes more significant. Immigrant policies determine how families are treated, supported or excluded from society by virtue of their deemed status, through access to services and welfare supports. These policies have a huge impact on a family's decision-making in relation to various aspects of life choices and can disproportionately affect women. The issues which relate to the family rights in the context of migration and the destruction of family life can often be the outcome of state policies rendering the people and, more particularly, women involved invisible. What is also often rendered invisible in the discussion and research is the resilience of migrant women; those who have had to make difficult choices when faced with unwielding policies which prolong separation and foster resentment of a host population.

The importance of adding the notion of resilience into the discussion here is not to negate the anguish and distress experienced by many families undergoing the risk of separation and the desire to reunite. But it is to reflect the spirit of a marginalized group; when the danger exists that the discourse becomes polarized into seeing migrant women as either abusers of a system or as victims in need of rescue. The reality for those of us who have been privileged to meet and work with families caught in the quagmire of immigration law and policy; through the shifting sands of suspicion, is that we have met people who are neither 'spongers' nor 'charity cases'. Advocacy can only be developed in a spirit of consultation and participation and the need for this to have a gendered element is hugely important if any real and meaningful discourse is to happen. 'All migration is courageous. Whether through coercion, persecution, war or indeed poverty, the past and present movement of people … is littered with painful stories, many too awful to recount. But they are also stories of strength and hope, of survival in (an) … often unwelcoming atmosphere' (Hayes 2004: 11). Research in order to guide policy needs to ask questions of the experiences of those in the process, and to truly analyse the discourse and understand the dilemmas, it will be crucial to look at the issues through a women's rights lens.

References

Anderfuhren-Wayne, C. (1996), 'Family Unity in Immigration and Refugee Matters: United States and European Approaches', *International Journal of Refugee Law* 8:3, 347–82.

Bayefsky, A., Farrior, S. et al. (2002), 'Protection Under the Complaint Procedures of the United Nations Treaty Bodies' in Fitzpatrick J. (ed.).

Bhabha, J. (2003), 'Children as Refugees and Displaced Persons: 'More than their Share of sorrows International Migration Law and the Rights of Children', *St Louis University Public Law Review* 22.

Cholewinski, R. (2002), 'Family Reunification and Conditions placed on Family Members: Dismantling a Fundamental Human Right', *European Journal of Migration and Law* 4, 271–90.

Coakley, A. (2005), 'Mothers, Welfare and Labour Market Activation' *Combat Poverty Research Working Paper Series*, <http://www.cpa.ie/publications/workingpapers.htm>.

Cohen, S. (2001), *Immigration Controls, the Family and the Welfare State* (London: Jessica Kingsley Publishing).

Council of Europe (2003), Directive 2003/86 of 22 September 2003 OJ 2003 L251/12.

Crosby, A. (2006), 'The Boundaries of Belonging: Reflections on Migration Policies into the 21st Century', *Inter Pares Canada Occasional Paper* No 7 June 2006.

Cubie, D. and Ryan, F. (2004), *Immigration, Refugee and Citizenship Law in Ireland: Cases and Materials* (Dublin: Thompson Round Hall).

De Hart, B. (2007), *The right to domicile of women with a migrant partner in European immigration law'* in Van Walsum, S. and Spijkerboer, T. (eds).

Demleitner, N. (2003), 'Conference on Marriage, Families, and Democracy: How much do Western Democracies Value Family Marriage? Immigration Law's Conflicted Answers', *Hofstra Law Review* 32, 273–311.

European Commission (2007), 'Communication form the Commission to the Council, the European Parliament the European Economic and Social Committee and the Committee of the Regions: Third Annual Report on Migration and Integration', <http://ec.europa.eu/justice_home/fsj/immigration/docs/com_2007_512_en.pdf> (Accessed 2 August 2008).

Fekete, L. (2005), 'The Deportation Machine: Europe Asylum and Human Rights', *Race and Class*, 47:1, Garda Siochana (2005), Annual Report, <www.garda.ie>.

Goode, A. (1997), title in J Heffernan et al. (eds).

Hammar, T. (1985), *European Immigration Policy* (Cambridge: Cambridge University Press).

Hammerberg, T. (2008), 'Refugees must be able to reunite with their family members' 4/8/2008. Viewpoints of the Council of Europe Commissioner for Human Rights available at www.coe.int/t/commisssioner/viewpoints/default_en.asp?

Hayes, D. (2004), 'History and Context: The impact of Immigration Control on Welfare Delivery' Chap 1 in Hayes D & Humphries B *Social Work, Immigration and Asylum: Debates dilemmas and ethical issues for social work and social care practice* Jessica Kingsley London).

Henriech, D. (1996), 'Family Law across Frontiers: Facts, Conflicts, Trends', in Lowe, N. and Douglas, G. (eds).

Human Rights Committee General Comment (1990), 19 UN Doc HR1/GEN/1/Rev.4 (Thirty-Ninth Session).

Immigrant Council of Ireland (2003), 'Handbook on Immigrants Rights and Entitlements in Ireland' (Dublin: Immigrant Council of Ireland Publishing).

Immigrant Council of Ireland (2006), 'Family Matters: Experiences of Family Reunification in sIreland', (Dublin: Immigrant Council of Ireland Publishing).

Jastram, K. (2003), 'Family Unity: The New Geography of Family Life' Migration Information Source, <www.migrationinformation.org/Featue/print.cfm?ID=118> (Accessed 1 August 2008).

Jones, A. (2001), 'Child Asylum Seekers and Refugees: Rights and Responsibilities', *Journal of Social Work* 1:3.

Kagan, S. and Weissman, B. (1994), *Putting Families First* (San Francisco: Jossey-Bass Publishing).

Lahav, G. (1997), 'International versus National Constraints in Family-Reunification Migration Policy', *Global Governance* 3.

Lambert, H. (1999), 'The European Court of Human Rights and The Right of Refugees and Other Persons in Need of Protection to Family Reunion', *International Journal of Refugee Law* 11.

Liddy, J. (1998), 'The Concept of Family under the ECHR' *European Human Rights Law Review* 1, 15–25.
Mullally, S. (2007a), *Ireland: Citizenship and Reproductive Autonomy* in Van Walsum S and Spijkerboer T (eds).
Mullally, S. (2007b), *Children, citizenship and constitutional change* in Fanning, B. (ed.).
Reid, L. (2005), 'Reconsider Deportation Cases Urges O'Rourke' Irish Times, 26 March 2005.
Rice, N. (1994), 'Local Initiatives in Support of Families' in Kagan, S. and Weissman, B. (eds).
Schibel, Y. (2004), 'Monitoring and Influencing the transposition of EU Immigration Law' Issue paper for the European Migration Dialogue MPG.
Starr, S. and Brilmayer, L. (2003), 'Family Separation as a Violation of International Law' *Berkley Journal of International Law* 21.
Van Bueren, G. (1995), *The International Law on the Rights of the Child* (The Hague: Martinus Nijhoff).
Van Walsum, S. and Spijkerboer, T. (2007), *Women and Immigration Law: New Variations on Classical Feminist Themes* (London: Routledge).

Cases

Amrollahi v Denmark (2002) 22 EHHR 585.
Case C-200/02, *Chen v Secretary of State for the Home Department.*
International Treaties.
African Charter on the Rights and Welfare of the Child 1990 OAU Doc. CAB/LEG/24.9/49.
American Convention on Human Rights 1969 OAS No 36 (1969).
European Convention for the Protection of Human Rights and Fundamental Freedoms 1950 ENTS No 5.
Universal Declaration of Human Rights UN Doc A/810 1948.
United Nations Convention Relating to the Status of Refugees 1951 189 UNTS 137.
United Nations International Convention on Civil and Political Rights ICCPR 1976.
999 UNTS 171.
United Nations International Convention on the Protection of the Rights of all Migrant Workers and Their Families 1990 UN Doc A/Res/45/158.
United Nations International Convention on Economic Social and Cultural Rights 1976 UN Doc. A/6316 1966 993 UNTS 3.
United Nations International Convention on the Rights of the Child GA Res 44/25, 44 GAOR 49 UN. Doc 1465 UNTS 85.
United Nations International Convention on the Protection of the Rights of all Migrant Workers and Their Families 1990 UN Doc A/Res/45/158.

Conclusion

Helen Stalford, Samantha Currie and Samantha Velluti

This collection has aimed to provide a fresh and multi-disciplinary examination of the interrelationship between migration and gender in contemporary Europe.

Individually, the chapters have explored the regulatory processes and gendered effects of migration in the context of social regimes, notably family and employment. Collectively, the chapters have illustrated and reinforced a number of issues. First, migration is a highly dynamic process, involving a variety of transitions; not simply between physical spaces, but legal, cultural, social, political and economic ones too – and sometimes at several points over the life course. Geographical moves are frequently accompanied and motivated by expectations of (life-changing) upward social and economic mobility and a greater degree of personal belonging and security. While for many such expectations are fulfilled, for others migration can trigger a gradual and, at times, unforgiving attrition of familial, legal, professional and economic status.

Of course, migration does not produce such effects of itself; rather, it provides the platform on which a number of variables interact, serving to both disaggregate and reinforce the status of different groups according to age, nationality, ethnicity, socio-economic status and gender. Indeed, migration functions on a number of different levels within a variegated regulatory framework, from the international human rights, European Union, national and regional legal and policy level to the more intimate community, social and inter-personal level; and this framework is, itself, informed by established presumptions as to the interests, capacities and responsibilities of each of these groups.

A number of chapters in this collection has revealed and critiqued the extensive and far-reaching legal and policy architecture governing migration that has emerged since the turn of the millennium. Developments at EU level have largely driven this process – but in a different direction than EU migration law of the pre-millennium era. For instance the established free movement provisions continue to mobilize the EU labour force across all sectors of activity but the chapter by Oliver illustrates that this is in pursuit of new objectives concerned with stimulating knowledge exchange and developing a globally competitive research and skills environment. A further, more recent undertaking in the field of EU migration law relates to the breakdown of intimate relationships as discussed by Lamont. This is, as Boyle, Cooke, Gayle and Mulder's analysis analysis confirms, one of the more poignant casualties of increasingly fluid migration, demanding harmonized measures to enable migrants to address the consequences of divorce and parental separation across international borders.

Conversely, the chapter by Currie highlights the more defensive operation of EU laws for EU migrants, through the introduction of more limited mobility rights for migrants from the more recent (and profitable) EU accession states. This stands in stark contrast to the highly preferential treatment afforded to migrants from more established Member States raising questions as to the currency of EU citizenship. A similarly defensive approach is evident in EU migration law governing the entitlement of third country national migrants, particularly asylum seekers, refugees and victims of human trafficking. This body of provision – which adopts a prominent securitization and criminalization agenda – obscures the distinctly gendered effects of such processes. For instance, Sherlock's chapter illustrates the dissonance between EU immigration law, human rights law, and the reality of family life in Europe; while EU law clearly endorses a right to family reunification and family unity, it is premised on an outdated, rigid and manifestly imperialist evaluation of 'family' which presumes fixed gender roles and relationships. We are not suggesting that traditional patterns of family life do not exist, or that they are any less valuable, but closer scrutiny of how family life is played out in different migration contexts presents significant and, at times uncomfortable, challenges to such presumptions. Skilled migrants, for instance, face significant practical challenges and choices when faced with juggling a demanding mobile career and caring responsibilities. Many other women choose to migrate without their children for lengthy periods, often to fulfil caring roles on behalf of other women in the host state. Scullion's chapter offers a bolder example of this conflict by drawing attention to women's role in facilitating (either consciously or otherwise) child trafficking for the purpose of domestic work. Sensitive analysis of the reality and diversity of these migration experiences force us to question whether such economically and culturally rationalized 'choices' are unequivocally repugnant to our understanding of women's instinct and responsibilities as mothers.

The chapters on trafficking offer a further illustration of the unhelpful tendency (of law and social policy in particular) to fix migrant groups into rigid categories. Askola and Scullion's contributions highlight that there is no neat, straight-forward categorization of 'trafficking victim'. Women and children shift seamlessly and usually reflexively between different migration statuses, perhaps beginning as trafficked persons and subsequently entering legal employment following regularization; or alternatively, beginning as an asylum seeker before entering the murky world of trafficking or the shadow economy. Such observations highlight the failure of the law as it is currently framed to represent the diverse vulnerabilities, capacities and migration trajectories of trafficked women and children.

A similar criticism relates to the failure of migration law and policy to extricate the needs of children from those of adults, and particularly women, or indeed, to consider the specific implications of migration for children according to their gender. This is evident in the international framework underpinning child trafficking which represents children as a distinctly homogenous group. But equally problematic is the tendency of migration law to frame children in a competing position to adults, thereby denying the complex interdependency that exists between migrant family members. Lamont's discussion, for instance, highlights how the legal framework surrounding parental child abduction, in seeking to protect the best interests of children, serves to undermine or even jeopardize the welfare of women. Similarly, Toner's exposition reveals that deportation orders against foreign national prisoners are more likely to be anchored in a desire to retain the *status quo* for their children, even if this is at the expense of the needs and interests of partners.

This brings us on to another essential factor to take into account in reviewing migration processes and practices; that of context. Accepting that multiple levels of governance intersect through migration, the gendered manifestations of such processes can only be fully explored within the systemic and cultural environment in which they are situated. Typically, nation states are the favoured contextual frame of reference, since they possess clearly defined territorial borders and distinct administrative and legal structures which are determinative of the rights and status afforded to migrants. This is particularly the case when researching European migration. EU immigration law, for instance, imposes a level of harmonization on the Member States but devolves decision-making as to the nature and scope of substantive rights (access to welfare benefits, associated family entitlement etc.) to the nation state. As far as individual entitlement is concerned, therefore, migration laws are dependent on national processes to give them teeth; and these teeth may eat away at migrants' formal entitlement in negative ways or, alternatively, chew over and digest it in a way that nourishes and fulfils the needs of different migrant groups. But to fully appreciate the true impact of EU and international immigration law on individuals, we need to delve further into its interface with domestic and regional policy and explore how resources are distributed internally – not just through state regulation, but in the private industrial and informal sectors too. 'Irregular' migrants are a case in point; they may be entitled to minimal rights under supra-national immigration and human rights law, but the added benefits that make such rights practicable and worthwhile (availability of decent housing, access to specialist language support and legal representation, for example) can vary significantly from state to state, and from region to region within each state. 'Higher status' migrants are equally subject to these contextual factors, with Raghuram's chapter demonstrating how location and sector determines the availability of resources and opportunities for highly skilled migrants.

By the same token a wide variety of cultural influences guide and shape migration experiences – and this is particularly evident when examined through the lens of gender. The value system within which migrants find themselves is as persuasive as the formal regulatory system, and can have a highly potent gendering impact on law, policy and society alike. Women with children who migrate to southern Europe, for instance, may have more limited access to public child care provision or early childhood education because of the value attached to and reliance on informal family care networks (sustained primarily by women) within those regions. Furthermore, Lazaridis' chapter demonstrates that other variables (such as race and ethnicity, for instance) interact with gender, creating multiple grounds for discrimination and further heightening the isolation of migrant groups.

In addition to the range of new perspectives presented in this collection the contributions have also applied a range of methodological approaches in order to capture the complexity of gender and migration. The regulatory framework exposed through doctrinal legal analyses reveals one part of the picture, while the statistical data offers valuable insight into the achievements of the law in stimulating or inhibiting migration, particularly for women. But law and statistics only reveal so much about the actual experiences of these migrants on the ground or about the multiplicity of factors that motivate migration decision-making. Appreciating the gendered dynamics of migration demands a more intimate look at the nature and 'quality' of the migration process in terms of social integration, professional ascendance, financial security, and general well-being.

Taken together, the rich body of research presented in this collection exposes, on the one hand, how migration persists in producing proportionately more negative effects for women. On the other hand, however, it represents the distinctly empowered status of women as protagonists of their own migration journey.

Index

For Product Safety Concerns and Information please contact our EU
representative GPSR@taylorandfrancis.com
Taylor & Francis Verlag GmbH, Kaufingerstraße 24, 80331 München, Germany

www.ingramcontent.com/pod-product-compliance
Ingram Content Group UK Ltd.
Pitfield, Milton Keynes, MK11 3LW, UK
UKHW020011200926
475702UK00014B/1821

* 9 7 8 1 1 3 8 2 7 9 5 5 1 *

For Product Safety Concerns and Information please contact our EU representative GPSR@taylorandfrancis.com
Taylor & Francis Verlag GmbH, Kaufingerstraße 24, 80331 München, Germany

www.ingramcontent.com/pod-product-compliance
Ingram Content Group UK Ltd.
Pitfield, Milton Keynes, MK11 3LW, UK
UKHW020011200926
475702UK00014B/1821

* 9 7 8 1 1 3 8 2 7 9 5 5 1 *